The Scots College Paris
1603–1792

To
My Mother

The Scots College Paris
1603–1792

Brian M. Halloran

Foreword by
The Right Revd Mark Dilworth, OSB
The Abbot, Fort Augustus

JOHN DONALD PUBLISHERS LTD
EDINBURGH

ISBN 0 85976 462 1

British Library Cataloguing in Publication Data.

A catalogue record for this book is available
from the British Library.

PostScript Typesetting & Origination by Brinnoven, Livingston.
Printed & bound in Great Britain by the Cromwell Press, Melksham.

Contents

Foreword

This study fills a notable gap in our knowledge of religion in Scotland since the Reformation. It was generally known that two Scottish medieval institutions on the Continent became recusant colleges, with the purpose of educating Roman Catholic priests to maintain their Church in Scotland. A hospice for Scottish pilgrims in Rome was greatly enlarged and became the Scots College there. The foundation for students from Moray diocese in Paris, having declined in the sixteenth century, was revived to become a college of some importance, significant not only for Scottish Catholicism but indeed for national affairs.

Various isolated parts of this story were known, but now, for the first time, Dr Halloran has given us the continuous history of the College with its shortcomings and vicissitudes and new beginnings and we can see the background of the episodes already known.

In the Jacobite period, from the flight of James VII in 1688 to the crushing defeat at Culloden, the Scots College in Paris played an important role, and at the centre were the brothers Louis and Thomas Innes. Louis was the confidant of the exiled monarch, whose court was at Paris. Thomas embarked on his scholarly career by examining the archives of the medieval diocese of Glasgow brought to Paris by Archbishop James Beaton, and almost at once he had the good fortune to discover, and the expertise to evaluate, a document proving the legitimacy of the Stuart dynasty against those who impugned it. The connection between the College and the exiled Stuarts was thereafter of the closest.

Thomas Innes is a key figure in Scottish historiography. He was also deeply involved in the Jansenist controversy, which endangered the whole Catholic mission in Scotland. Indeed the effects of Jansenism, with its stress on the more legal and gloomier aspects of religion, have remained to this day.

Dr Halloran's wide researches have unearthed an astonishing number of students at the College, by no means all of them clerical, a further reminder that Scottish history cannot be adequately studied without taking the Scot abroad into account.

Fort Augustus, 1997   *M D*

Preface

The Scots College Paris has been an enigma to Scottish Catholic historians, sometimes being seen as extremely beneficial to the Scottish Catholic Mission, and at other times regarded as the source of many woes. Many articles have been written about various facets, which include its early foundation, its library and archives, and the Jansenist quarrels associated with it. What has not been presented is an overall picture of the college. One reason for this is the loss of the College Register if one ever existed. Without it, it has been difficult to determine student numbers, their composition (whether ecclesiastical or lay), their age, their provenance and their social background. This study is an attempt to gain a comprehensive view of the history of the Scots College Paris from the beginning of its second foundation in 1603 until its demise at the French Revolution in 1792.

My thanks must be expressed to the Right Revd G. Mark Dilworth for suggesting this topic for a doctoral thesis, and for his inestimable archival assistance while he was Keeper of Columba House, Edinburgh. I wish to thank also my supervisors at the University of St Andrews, Professor T. Smout and Professor D. Stevenson, for their invaluable assistance and encouragement. Dr Christine Johnson, the present Keeper of Columba House, has given me untiring assistance for six years, and to her also I am deeply indebted.

I am also grateful to Mr Peter Woodward and to Mr Gordon Beamish for translations of Latin and Italian documents, to Mr Andrew Wedderburn and Sir Alexander Sharp for information on the history of the Bethune family, and to Mother Patrice who showed me the chapel and environs of the Scots College Paris.

Without the help and encouragement of all these people, and many others, both within and without the University of St Andrews, this work could not have been undertaken, and I am very grateful to all of them.

St Andrews, 1997 *B M H*

CHAPTER 1
The First Foundation

In the reign of Robert Bruce, David, Bishop of Moray decided to provide a university education for youths from his own diocese, After Bannockburn, it was unthinkable that they should go to Oxford or Cambridge, especially after the bishop's own part in the patriotic war. He was said to have been like a human Fiery Cross, preaching throughout his diocese that a campaign against the English King was every bit as laudable as a crusade against the Saracen.[1] Besides, the Bishop himself had been educated at Paris[2], and his country was just about to renew her alliance with France in the Treaty of Corbeil of 1326. Bishop David anticipated this by his provision for Scottish students studying in France. On the 28 February 1325 he purchased a farm at Grisy-Suines, seven leagues from Paris so that the revenues could provide bursaries for four students from his own diocese who would study at the University of Paris, an arrangement that was confirmed by King Charles IV of France in 1326. This was the first foundation of the Scots College Paris which over three centuries later was to be legally united with the foundation of Archbishop James Beaton. Hence the Scots College Paris was often called 'Grisy' which was not just a nickname since the first foundation, with which the Scots College always claimed to have continuity, was called the 'College of Grisy' in official documents.[3]

At first the bursars were to reside in the College of Cardinal Lemoine, but this arrangement was legally terminated on 8 July 1333, when the masters of the college claimed that the revenue was insufficient to maintain four scholars honourably according to their station, and John, Bishop of Moray maintained that the masters had acted illegally in continuing the arrangement after his predecessor's death.[4] It has been argued that the Grisy foundation was a college only in the sense of being a collegiate body with its own revenues, and that the bursars had no corporate dwelling from 1333 until Beaton's bequest of 1603,[5] but this is not certain. Felibien said that the scholars eventually came to reside in the *Rue des Amandiers*,[6] now *Rue la Place*, and Émile Raunié explicitly stated that Archbishop Beaton bought the house in which the college of the Scots was installed.[7] Neither of these statements gives any indication as to when the scholars moved there, but it does seem probable that the bursars were in the *Rue des Amandiers* for at least some time before 1603.

Although we tend to think that the Bishop of Moray would have made such provision only for the education of future priests, it is highly unlikely

1

that a fourteenth century bishop would have made a sharp distinction between ecclesiastical and secular students. The original provision was for three students in arts and one in theology, and the first bursar whose name we know was William de Camera, a student in arts, who was assigned his bursary by Alexander Bur, Bishop of Moray, in 1384.[8] In later times the Scots College Paris was to insist that there never had been a requirement that the beneficiaries of the burse should be students for the priesthood.

Bursaries appear to have been granted in a little ceremony in which the Bishop placed his ring on the finger of the beneficiary, as when Bishop David Stuart gave a bursary to William Winchester in 1467, or Bishop Andrew Forman gave his bursary to John Hervey in the collegiate church of Stirling in 1502.

It was in Hervey's time that John Major complained in 1512 that the bursaries had been amalgamated into one, and that a Moray man had not received a bursary for a century.[9] This was not quite accurate as William Winchester, who had received a bursary in 1467, had been a canon of Moray. When, however, Walter Forrester had received Grisy bursaries in 1486, a dispensation had been granted in respect his belonging to the diocese of St Andrews,[10] and John Hervey was certainly the only bursar in 1509.[11] Being on his own, made him an easier prey for the predator when in 1510 John Hervey was abused and misled by John Coqbourne, an archer of the Scots Guards, into leasing the lands to Coqbourne for a term of 22 years at an annual rent of 25 pounds Tournois. Coqbourne died in 1531, but had previously stolen the title deeds of the property.

This must have made things difficult for George Lokert, one of Major's brilliant pupils, who in 1526 was appointed by Robert Shaw, Bishop of Moray to be the overseer of those who held Grisy bursaries, and was to correct and reform them when necessary.[12] The arrangement has the appearance of reconstituting the foundation as an authentic collegiate body which was not, however, sufficient means to prevent advantage being taken of Lokert's successors by André Foulorton, also archer of the Scots Guard, and his wife Catherine Hogg to whom they leased the property.[13] After Foulorton's death in 1547, four Grisy bursars, William Cranston, John Stuart, John Matthieson and John Rule were involved in litigation to recover their rights. The case was concluded in 1549 when Catherine Hogg agreed to abandon and annul all previous leases and to make repairs to the property within one year. She was then granted a new lease for a period of nine years.[14]

Despite the court decision of 1549, Catherine Hogg, now married to Alexander Lesque, another archer of the Scots Guard, was, in 1557, again in litigation with Thomas Wynterhop who had been granted a bursary by the Bishop of Moray in 1556.[15] (Wynterhop was a native of Galashiels and a Master of Arts of Glasgow University. In a chartulary of the University of Paris he is described as *Nationis quaestor,* and he was several times procurator of the University of Paris. Thomas Dempster said that he was well known in Paris, claiming that he had written two books, *Moralis Compendium* and *Apologia pro Epicuro.*[16]) Wynterhop won his case, only to find later in the year that his possession of the bursary was challenged by a priest called Robert Straloche, who claimed to have it from the Archbishop of Paris. In a subsequent court case, the judge found in favour of Wynterhop on the grounds that the bursary was in the gift of the Bishop of Moray, the Bishop of Paris having no right to make such provision, but he gave Straloche the right to appeal.[17] Straloche, however, failed to appear at the hearing which was held in the Church of Grisy on 21 December 1557.[18] Whereupon Wynterhop was put in possession of a quarter of the lands and revenue of Grisy.[19] His fellow bursars, John Stuart, David Henderson and a youth called John Scot; having in 1558 delegated him to act for them, Wynterhop was then instrumental in repairing the farm buildings, and doubling the revenue from the holdings. In addition to this, he managed to get grants from Mary, Queen of Scots and Archbishop Beaton. The charters of his achievement, or copies of them, he had bound together in the chartulary that is known as the 'Book of Grisy', now kept in Columba House, Edinburgh. Thus Thomas Wynterhop saved the foundation from extinction.

Not many names of bursars are known to us with certainty, but a claim that they included a great number of eminent persons is made in an undated letter of Alexander Gordon, Principal of the Scots College from 1777 to 1792, to a Scottish Bishop, probably John Geddes. The letter, which has a docket 'Principal A Gordon Paris Early in 1782 Febry', reads,

Mr Thos Gordon Professor at King's college Aberdeen put some queries to me which led me to look into our records. He mentioned a John Hervey who was said to have been rector in the University of Paris & to a Mr Rait Bp of Aberdeen who as well as Hervey was supposed to have belonged to our College. This set me upon examining what number of our College had been Rectors of the university or Bps. These Rectors & Bps I shall here insert as you are fond of Scotch worthies.

Rectors

1328 John Pilmore
1334 John de Waltustona what name this is guess if you can
1339 Philip Scot
1341 John Kinhard or Kinnaird
1345 Month of March Willm Greynlaw
1345 In Sepr Walter Wardlaw
1467 Patrick Leche

1469   Jan[r] 13 John Ireland & again in 1475
1469   3rd Thos Kennedy
1482   Richard Murehed
1523   Will[m] Manderston. M.L.
1538   Rob[t] Herriot
1542   Will[m] Cranston
1550   John Stuart
1568   Henry Blackwood
1598   John Fraser
1604   James Leith

Bishops

Walter Wardlaw Bp of Glasgow & Cardinal the same that was rector
Gilbert Greenlaw Bp of Aberdeen Chancellor of Scotland
John Rait Bp of Aberdeen
Matthew Glendonwyn Abp of Glasgow
Will[m] Turnbull or Durisdeir Abp of Glasgow & founder of the university there
Henry Wardlaw Bp of St Andrews founder of the university there and of that at
Paris from whence it had its first professors & in Particular Laurence of Lindoris
one of our Eleves.
Walter Forrester Bp of Brechin
Robert Strabrock Bp of Caithness
Robert Schaw Bp of Murray
David Panthin Bp of Ross
to these add our two historians Hector Boece & Geo. Buchanan.[20]

The names of four out of the last five rectors mentioned in this list are
recorded in the *Necrology* of the college, and in the case of two of these,
William Cranston and John Stuart, there is no doubt that they were Grisy
bursars, as they are described as such in the 'Book of Grisy'.[21] One would
not put too much reliance on the others being students of the Scots College
Paris unless there was supporting evidence, although Bellesheim claimed
that George Buchanan graduated in the Scottish College in 1527.[22] A
bishop that Alexander Gordon did not claim for the college, but who is
mentioned in the *Necrology* is Robert Wauchope, Archbishop of Armagh.
Although the *Necrology* was begun only in 1694, and on account of this
late date might be mistrusted as regards earlier information, there are very
few priests listed as *socii* for whom there is not corroborative evidence
that they were in the college.

In 1580 (Sept 26th), Gregory III, at the request of James Beaton,
Archbishop of Glasgow, granted an indult enabling the Bishop of Paris
and Meaux to ordain priests for the Scottish Mission without dimissorial
letters,[23] a concession that would be needed when the Scottish hierarchy
became extinct.

On 20 February 1602 Archbishop James Beaton purchased the house
in the *Rue des Amandiers* which in his will of 24 April 1603 he bequeathed,

with the residue of his estate, to the poor Scottsh scholars, placing his new college under the supervision of the Carthusian monks of Vauvert, Paris.[24] Thus began the second foundation of the Scots College Paris, over which one of the Grisy bursars, William Lumsden was appointed first Principal on 21 December 1604.

NOTES

1. MacKenzie, A.M., *Robert Bruce King of Scots* (London 1935), p.198 & p.167.
2. SCA/CA 1/1, Book of Grisy (unpublished), f.50r.
3. Ibid. f.ir, f.iii, f.iv.
4. Felibien, M., *Histoire de la Ville de Paris* (Paris1725) T. 5, p.634.
5. Durkan, J., 'Scots College Paris', *Innes Review* 2 (1951), p.112.
5. Felibien, M., op. cit., Vol I, p.561.
6. Raunié, E., *Epitaphier du Vieux Paris* (Paris 1901), Vol III, p.520.
7. *Registrum Moraviensis,* p.322.
8. *Quartus Sent.*, 1512, Dist. xxiv, q.v, f.cxxxix D.
9. Durkan J., 'Grisy Burses at Scots College, Paris', *Innes Review* 22 (1971), p.50.
10. SCA/CA 1/1, Book of Grisy, f.50.
11. Durkan, J., 'Scots College, Paris', *Innes Review* 2 (1951), p.112.
12. SCA/CA 1/1 Book of Grisy, ff.50r–54r.
13. Ibid. ff.10r–13v.
14. Ibid. f.14.
15. Dempster, T., *Historia Ecclesiastica Gentis Scotorum* (Edinburgh 1829), Tom II, p.665.
16. SCA/CA 1/1, Book of Grisy, ff.15r–16v.
17. Ibid. f.17r.
18. Ibid, f.18.
19. SCA/BL 3/357/2, undated, A. Gordon (Paris) to Bishop Geddes.
20. SCA/CA 1/1, Book of Grisy, ff.10r–13v, 19r–22r, 24r–25r, 29v–36r, 42v–44r, 47r–48v.
21. Bellesheim, A., *History of the Catholic Church in Scotland* (Edinburgh & London; 1887–1890), Vol. III, p.262.
22. Appendix ad Bullarium Pontificium Sacrae Congregationis de Propaganda Fide T. 1, p.124, Romae Typis Collegii Urbani. Found in SCA/GC 13/1 (Avery) f.72.
23. *Diocesan Registers of Glasgow* (London 1875), Vol. I, pp.229–233.

CHAPTER 2

Nature and Organisation of the College

The Composition of the Student Body

The Scots College in Paris was not exclusively for seminarians destined for the priesthood. We have seen that the first foundation of David, Bishop of Moray, made no stipulation that bursaries should be given only to students for the priesthood. Neither was the second foundation in 1603 only for theologians, but explicitly in his will, James Beaton left his house in the *Rue des Amandiers* for the poor students of the Scotch nation 'to study either in humanities or in theology.'[1] It is, therefore not surprising to find in Louis XIV's Decree of Ratification in 1688 that the College is 'just as much for the education and formation of ecclesiastical missionaries to be sent to the kingdom of Scotland as for the education of the youth of the said country in science and virtue'.[2]

In this respect, the Scots College, Paris differed from the Scots College, Rome. The latter had indeed been founded in 1600 for both ecclesiastical and non-ecclesiastical students, but Pope Paul V, who had been Protector of the Scots College Rome when he was Cardinal Borghese, decided that this pontifical foundation must be entirely for the education of priests The Roman College did, however, continue to take a few *convictores* (as non-ecclesiastical students were termed) as can be seen from the Roman Register,[3] but very much by way of exception.

Notwithstanding the prescriptions of foundation and union of the Scots College Paris, we find in the Statutes of the College, drawn up by Louis Innes in 1707, that no one is to be admitted as a student unless there is hope that he will reach sacred orders for the good of the mission in Scotland. This rule may have been included to impress the Roman Church authorities (the college had shortly before this time been under some criticism), but it was scarcely a reality.[4] Although it could be argued that the college had some hopes that all its students might become priests, Louis Innes readily admitted youths who had no explicit intention of becoming priests. Indeed he was anxious to get them so that their fees would contribute to the College, and seminarians could, if necessary, be taken free. Thus we find a Scottish priest, George Gordon, writing to Innes in April 1683 thinking that he might get 100 livres each from Strachan's and Gordon's parents, so that George Adamson, a seminarian, might be taken free.[5]

While the mixture of students must have had advantages, particularly in broadening the perspectives of the youths, it must have been difficult, especially in such a small college, to maintain the discipline suitable to each group. Imagine, for example, how unsettling it could be for seminarians to hear their table companions discussing their fencing or dancing lessons. Since the Council of Trent, seminarians were expected to follow a rigid discipline; it was harder to be so strict with those not destined for the priesthood. Moreover they were often from the lesser nobility whom the college was loath to offend, for fear of upsetting the gentry was a real anxiety. When, for example, John Urquhart, the son of Lady Meldrum, a daughter of Lewis Gordon, 8th Earl and 3rd Marquis of Huntly, caused his superiors grave anxiety in 1684, the Principal, Louis Innes, was at first afraid to dismiss him and wrote to Charles Whyteford, 'I could not for my part gett him off our hands now except we had her & all that family for our enemies.'[6] Later, however, Innes changed his mind.[7] A similar dread of offending the family was experienced in the case of Dr Irvin's son. Innes wrote to Whyteford from Drummond Castle in September 1687:

> as for Dr Irwins Sone I wish I had payd 100 crowns on condition he had never seen our Coll. you cannot imagin how clamorous his parents are & what harme ther talking may do in this country,...I think best you writ directly to the Doctor & tell him what trouble you have had wt his sone, & in plain terms that he must dispose of him otherwyse becaus he will not obey by fair means & you know the Dr wold not be content any severity were used, besyds that it is not much the custome of our Coll & tell him that at my desyre you have born more wt him than otherways you wold, but can no longer wtout altering the discipline of the house wch cannot be done, & therfor you expect to hear by first post how to dispose of him, I know I shall have trouble by this matter, but as good have it now as afterwards, so presse the Dr to remove his Sone, tell him plainly how things goes & that tis not in yr power to keep him wtout disturbing yr wholl house.[8]

Numbers of Students in the College

As the Register of the college has been lost, it is difficult to assess the number of students in the college. Over the one hundred and ninety years of the college's existence, twenty-three references to numbers were found, the numbers varying from 2 to 14. These gave an average of about eight students, but here caution has to be exercised since it is not always clear whether the references were to total numbers or to ecclesiastical students only.

It is exceedingly difficult to determine the proportions of seminarians and non-ecclesiastical students. Of 233 students known to be in the college,[9] 134 were probably ecclesiastics, 31 were probably not, leaving 68 cases in which we do not know. Although this at first suggests a high percentage of seminarians, it must be borne in mind that the church students would be of special interest to the bishops, and to priests in other colleges, and so they would naturally appear more often in letters. Unless *convictores* were nobility, or misbehaved very badly, or did not pay their fees, there was very little reason to write about them. If there is any accuracy in our estimate of an average of eight students in the college at any one time, this would amount to 1520 student years in the 190 years of the college's existence. Although the length of time spent in the college by ecclesiastics varied immensely, from less than a year up to twelve or fourteen years (two were even longer), the average for church students was about 6.3 years. 134 seminarians would therefore account for 844 student years. This would leave 676 student years. Supposing all these to be occupied by *convictores* who ordinarily spent three years each in the college, this would put the number of non-seminarians at about 225. The very tentative conclusion might be that more *convictores* than seminarians entered the college, but since seminarians generally spent more than twice the other's time in the college, there would usually be more seminarians than *convictores* in the college at any one time. The ratio, however, did not remain constant. There appear to have been a large percentage of *convictores* in the 1670s, and in the pre-Revolution days of Louis Innes, whereas in Charles Whyteford's principalship, although the number of ordinations had greatly diminished, there appears to have been a high percentage of ecclesiastical students.

Age of Students

By the statutes of the College drawn up in 1707, a student had to be fifteen years of age before entering. [10] This rule reflects the opinion of Louis Innes who thought that boys under fifteen were too young to enter the college. There had been no such rule before his time, and several cases of younger students are to be found. In 1627, a fourteen year old student, John Abercromby was sent by Alexander Pendrick from Paris to Douai to study grammar. [11] One, John Gordon sent the previous year at the age of fifteen may have been younger when he entered Scots College, Paris. [12] Alexander Leslie was thirteen when he entered in 1663, John Irvine of Cabrach (entered 1666) was no more than fourteen, and Richard (Augustine) Hay (entered 1773) was twelve. Louis Innes tried to introduce the rule that entrants had to be fifteen shortly after he became Principal. George Adamson had been sent to Paris by George Gordon on May 20 1683, and probably arrived there the following month. [13] He was only twelve. Innes must have felt that he was too young, and must have advised George Gordon not to send any more that age, for we find George Gordon writing to Innes in July of the same year, 'Nor shal any be sent who ar not 15 or 16 years of age & capable of the 3d school if any such can be had in the country.'[14] (Despite the misgivings about receiving one so young, George Adamson proved himself a credit to the College.) The attempt to enforce the 'aged-fifteen' rule, however, was not successful, and Louis Innes was not consistent. In 1684, he personally recruited Alexander Gordon, son of Lord Auchintoul who was only fourteen and his brother who was younger; two years later, one of his recruits was Lord James Drummond who was thirteen,[15] and in 1687, Innes was very happy to receive John Fleming, Earl of Wigton, and his brother Charles who were respectively fourteen and twelve.[16] Lord Edward Drummond was only eight when he was received in 1698, and with him came a younger brother, William. When it came to receiving the sons of peers, it would appear that the college was happy to have them at any age. Peers were not, however, the only ones to enter the college at a younger age than fifteen. James Brown came in 1687, and his father, Hew Brown, wrote to Charles Whyteford saying that his son 'is not yet thirtine years of age.'[17] Louis Innes was very happy to get Gilbert Wauchope, Niddry's son, as an ecclesiastical student in 1693, and he was only nine. John Caryll, grand nephew of Lord Caryll was admitted at twelve, and George Gordon was eleven when he entered the college in 1712. The youngest of all was probably George Napier, Wrighthouse's son, who was described as 'being so young that he can not put on his own cloaths, & kn[ows] nothing at all';[18] at first he was to be sent home as unsuitable, but then it was thought that it would be bad for the college reputation to send him home,[19] and so they kept him. After Louis Innes' principalship, several students under fifteen years of age were received into the college. These included John Farquharson (aged 11), James Drummond (aged 8), John Drummond (aged 7), Alexander Gordon (aged 14), John Gordon Dorlaithers (aged 14), James Gordon (aged 11), Seignelay Colbert (aged 11), Henry Innes (aged 11), John Baptist Gordon (aged 13), Alexander Innes (aged 14), and Alexander Macdonald (aged 14). Thus it can be seen that the college statutes are an uncertain guide as to the age of students. From about fifty-four instances where we know the age of students, it would appear that the age at entry generally ranged from eleven to twenty-one with exceptions both younger and older.

Junior and Senior Seminary[20]

From the number of young students, it can be seen that the Scots College, Paris acted as a junior seminary as well as a senior seminary, a provision that was necessary as there were so few opportunities for Catholic education in Scotland. This in an aspect that is often overlooked in attempts to evaluate the achievement of the Scots College Paris. It is worth remembering that before Louis Innes' principalship, at least twenty students of Scots

College Rome had undertaken previous studies at Scots College Paris, and fifteen of these twenty became priests. It is not always clear how the selection for Rome was made, but it sometimes appears to have been determined by the desires of the students, not overlooking the wishes of their parents.

Very soon after Louis Innes became Principal, there was a demand for students from the Scots College Rome that threatened to reduce the Scots College Paris to an exclusively junior seminary. In January 1683, in the first letter that William Louis Leslie, Rector of the Scots College, Rome, sent to Innes, he asked the Paris Principal to send him two students fit for Philosophy, thus leaving room in Paris for two Highland students.[21]

Innes first stalled for time; he wrote back that he had no Highland scholars, but meantime was consulting the priests on the Scottish Mission. Rector Leslie replied in March:

> It seems I did not explicate my self weale about the Scolers I desyred to have, for I knew very weale you had not highland youths at present to send us, But my intentione was that you should send us now such as you have, and take therafter highland youths in their places.[22]

This was followed in April by a back-up request from the Scottish agent in Rome, who was also called William Leslie, urging Innes to comply, and very uncharacteristically praising the Jesuit plan:

> I ame most glade of this good disposition of the Jesuits to receave alumni out of the hands of the clergie: so wee must not neglect it, but nourrish it as much as wee can.[23]

Shortly afterwards, Innes had a reply from Scotland, sent from Speymouth on 28 April 1683 by Alexander Leslie, brother to the Scots Agent in Rome, who signed himself 'Bootes'; Bootes did not share the view expressed by his brother about the 'good disposition' of the Jesuits whom he spoke of with the current pseudonym of 'birlaymen'.[24] He wrote:

> I shal only make bold at this tym to give you my advyse concerning what ye wrott of the birlaymens designe for making your Cought subservient to theirs in the old toune. I would grant to the barkers what the Birlaymen desyres upon condition they would immediatly remove altogether Birlaymen shipheards from our Cought in the old toune, and establish in their place thos kind of shipheards whom ye think ought to be their. otherways I would absolutely refuse and reject their request or proposall as a thing ye could noways accept off, unless yee were fully resolved to ruine and emptie your own cought for to serve them, but if they cannot find Lambs, lett them give the Cought to thos shepheards who will find them and food as weil as they and better two. I believ ther is non of my comerads refractory to this advyse, and assure your self that whatever lyes in our power to assist you in this shal not be wanting, and whatever your prudence shall suggest unto us for to stope their designe shall be accomplished to the utmost of our power.[25]

In June, the agent in Rome made an impassioned plea,[26] but this letter must have crossed with one in which Innes declined the proposals. Only eight days later, the agent in Rome accepted Innes' decision, although he still argued the case, pointing out the advantages of youths being prepared in Paris. His second point was that screening the youths in Scotland would be difficult, and would leave their selection in the hands of the Jesuits. He then warned that in the future there might be discord between Roman priests and Paris priests, and made the unrealistically optimistic suggestion that Innes could send three to Rome and keep three for himself, adding that Innes could have all the Roman priests for their practical training after ordination.[27] The agent was clearly embarrassed at having to tell those in Rome that the scheme had ganged aglee, and was pleading for a reconsideration. Innes, however, did not change his mind. He was not opposed in principle to students going to Rome, and during his time, there were five who proceeded to Rome after a considerable number of years in Scots College Paris, and a further seven wintered at the Paris college before going on to Rome. What Innes objected to was being obliged to send students when Rome demanded. The missioners were afraid that too many would join the Jesuits and not return to Scotland, and no doubt Innes wanted his College to keep the status of a major seminary. This it did, and although its numbers were few, it had ordinations until 1788, while it remained also a minor seminary.

William Leslie, the Scots agent in Rome, tried again in 1702 to get a constant supply of students from Paris when he wrote proposing that the Scots College, Paris should regularly send its three best students to Rome, and replace them with others from Scotland. The reply from Paris was the same as before, this time given by the Prefect of Studies, George Adamson, who had started his studies in Paris, and then, at his own wish, gone to Rome for his philosophy and theology. He pointed out that students could not be forced to go to Rome against their wishes and those of their parents, even by Cardinals, and he added 'nor has this colledge any obligation to furnish Rome wt scholars' and 'I pray you doe you think it fitte that Paris should serve for no other use for the mission but to be a grammar school to Rome, I doe nott thinke itt.'[28]

Religion of the Students

As Archbishop Beaton's legacy was intended to further Catholicism in Scotland, it is not surprising that the college was exclusively for Catholics, and when the statutes of the college were drawn up in 1707, the rule that only Catholics should be admitted was included.[29] This policy, later a rule, was not, however, absolutely enforced. In October 1638, a non-Catholic called Forrester was admitted to the college.[30] In 1655, an Alexander Gordon was admitted, and joined the Catholic Church soon afterwards. Robert Barclay, the future Quaker apologist and nephew of Principal Barclay was a student in the college in the 1660s. Although his uncle wanted to convert him, the younger Robert Barclay was strongly opposed to the idea. John Fleming, Earl of Wigton, and his brother Charles, although converts soon after joining the college community, were probably not Catholics at their entry in 1687.[31] John Stuart, brother of the Earl of Bute, entered the college in 1717 before his reception into the Catholic Church. The same was probably true of a student called Drummond, nephew of Abbot Cooke, who received his first communion in the college in April 1699.

Most of the students were from Catholic families, although there were at least twenty-two converts to Catholicism, eighteen of them ecclesiastical students, fifteen of whom became priests. One of them was the future bishop, John Wallace, who was an episcopalian minister before his conversion.

Preferences for Acceptance

At the union of Beaton's foundation with that of the Bishop of Moray in 1639, the Archbishop of Paris reserved the right to appoint to two places in the College,[32] but in the statutes of 1707, this proviso had disappeared. There is, however, an order of preference for the selection of students which reflects earlier foundations and legacies. Theologians are to be preferred to philosophers, and philosophers to humanists, and in each kind of study, all things being equal, preference is to be given to (1) two from the Diocese of Moray, then those who are Bethunes, whether they are from the Bethunes of Balfour in the province of Fife from which family our second founder came, or merely Bethune by name; (2) those from the family of Bethune of Creich; (3) one from the family of Gordon of Letterfurie in the Enzie; (4) one presented by the Duke of Gordon.[33]

In regard to these categories, we know of fourteen students who came from the diocese of Moray. There was at least one from the family of Bethune of Balfour. He was James Bethune who after his time at Paris 'did practiss medicine wt very good success at Coupar in Fyfe'. He would have entered the college c.1645, and his grandson George visited Paris in 1730.[34] Another of the name was Neil Beaton (Bethune and Beaton being variants of the same name) who was a Highlander who came to the college in 1702. We know of three students from the family of Gordon of Letterfourie, James Gordon who came in 1678, his eldest son, Patrick, who was in the college from 1713 until 1716, and James' fourth son, Alexander who entered the college in 1730.

Provenance

A complete analysis of student background is impossible, but the known region of origin of a hundred and forty-four students, helps to provide a pattern. All Scots Colleges abroad continued to designate students as coming from the dioceses as they had existed before the Reformation, and it may be useful to follow this pattern. It must be borne in mind, however, that these dioceses are not co-terminous with those set up in 1878 with the restoration of the Scottish Catholic hierarchy, and in some instances, the old divisions may seem strange to us. Galashiels and Melrose, for example, belonged to the diocese of Glasgow, while St Andrews had enclaves bordering on, and even inside the dioceses of Dunkeld and Brechin, so that Perth and Arbroath belonged to the diocese of St Andrews. From those of known provenance, the largest group came from the north east of Scotland with sixty-two students coming from Aberdeen diocese, and fourteen from the diocese of Moray. The diocese of St Andrews provided twenty-five students which is perhaps more than one would have expected, but with its peculiar boundaries, this included five from the titular Duke of Perth's family and John Wallace who came from Arbroath. Glasgow and Galloway provided seven students each, and there were six from Brechin, five from Ross and three from Dunkeld. Highlanders were always a small percentage, although in numbers of Catholics, the Highlands far exceeded the Lowlands. At least three came from the diocese of the Isles, and a further twelve were either described as from the diocese of Argyll or as Highlanders. We know of no students from the dioceses of Orkney and Caithness, and rather surprisingly, none from the diocese of Dunblane.

A statute of the college decreed that students had to be Scots, either born in Scotland or having both parents Scots. This rule was well observed. The exception was John Caryll, great nephew of Lord Caryll, the Jacobite Secretary of State, who was reluctantly received in 1699 to avoid giving offence to the Jacobite court. (It would have been hard to refuse him since a legacy of John Caryll provided the Prefect of Studies' salary, as will be noted again in the section on 'Staff.') Three others born outside Scotland, James Kennedy, born in Brussels, Alexander Leslie, born in Paris, and an unnamed student born in York, probably had Scots fathers and mothers. A youth named Benjamin Forbes who was living in the college in 1791 did not quite meet the requirements of the statute as he was born in France and his mother was English, but he may not have been strictly speaking a student of the college, but may have been one of the French boarders brought into the College by Principal Alexander Gordon.

Social Status

Very few ecclesiastical students came from families of rank. Some of them, such as George Con, John Menzies & Alexander Gordon, were described as coming from noble families, and some like Robert Barclay could trace a long and distinguished ancestry, but none were from the peerage. One, however, who was to become clan chief, Ranald Macdonald, later 15th of Clanranald, was in the college from 1739 until 1742, and appears to have been an ecclesiastical student. Colin and James Campbell were brothers of Sir Duncan Campbell, and were close relatives of the Duke of Argyll.[35] Thomas Fleming who was ordained in 1671 as a Benedictine monk with the religious name of Placidus was a descendant of the earls of Wigton.[36] James Gordon and Alexander MacDonald are described as cadets of Letterfourie and Keppoch respectively.[37] Charles Whyteford, who became Principal of the College, was the son of a Colonel, and grandson of David, Bishop of Brechin.[38] The father of Louis and Thomas Innes was a wadsetter.[39] Two students not ordained, Angus MacDonald[40] and Robert MacLean,[41] were sons of merchants. The majority, however, at least among the ecclesiastical students, were of very humble birth.

The *convictores*, however, who were always obliged to pay fees, tended to be of higher social station, and we find amongst them ten sons of peers, five from the family of the titular Dukes of Perth, two from the family of the Earls of Traquair, two Earls of Wigton, and a son of the first Earl of Bute. There was also one clan chieftain, Alastair Macdonnell, 12th chief of Glengarry. Archibald Blaccader, whose son John left the college in 1683, should have been a baronet as he was heir to his grandfather, John Blaccader of Tulliallan, but he resided in Cadiz as a merchant factor, and the Baronetcy had become dormant after the death of his grandfather (c.1675).[42] Most of the non-ecclesiastical students were sons of the landed gentry, often prominent enough to be referred to by the name of their estate.

Political Allegiance

Politically, Catholics of the seventeenth century tended to be on the royalist side, and there is no reason to believe that it was otherwise in the Scots College Paris. David Chambers, who was Principal from 1637 until 1641, dedicated his book *De Fortitudine Scotorum* to King Charles I.[43] An exception to royalist allegiance, however, was Thomas Chambers, junior, who had been a student in Paris, probably between his leaving Braunsberg in 1625 and his entering Rome in 1629. Thomas Chambers was almoner to Cardinal Richelieu who having failed to gain Charles I's support for the King of France, provoked the Scottish Presbyterians against the British monarch. To this end he sent Thomas Chambers to

Scotland in 1637, under the pretence of recruiting in Scotland for the Scottish regiments in France.[44] After the Revolution, the Scots College Paris fervently supported the Jacobite cause, and in a later chapter, we will see how the Scots College Paris became heavily involved in Jacobite affairs.

Priests on Pastoral Training

In addition to educating seminarians and *convictores*, Scots College, Paris became a centre of practical training for ordained priests before they proceeded to the Mission. This began in 1683, very soon after Louis Innes became Principal. In February that year, William Leslie, the Scots Agent in Rome, asked Innes to give hospitality to James Nicol who was newly ordained.[45] Innes not only welcomed Nicol, but got the idea of giving pastoral formation to other priests. The Scots agent in Rome endorsed the plan. In June, he wrote to Innes:

> thank you most kindly for yr kindnesse to Mr Nicoll, so much the more becaus you promise the lyke to others of his character who shall come to Paris. I ame most glade you are so zealous for the establishing of some way to have our Scots priests stay some tyme in Paris to learne some practicall things befor they go to the Mission.[46]

To help with the financing of the project, Leslie suggests how a 70 crown allowance from Propaganda could be applied to the college:

> unless you assigne to our priests ane appartement, or some two or three chambers in the college itself, which may have the title of ane hospitium for them, Rome will never consent to imploy that 70 crowns dessinated alreadie for such ane use to another, but if you will consent to assigne them the said chambers, and give them the baire title of ane hospitius, Rome will not grudge what use wee make other ways of the same money.[47]

Thereafter, the pastoral training of ordained priests became a regular task of the College.

The Staff of the College

The Superior of the Scots College, Paris, was the Prior of the Carthusians. This was in accordance with the terms of Archbishop Beaton's foundation in 1603;[48] it was customary at that time for seminaries to be placed under the supervision of a religious order, and from a practical point of view, it provided continuity for the government of the college and ownership of its property. In the Scottish case, with the extinction of the hierarchy at Beaton's death, it provided an authority who could appoint a Principal. Usually the Jesuits were chosen as the supervisory authority, but the Jesuits had been expelled from France in 1594, and did not return until 1604.[49] The choice of the Carthusians may have been suggested by Beaton's adviser, William Chisholm of Vaison whose uncle died as Prior of the

Charterhouse of Rome in the year 1593. The Paris Charterhouse had the advantage of being very close to the college, and the Carthusians were men of great distinction, less likely than the Jesuits to want to incorporate the college into their own order.[50]

For the practical running of the college, there were Scottish secular priests appointed by the Carthusian prior. By the 1707 Constitutions of the College, there were three offices of Principal, Procurator and Prefect of Studies. All three titles pre-existed the Constitution, but with the exception of the Principalship, there was not always a formality of designation before 1707. In the early days, the office of Principal and Procurator were combined. The duties of each office are detailed in the Statutes of the College:

> The Principal has to ensure that the Procurator and the Prefect of Studies carry out all the duties of their office, that all the students observe the rules, and that all is done according to the statutes of the college, and in accordance with the intentions of Founders and Benefactors. Each month he has to inspect the accounts of the college. Each month he has to find out from the Prefect of Studies how each student is progressing in piety and in studies, and determine what must be done for each. Twice a year, once in the second week of Lent and again in the last week of vacation, the students are to be examined by him or in his presence.
>
> On Festivals, the Principal is to offer Mass in the Chapel, and administer Holy Communion to the students. If disputes arise between Procurator and Prefect, he is to resolve them in accordance with the statutes of the college. Twice a year, in the second week of Lent and in the last week of vacation, along with the Procurator and Prefect, he has to inspect the inventory of the archives and library, and add recent accessions. He is also to keep an inventory of all movables in each room and office of the college, including the sacristy. He is also to inspect the daily register and anything else of moment.
>
> In case the statutes of the college be forgotten or fall into desuetude, they are to be read by him in the presence of the Procurator and Prefect and students on the Mondays of the second week of Lent and the last week of vacation. After each examination of the spiritual and temporal state of the college, he is to visit the Carthusian Prior to discuss matters with him. Each year he has to assist the Procurator in rendering the college accounts to the Prior. If disputes arise between the Principal and Procurator which cannot be resolved, the Principal must refer the matter to the Prior whose decision is final. The Principal must ordinarily reside in the college.
>
> The Office of Procurator is to care for the temporal affairs and goods of the college, to receive income and deal with expenditure, to visit the houses and villas owned by the college lest they fall or perish through age or lack of repair so that they can be repaired as soon as possible, and hired out when this can be done usefully. In matters of moment, such as the moving of houses, their repair and similar cases, the Procurator is to do nothing without the consent of the Principal. Things of greater moment such as demolitions or major restorations of buildings, and other extraordinary business of which the expense exceeds £200, cannot lawfully be undertaken by the Principal or Procurator, unless they have a signed permission from the Prior Superior which must be shown in the annual accounts. In matters of greater moment, such as the making

of financial contracts and changing money in the name of the college or other matters which relate to altering the credit of the college by alienation, acquisition or changing, the Procurator cannot act without the consent of the Prior Superior and of the Principal; without their written consent, the college will not be bound to honour the contract. In the interest of efficiency, matters to be presented to the Prior Superior should first be discussed by the Principal and Procurator.

The Procurator is to be experienced in the art of counting, and must enter transactions immediately, or at least on the day they occur, and he must keep registers which are to be inspected, checked and signed by the Principal every six months. The Procurator must demand and keep receipts which will be shown to the Prior Superior at the annual audit.

The daily economy of the college is in the hands of the Procurator, not only as regards food, but also as regards the clothes of each which must be kept up to standard by renewing with clothes which are good, decent and not easily deteriorated. He is take care of household furniture in common rooms, bedrooms, offices and other places. From time to time he will visit the rooms and when expedient renew the furniture, and keep an exact inventory to be examined by the Principal every six months.

Each night at about nine o' clock, the procurator is to visit the main door and offices of the college. He will keep the keys in his possession. Then he will visit the school offices, and even the kitchen, lest any danger befall the college by his neglect. In the absence of the Procurator, the Principal or the Prefect will care for what is needed scholastically or domestically.

The Procurator is to care for and supervise the domestic staff. In hiring and dismissing, he must consult the Principal. He is not allowed to leave the domestic economy in the hands of the domestic staff lest fraud or detriment occur. He will assist in the buying when he can, lest there be cheating in the price. He will also keep the keys of the provision cellar lest anything be taken or destroyed without his knowledge, unless he is certain of the probity of the domestic staff.

The Procurator is to keep the money for the daily and ordinary needs of the college. Greater sums of money which exceed 1000 livres or are not necessary for ordinary use are to be kept in a safe in the archives under two keys, one in possession of the Principal and the other in the possession of the Procurator. The Procurator must not get involved in the business of outsiders, especially in money matters.

In the absence of the Principal, the Procurator will govern the college. The Procurator must be a Scottish clergyman. He is to be appointed by the Prior of the Carthusians, Superior of the College, by instrument in the presence of notaries; his office will be for three years to be renewed as often as the Prior wishes.

The Prefect of Studies is responsible, under the Principal, for the care of the students in piety, education and the observance of discipline. Since the eternal salvation of the youths, the progress of the Catholic religion in Scotland, and the good state and reputation of the college, depend on correct direction by the Prefect, he must not be involved in other business or even studies which in any way would deter him from fulfilling the office which requires constant vigilance and attention and the whole man.

The office of Prefect has three priorities:
1. to form the students in piety
2. to instruct their minds in the knowledge of religion
3. to develop their characters.

As to the first, which is the chief duty of the Prefect, he must supervise the habits of the youths, so that he can dispose them to piety, observance of discipline, temperance, even urbanity, and other duties of society, and he must diligently correct vices and defects by advice, exhortation, timely correction and example. His constant task is vigilance, so that he knows where they are, with whom they are and what they are doing. He himself is to walk with the students when they are outside the college grounds, and if prevented by some grave cause (which should rarely occur) he is to entrust this task to a student on whom he can rely. Inside the college, he will always be present during recreation. He is to take care that the rules and discipline are exactly observed.

The second part of the duty of the Prefect is to form, in the minds of the students, solid principles of knowledge of the chief dogmas of the Christian religion, both those which relate to the Catholic faith and those which pertain to the rules of morality, and even especially those which relate to controversy against heresy which flourishes in Scotland. Over and above private instruction according to the need of each, each week on a stated day and hour, he will give instruction on the Catechism, on piety, and about controversies.

The third part of his duty lies in the correct fostering of judgement and cultivating knowledge in sciences both secular and sacred. Theologians and philosophers are to repeat lessons before the Prefect, and he is to examine students in humanities and other matters. He is to prescribe the order and method of studies and the books chosen for each. He is not allowed, unless with advice and permission, to make any innovations in studies. In all things, he must take account of age and needs.

The main quality required in a Prefect is discretion. It is necessary to explore and discern with great attention and judgement the characters, virtues, defects and intentions. Some will be motivated by leniency who with severity would be despondent; others progress faced with severity who with leniency might become insolent; some excel in memory, others in judgement. It will help not a little to remember that those who are admitted to the college can be divided into four classes. The first are clerics [this means that they have embraced the clerical state by receiving the tonsure], the second are those who aspire to the clerical state, the third are those who have been sent by their parents to be instructed in religion, good morals and the sciences, who do not now desire the ecclesiastical state, but may later receive a vocation to it, and the fourth are those who are reasonably certain to remain laymen.

For those in the first category it is entirely the duty of the Prefect to prepare them through solid piety and knowledge of holy things for the duties of missionary and pastoral tasks. For those in the second category, it is the duty of the Prefect to probe their vocation, morals and purpose, and to foster in them sincere piety, and love of God and neighbour. Irrespective of good references from Scotland, they are not to be admitted to the ecclesiastical tonsure until they are proved worthy. With youths in the third category, great caution is to be exercised, since there is already in many parts of Scotland an unfortunate prejudice that superiors of colleges abroad take advantage of the simplicity and ingenuity of the youths and persuade them by enticing words to embrace the ecclesiastical state. The Prefect and other superiors must take the greatest care lest they confirm suspicions in this pernicious prejudice which the students have enough of themselves. The main care of the Prefect for this category is to inspire sincere and solid piety and the highest dependence on the divine will, and then leave them to the divine disposition, since it is certain that if they seek God with all their hearts and souls, and if they are truly called, God will make this known to them.

To youths in the fourth category the Prefect will hand over the rules of true Christian life, inspiring fear of God, and especially he will studiously inculcate how much even a layman can bring about the conversion of heretics, amongst whom they will have to live, by a sober and just mode of life and piously living according to the gospel norm. To these ends he will religiously dispose the family, for experience constantly proves that the morals not only of priests but also of the Catholic laity serve more to convert heretics to faith than controversies on Christian doctrine or disputations about dogma, and nothing impedes true religion more than the scandal of Catholics. The Prefect, however, will not omit to give the youths instruction on the controversies of the faith.

If there is any defect in food, clothes, health, studies, recreation or anything else, Students will have immediate recourse to the Prefect, who, if the request is seen to be just, will call upon the Procurator with the matter, and with common council, they will decide what is to be done. Each week on Saturday at a stated hour, the Procurator and Prefect will meet with the Principal to confer about all the affairs of the College or the discipline and necessities of the students.

Twice a year at the time of the exams, he will give an account to the Principal of each and every student. The Prefect will then visit the Professors both of humanity and philosophy, and diligently enquire of them the progress, diligence and assiduity of the students.

The Prefect is to take care of the library according to the statutes laid down which he will diligently observe. He will also seriously adhere to the admission procedures in the Statutes, and all the general statutes of the college, the highest execution of which depends on his vigilance, and he will diligently and with solicitude take care that these statutes are observed.[51]

It is sometimes said that a code of law is a history of misdemeanour. Some of these statutes reflect the chief faults of the three office-bearers at the time of their composition (1707). The Principal should ordinarily reside in the college, which Louis Innes seldom did from the Revolution of 1688 until his resignation in 1713, as he was constantly staying with the Jacobite court at St Germain. The Procurator was not to be involved with outside business, especially financial, which Charles Whyteford constantly was, and this was his chief fault. The Prefect of Studies was not to be distracted by other tasks, even studies, a fault very apparent in Thomas Innes who amongst many other tasks devoted himself to the care of the college library and archives and to the writing of history much to the detriment of his task as Prefect of Studies.

The Principal's salary was £250 per annum, the procurator's £200 with a further £50 for incidental expenses. The Prefect's salary was £200, paid from the foundation of John Caryll, Baron of Dunford (who was still alive when the statutes were drawn up).

We have the full list of Principals from 1622. Before that we are not absolutely certain, but William Lumsden was definitely the first Principal, appointed in 1604. This is the list of Principals:

1. William Lumsden	1604–
2. Under the care of Robert Philip and Alexander Pendrick	–1617
3. Alexander Pendrick	1617–1637
4. David Chambers (or Chalmers)	1637–1641
5. George Leith	1641–1655
6. Gilbert Blakhal for few months in	1653
7. Robert Barclay	1655–1682
8. Louis Innes	1682–1713
9. Charles Whyteford	1713–1738
10. George Innes	1738–1752
11. John Gordon	1752–1777
12. Alexander Gordon	1777–1792

The offices of Principal and Procurator were made distinct in the principalship of Robert Barclay, and the first known to hold the office of Procurator is Thomas Lumsden. The following is the list of Procurators:

Thomas Lumsden	1664–1671
Charles Whyteford	1682–1713
Robert Gordon	1713–1718
Alexander Smith (later Bishop)	1718–1729
James Carnegie	1729–1734
George Innes	1734–1738
Andrew Riddoch	1738–1772
Alexander Gordon	1773–1774
Henry Innes	1774–1789
Alexander Gordon (also Principal)	1789–1792
Alexander Innes	1792–

The first mention of a Prefect of Studies is that of Robert Barclay in 1653. Short gaps will be seen in the list; it seems likely that there were times when the office was not formally filled, or there may simply be some information missing. This is the list of Prefects of Studies:

Robert Barclay	1653
William Ballantine	1658–1660
Thomas Lumsden	1660–1672
David Burnet	1676–1680
Louis Innes	1680–1682
Charles Whyteford	1682–1696
Alexander Drummond	1696–1697
George Adamson	1697–1703
James Paplay	1703–1704
Thomas Innes	1704–1712
Robert Gordon	1712–1718
Thomas Innes	1718–1727
George Innes	1727–1735
Alexander Gordon (Coffurich)	1735–1737
John McKenzie	1738–1743

John Gordon	1743–1752
Robert Gordon	1753–1756
William Duthie (or Dorthie)	1759–1761
Alexander Gordon	1764–1772
Henry Innes	1772–1777
Peter Hay	1777–1781
Alexander Innes	1781–1792

There was not regularly a Vice-Principal of the college, though David Burnet held this title from 1676 until 1680, and Charles Whyteford is often given this title with the address on letters, and Thomas Innes was appointed vice-principal in 1727, presumably on account of the age of Charles Whyteford who was then about 79.

In addition to those who formally held office, there were from time to time other priests helping with the running of the college, sometimes sent for the task and at other times fulfilling a need when they happened to be there. Thus we find Angus McDonnell (or McDonald) in the college in the first half of 1683;[52] he went to the Highlands and Islands in June, but died on the 27 December 1683. John Irvine who stayed at the college on his way from Padua to Scotland did staff duties in the first half of 1684.[53] James Devoir and James Cahassy, both Irishmen recruited for the Scottish Mission by Alexander Leslie, were appointed to the staff from July 1685 until July 1686.[54] This time in Paris gave Cahassy the time to write two very interesting letters which give an Irishman's impression of the mission in the Highlands and Islands.[55]

Servants in the College

Other residents in the College were the servants, normally two, and they seem always to have been male. A high priority here was a resident tailor. Louis Innes was looking desperately for one in 1684. In July, he wrote, 'I have done & am doing for a taylor I have found non as yet fitt.'[56] In August, 'I could not for my hart find a tayllor in Scotland fit for us…must be found…before all these youths come.'[57] It was the missioner, John Irvine (known as Cabrach) who found one; in September 1684, Innes wrote to Whyteford, 'Cabrach has found a tayllor. he has engaged wt this tayllor to stay wih us all his life, he has 4 years at ye trade & will come by first ship.'[58] We may surmise that the tailor did not make it a life-long contract, for we find Innes getting another tailor (Alexander Dumbreck) three years later. In August 1687, he wrote from Preshome, 'I bring a tayllor & another boy for servants to our house. I hope they will do wealle.'[59] When in 1699 Peter Fraser was deemed incapable of ever being proficient enough in his studies to become a priest, he was given a job as servant, but since the college was only allowed to have two servants, he was given the title of 'tailor'. There is mention of this post again in 1721 when George Clerk, the college tailor caused anxiety by going off to Rome against advice.

The Earl Wigton and his brother had their own servant living in the College; his name was Mr Crystie and he was provided with a 'draw bed'.[60]

The Daily Time-Table

The Council of Trent had decreed that seminaries be established for training future priests in piety and learning.[61] In practice, the discipline and routine followed a monastic pattern, and we have the daily programme of the College outlined in the Statutes. Students rose at five, and had to be present at morning prayers at five-thirty exactly. From six till seven was a study period. At seven a bell summoned them to the chapel for Mass, after which they returned to their rooms without noise. When the bell rang again, they went down to the refectory where they had each assigned places, and they breakfasted without noise or gossip. After breakfast, they went to the public schools of the university, the philosophers all going together, and similarly, the humanists went as a group with the Prefect of Studies. After classes, they had to return together without delay. (The same procedure was to be followed for afternoon classes.) On return to the College, students were to study until lunch time; when the bell sounded, they went first for a visit to the chapel, and then to the refectory. During lunch, each had to sit in his assigned place, sit properly, and in silence listen to the reading. After lunch, there was an hour's recreation either for a walk or for some other honest recreation or for a game. The Prefect was to be present, and students were not allowed to be by themselves, or in companies of two, or to separate themselves from the others without permission. Games of chance, such as cards or dice, were entirely forbidden by the statutes of the University and those of the College. When the bell rang after recreation, all had to go to their rooms for study until the customary time to go to the schools. When they returned from the schools, they had to study or write exercises until supper at seven. After supper, there was an hour's recreation as there was after lunch. Eight was the hour for the prayer of Vespers, after which they retired in silence to their rooms where they were to be in bed, with candles extinguished, by a quarter past nine.

On feast days and non-study days, there was more recreation, but still a detailed programme. They rose at five-thirty, and if they did not go for a walk in the morning, they could play games from eleven to midday. In the afternoon, they could either go for a walk, play games or take honest recreation until about four. Those who wished were free to go to their rooms at two in the afternoon. Once a week, there was a compulsory walk. They had to go with the Prefect, and stay with him, unless he split the walk into two or more groups, in which case each had to stay in the group allocated. Special permission was needed to absent oneself from this walk. All had to return home about six o' clock in summer time, and before five from the Kalends of October until Easter. On Sundays and feast-days, they could enjoy an hour's walk or modest recreation, without loud noise, after returning from the office of Vespers. Fifteen feast-days were specified on which by custom, the students were entitled to a more festive lunch, and in the holiday month of September, they were entitled to a more festive lunch four times a week.

The Finances of the College

One may wonder how the Scots College in Paris was financed, especially as Scotland had so few Catholics, and many of these were in pecuniary difficulties. Although we are far from knowing all the details of benefactions, we can piece together a general idea of the college finances. The basic income of the first foundation in 1325 was the revenue from the farm at Grisy. The college Necrology[62] lists all but four of the subsequent sixteen bishops of Moray as 'benefactors' of the college, but as the 'Necrology' was first compiled in 1694, not too much reliance can be put on the historicity of this claim. Thomas Randolf of Moray patronised the first foundation in 1339, and one, Andrew Ramsay, who died in 1581 is also mentioned in the Necrology as a benefactor. The farm continued to be a source of revenue for the college after the Bishop of Moray's foundation was joined with Archbishop Beaton's. Archbishop Beaton, in addition to bequeathing a house to the poor scholars from Scotland, also left them in his will the residue of his estate which amounted to 80,000.[63] Further bequests were made both by priests and by *ex-convictores* of the college. Principal Robert Barclay contributed from his own resources towards the building of the new college (1662–1665), and in his will he left all his money to the college. John Law, the famous banker, gave the college fifty shares in his East India Company. Each share was then quoted at 9,000 livres tournois, making a total value of 450,000 livres, a very large sum in that day. Ill-fatedly, however, after the fall of Law's system, the French government nullified the bequest, and although Chevalier Andrew Michael Ramsay managed to get the actions restored to the college, the shares had dropped to one-fourteenth of their original value.

Besides the college building, the Scots College Paris owned another six houses, of which more will be said in the next chapter. These houses were hired out, and it was ordinarily expected that between a third and 40% of the revenue would be spent on maintenance, and that the remainder would contribute to the finances of the college. King James VII gave a grant in 1687 of £1000 sterling, the equivalent of 12,000 French livres, and in 1698, his son[64] James Edward, despite the straightened circumstances of the court, donated a thousand livres. The salary of the Prefect of Studies came from a foundation made by John Caryll, first Baron of Dunford.[65] The French clergy also made a voluntary contribution, and there are extant receipts of 1600 livres per annum from 1704–1724.

The families who could afford it were charged fees for their sons in the college. These were variable and subject to negotiation as is instanced in 1684, when Innes wrote to Whyteford, 'Coats payes 300l all the rest pay something but little.'[66] In practice, great difficulties were experienced in collecting the fees, letters of excuse were sent to the college, and often fees did not materialise. Nevertheless this was an important, and more or less constant, source of income.

Louis Innes must have had a good salary when he was at the court of St Germain where he acted as a kind of personal secretary to James VII, and as almoner to Queen Marie d'Est, and from 1713 until 1718 as almoner to James Edward. Innes often paid for the education of a seminarian, especially when circumstances would not ordinarily warrant the student's acceptance into the college. He contributed from his own resources to the Scottish seminaries at Scalan and Guidal, and to his brother's publication of the History of the Picts. It seems likely that he may also have contributed to the Scots College, Paris, in a more general way.

The College Building

Until 1665, the college was in the house bequeathed by Archbishop Beaton in *Rue des Amandiers* (now *Rue La Place*). Principal Robert Barclay, however, acquired ground in 1662 and built a new college in the *Rue des Fossés-Saint-Victor* (now *Rue du Cardinal-Lemoine*) which was completed in 1665, and the chapel was added in 1672. It has a very impressive facade, being four storeys high, with five windows, each side of the main door, and eleven windows on each of the other floors. There are also attic windows which look as if they had been added later, and the north wing which was added in 1672 has on the front of the building one window on each floor, a feature which upsets the symmetry of the facade. Being built literally where the fosse was, there is a difference in ground level between the front and the back, the first floor on the street side being level with the ground of the garden (now yard) at the back. Thus what is the ground floor at the front or street side served as a basement in which was installed the kitchen, store-rooms etc, and presumably the rooms of the servants and the tailor. A very fine wooden staircase leads up to the first floor, and on the landing to the left is the door of the chapel which is partly inside the original building and partly built out into the garden at the back. The sacristy is behind the sanctuary and further into the garden. On the right of the first floor landing, there was a passage between two classrooms which led to the library and to the refectory.

The floor above was reserved for the staff, and presumably the visitors' rooms were also on this floor, as also the rooms of priests on Pastoral training and of those priests who were given refuge from persecution in Scotland. The students rooms were on the floor above this,[67] the top storey. There were twenty student rooms, ten to the front and ten to the back, but there is no evidence that there were ever more than fourteen students in the college at any one time.

NOTES

1. SCA/GC 13/1, Avery, 'A collection of documentary information about the Scots College, collected in Paris by Fr Avery', now in Columba House, unpublished, ff.44–53.
2. SCA/GC 13/1, Avery, f.152.
3. *Records of the Scots Colleges I*, (Aberdeen 1906), pp. 185–189.
4. SCA/CA 1/10, Statutes of the College.
5. SCA/BlLett 1/77/2, George Gordon to Charles Whyteford, Paris, 24 April 1683.
6. SCA/BlLett 1/84/10, Louis Innes, Edinburgh to Charles Whyteford, Paris, 12 June 1684.
7. SCA/BlLett 1/84/18, Louis Innes, to Charles Whyteford, Paris, 29 Sept 1684.
8. SCA/BlLett 1/103/1, Louis Innes, Drummond Castle, to Charles Whyteford, Paris, 12 September 1687.
9. cf. Reconstructed College Register in Appendix pp.388–408.
10. SCA/CA 1/10, Statutes of the College.
11. 'Douai Diary', No.192, *Records of the Scots Colleges*, p.22.
12. Ibid. p.19.
13. SCA/BlLett 1/77/5, Geoorge Gordon to Louis Innes, Paris, 20 May 1683.
14. SCA/BlLett 1/77/7, Geoorge Gordon, Boyne, to Louis Innes, Paris, 26 July 1683.
15. Paul, J.B. (Ed.), The Scots Peerage, (Edinburgh 1904–1911).
16. Ibid. Vol 8, pp.554f.
17. SCA/BlLett 1/97/5, Hew Brown to Charles Whyteford, Paris, April 1687.
18. SCA/BlLett 2/51/2, Louis Innes to William Leslie, 9 Feb 1699
19. SCA/BlLett 2/43/2, George Adamson to Louis Innes, 6 Jan 1699.
20. Although anachronistic, the term 'senior seminary' or 'major seminary' is a convenient shorthand for describing a college of training for the priesthood where the students studied philosophy and theology, and 'junior seminary' or 'minor

seminary' is likewise apt to describe a college where preliminary subjects (mainly the liberal arts) were taught.

21. SCA/BlLett 1/79/22, William Leslie, Rome, to Louis Innes, Paris, 6 January 1683.

22. SCA/BlLett 1/79/23, William Leslie, Rome, to Louis Innes, Paris, 9 March 1683.

23. SCA/BlLett 1/79/13, William Leslie, Rome, to Louis Innes, Paris, 20 April 1683.

24. 'Birlaymen' is possibly a corruption of 'birlawman', implying that the Jesuits adhered to the letter of the law.

25. SCA/BlLett 1/78/18, Alexander Leslie, Speymouth to Louis Innes, Paris, 28 April 1683.

26. SCA/BlLett 1/79/14, William Leslie, Rome, to Louis Innes, Paris, 29 June 1683.

27. SCA/BlLett 1/79/16, William Leslie, Rome, to Louis Innes, Paris, 5 July 1683.

28. SCA/BlLett 2/74/1, George Adamson [to William Leslie] 7 August 1702.

29. SCA/CA 1/10, Statutes of the College.

30. SRO, Edinburgh GD 18/2364 6, John Clerk, Paris, to William Forrester, 12 Nov 1638.

31. SCA/BlLett 1/106/15, Earl of Perth, Edinburgh, to Charles Whyteford, Paris, 12July 1687.

32. SCA/GC 13/1, Avery, f.96.

33. SCA/CA 1/10, Statutes of the College.

34. SCA/BlLett 2/327/2 Dr Bethune Balfour to Thomas Innes, 25 May 1730.

35. Gordon, J.F.S., *Catholic Church in Scotland* (Glasgow 1869), p.531.

36. Dilworth, M., *The Scots in Franconia* (Edinburgh & London 1974), p.104.

37. Gordon, J.F.S., op. cit., p.3. M. Taylor, *The Scots College in Spain* (Valladolid 1971), p.320.

38. M. V. Hay, Winston Churchill and James II of England (London 1934), p. 21n.

39. Innes, T., *The Civil & Ecclesiastical History of Scotland* (Aberdeen 1853), p.ix.

40. Gordon, John of Glencat, *Memoirs of the life of John Gordon of Glencat* (London: 1733)

41. 'Douai Diary', no. 166, *Records of the Scots Colleges*, p.18.

42. *Complete Baronetage* Vol II 1625–1649 (Exeter 1902), pp.315f.

43. David Chambers, *De Fortitudine Scotorum* (Paris 1631).

44. M.V. Hay, *Blairs Papers (1603–1660)* (London & Edinburgh 1929), p.126.

45. SCA/BlLett 1/79/12, William Leslie, Rome, to Louis Innes, Paris, 5 February 1683.

46. SCA/BlLett 1/79/14, William Leslie, Rome, to Louis Innes, Paris, 29 June 1683.

47. Ibid.

48. SCA/GC 13/1, Avery, ff.44–53.

49. Hay, M.V., *The Blairs Papers (1603–1660)* (London & Edinburgh 1929), p.76,n.1.

50. McRoberts, D., 'The Scottish Catholic Archives, 1560–1976', *Innes Review* 26 (1977), pp. 59–128.

51. SCA/CA 1/10/2, Statutes of the College, pp.15–34.

52. SCA/BlLett 1/76/15, Alexander Dunbar, Edinburgh, to Louis Innes, Paris, 31 January 1683.
SCA/BlLett 1//77/8, George Gordon to Louis Innes, Paris, 22 June 1683.

SCA/BlLett 1/79/18, William Leslie, Rome, to Louis Innes, Paris, 24 August 1683.

53. SCA/BlLett 1/86/2, William Leslie, Rome, to Louis Innes, Paris, 5 January 1684.
SCA/BlLett 1/86/5, William Leslie, Rome, to Louis Innes, Paris, 4 April 1684.

54. Gordon, J.F.S., op. cit., p.628.

55. SCA/BlLett 1/90/1, John Cahassy, Paris, 8 November 1685.
SCA/BlLett 1/90/2, John Cahassy, Paris, 31 December 1685.

56. SCA/BlLett 1/84/12, Louis Innes, Leith, to Charles Whyteford, Paris, 31 July 1684.

57. SCA/BlLett 1/84/13, Louis Innes, London, to Charles Whyteford, Paris, 25 August 1684.

58. SCA/BlLett 1/84/16, Louis Innes, London, to Charles Whyteford, Paris, 4 September 1684.

59. SCA/BlLett 1/102/20, Louis Innes, Presholme, to Charles Whyteford, Paris, 25 August 1687.

60. SCA/BlLett 1/102/5, Louis Innes to Charles Whyteford, Paris, 28 April 1687.

61. *The Canons and Decrees of the sacredand oecumenical Council of Trent*, tr. Rev J. Waterworth (London & New York 1848), p. 187ff.

62. SCA/CA 1/7, Necrology of Scots College Paris.

63. Blakhal, G., *A Breiffe Narration of the Services done to Three Noble Ladyes*, 1631–1649 (Aberdeen 1844), p. xxvi.

64. SCA/BlLett 1/102/7, Louis Innes, Windsor, to Charles Whyteford, Paris, 23 May 1687.
SCA/BlLett 1/102/10, Louis Innes, Holyrood House, to Charles Whyteford, Paris, 21June 1687.
SCA/BlLett 1/102/11, Louis Innes, Holyrood House, to Charles Whyteford, Paris, 28June 1687.

65. SCA/CA 1/10, Statutes of the College.

66. SCA/BlLett 1/84/11, Louis Innes, Castle Gordon, to Charles Whyteford, Paris.

67. Emile Raunie, *Epitaphies du Vieux Paris,* Tom III (Paris 1901), pp.524f.

CHAPTER 3

The First Fifty Years

After Archbishop Beaton's bequest, the bursars of the second foundation lived in the same house and under the same discipline as those of the ancient foundation of Grisy,[1] each group having their separate funding. Three of the early Principals, William Lumsden, Alexander Pendrick and David Chambers, were Grisy bursars. At first sight, this may seem to have been simply an abuse, since the bursaries were first intended for poor scholars, but further consideration shows this to have been a virtual necessity, since the Grisy bursars were not under the jurisdiction of the Carthusian Prior, and they could only be made subject to the Principal if he was the chief Grisy bursar.

William Lumsden (1604–)

The first Principal appointed on 21 December 1604 was William Lumsden,[2] but apart from the fact that he was a doctor of law who had received a bursary of Grisy on 3 September 1600, we know little else about him. He died on 5 June 1624, no longer Principal, but we do not know when or why he demitted office. David Chambers who became Principal in 1637 may have been one of his pupils, as may have been William Fraser, younger son of the second laird of Techmuiry, who entered the college on 1July 1611,[3] and later became a benefactor of the college.[4]

Robert Philip[5] (–1617)

With some sort of sixth sense, Malcolm Hay thought that there might have been a principal in between Lumsden and Alexander Pendrick whom he knew to have been principal in 1622, but he had no idea who it was. A letter in the Vatican Library[6] reveals the presence in the college of Robert Philip who had been banished from Scotland in 1613 for the crime of celebrating Mass. The letter is written by David Chambers to a Cardinal in Rome (presumably Cardinal Maffeo Barberini, Cardinal Protector of Scotland) requesting permission for a chapel in the college, and for the privilege of having students ordained to sacred orders without dimissorial letters. The letter is undated, but as both requests were granted by Pope Paul V on 27 May 1617,[7] it seems reasonable to assume that it was written a short time before that. The letter stated that Robert Philip and Alexander Pendrick were in charge of the college. At first it seems strange to find that two priests are in charge of the college, but the likeliest explanation is that one was the chief Grisy bursar, and the other was in charge of the Beaton bursars. As Alexander Pendrick certainly had a bursary when he was Principal, though we do not know when he received it, it seems more likely that he was the Grisy bursar, with Robert Philip in charge of the others. Certainly Robert Philip was on the staff of the college, and this explains why he is described in the Necrology of the Scots College Paris as a *socius* although he was trained and ordained in Rome.[8] An interesting feature of David Chamber's letter is that it gives the earliest indication of numbers in the college, by stating that there were in it three priests (very possibly he himself was the third) and five theological students.

The college could have justly been proud to have had Robert Philip on its staff. Later, after he had joined the Oratorians, he achieved some fame as the chaplain to Henrietta Maria, the Queen of Charles I.[9] He was renowned for his conciliatory approach to the Anglicans, was consulted by the Holy See on the possibilities of unity, and had personal talks to that end with King Charles I. Friendship and good will towards those of other faiths was to be a characteristic of the Scots College Paris, and may well have been the heritage of Robert Philip as the founder of that tradition.

Alexander Pendrick (1617–1637)

Robert Philip joined the Oratorians in 1617, and it is a fair assumption that we can place the beginning of Alexander Pendrick's principalship in that year. Alexander Pendrick was from the diocese of Aberdeen, he had been educated at Scots College Rome which he had entered in 1608, and he held a priory *in commendam* which he kept until 1637. Although he was Principal for twenty years, he does not seem to have been very successful. In 1623, two Franciscan Fathers wrote to Rome to complain about the state of the college, saying that although the college had space for twenty students, it had only two, ad that the college had almost ceased to exist under Pendrick's rule.[10] Probably as a result of this complaint, the Nuncio at Paris in 1624, acting on instructions from Propaganda, sent his auditor, Signore Sforza, to inquire into the state of the college. His report was unfavourable, and it was suggested that the Jesuits be put in charge of the college, but Alexander Pendrick was able to show that this contravened Beaton's last will and testament.[11] What is even more telling against Pendrick is that he was dismissed from office on 9 September 1637. The grounds of dismissal are not too specific, but do suggest that his administration had not been satisfactory. The Prior of the Carthusians relieved him of office

on account of different and continual infirmities which have beset him for some time and other occupations he may have besides which no longer allow him to fulfil the said office and function with the necessary care and diligence.[12]

A contemporary Scots priest, Gilbert Blakhal, did not have a high opinion of him either, maintaining that Pendrick had conspired with a Mr Forbes to make out that Blakhal was a liar, but we have only one side of that story. It is perhaps a cruel chance that we have only negative reports on Pendrick. It seems most likely that numbers had risen before his dismissal, and a priest by the name of George Galloway donated a house in the *rue des Postes* to the college in 1636, which he would hardly have done if he had considered the college to be a complete failure.

David Chambers (1637–1641)

David Chambers was appointed as successor; he was a man of action and of influence. The son of Patrick Chambers of Fintray, he had been at Aberdeen University, and was a convert to the Catholic faith.[13] It is quite possible that he had been a student in the Scots College Paris, as no other college has record of him, and it was from Paris that he was recommended to Cardinal Barberini in 1609 by both George Strachan[14] and the Jesuit, Fr William Crighton.[15] David Chambers was the one who, before the missionary expedition of 1613, advised the Jesuit James Moffat, and in all probability John Ogilvie as well, to visit William Sinclair, the lawyer in the Canongate who reset priests.[16] Between 1610 and 1623,[17] he had been entrusted with various missions by the Holy See, after which he had written and published two books, *De Statu Honinis Veteris* (Chalons 1627) and *De Scotorum Fortitudine* (Paris 1631) thus responding to a great need as there was a dearth of writings by Scottish Catholics. After being in Rome in 1630, he went to work in Scotland in the following year, whence he sent a report to Propaganda in 1633, describing the state of the mission, and asking for the appointment of a bishop.[18]

For the better management of the college, and to correct the abuse of Grisy bursaries being in the possession of men who had finished their studies, Chambers got the Archbishop of Paris to amalgamate the foundation of David of Moray with that of Archbishop Beaton, and this was ratified by act of the French Parliament in 1639. To facilitate this action, three of the four bursars resigned their bursaries; the three were David Chambers himself, John Black and Patrick Con;[19] none of them had held a bursary for very long. Avery believed that the fourth bursary was held by Alexander Pendrick,[20] but Pendrick had in September 1637 resigned his bursary in favour of David Chambers,[21] and it seems unlikely that if he had held two bursaries, he would have resigned the one and not the other after his dismissal which was on 9 September 1637.

A fortunate discovery by Professor Christopher Smout, the Historiographer Royal, in the letters of the first John Clerk of Penicuik,[22] has revealed an incident in Paris in the principalship of David Chambers.[23] A son of Clerk's friend William Forrester had been received into the Scots College Paris in October 1638. Within eight days Clerk had written to his friend in some alarm, fearing greatly that his son would be converted to Catholicism, since he deemed it impossible that a young man who was a Scotsman and scholar could live besides Scotsmen who were papists without being persuaded to change his religion. By the following February, young Forrester, who had since left the college, had been back at the college to tell his old student friends about Clerk's letter. Whereupon several students from the college mustered at Clerk's house to protest that Clerk 'had called them all Begars and poore mens sons'. In Clerk's words:

> sum of thos young men cam doun to the house where I lodged and told a frind of myne that you had put bak on of my letters which I wroat to you concerning your sonne — and that they would produce it befor me, and that they would have amends of me.[24]

John Clerk was so annoyed that in asking Forrester if had returned the letter to Paris, he declared 'for if it be so, you have done to bring me in trouble and in great hazard of my life'.[25]

Although John Clerk does not name any of the '10 or 12 Scotts men' at the college, we do know the names of seven who were at the college at least close to this time — William Ballantine, later Prefect of the Scottish Mission, who was a student in Paris before going to Rome in 1641,[26] James Crighton and Thomas Lumsden who were to accompany Ballantine as missioners to Scotland in 1653, James Ramsay and John Black who later worked as priests in France, Robert Barclay, later Principal of the College, and Patrick Con who did not reach the priesthood but became a distinguished layman in the service of Cardinal Barberini. Thus we have evidence of a remarkably good set of students in David Chambers' principalship, and four of these, William Ballantine, Thomas Lumsden, James Crighton and Robert Barclay were in the team that put the secular mission on a completely new footing in the early sixteen-fifties, as will be recounted in the next chapter. They would appear to have been influenced and inspired by David Chambers.

George Leith (1641–1655)

David Chambers died in office in 1641, and was succeeded by George Leith. He was from the diocese of Aberdeen, had been a student in Scots College, Paris before going to Scots College Rome in 1634.[27] Since he left Rome as a priest in 1641, and the date of his appointment to Paris was 31 January 1641,[28] the principalship must have been his first appointment. We know little about his administration, but it does not seem to have been outstanding.

In 1649, the Jesuit Father Christie wrote to Rome, complaining about the 'imperfection and abuse of this Scottish hous…discredite to catholiks and to our nation.'[29] This was followed by a serious attempt by the Jesuits to take over the college. Fr Gall who was in charge of the Jesuit college in Paris hoped to obtain the help of the Marquise de Sécence, niece of Cardinal Rochefoucauld, first Lady of Honour to the Queen-Regent, whose spiritual directors were Jesuits. Gall hoped that Pope Innocent X could be persuaded that the Carthusians, being an enclosed order, were unsuitable overseers. Disappointment at finding no mention of the Jesuits in Beaton's will, did not prevent Father Christie S. J. from suggesting to Fr Gall that a direct approach should be made to the sovereign pontiff. The Carthusians and the staff of the college were, however, united in opposition to the Jesuit scheming, and they gained the support of the University of Paris, so that nothing came of the Jesuit intrigue.[30]

George Leith resigned his office, and left the college in either July or August 1655. He may have been handicapped by poor health, and this could explain both the brief principalship of Gilbert Blakhal and the later confusion about the length of Robert Barclay's principalship, if these two had alternately stood in for him during illness.

Gilbert Blakhal (1653)

Malcolm Hay listed Gilbert Blakhal as Principal, tentatively dating his spell of office from 1651 until 1653. There are three pieces of evidence pointing to Blakhal being Principal for a short time:

1. Father Richard Brown, S. J., writing from Clermont College to Rome on 5 September 1653 stated that, 'Monsieur Leith is master againe in the College heere, Monsieur Barclay prefect under him, and Monsieur Blakhal retired.'

This would appear to mean that Blakhal was retired from the position of Principal.

2. There is a document in the Archives of Propaganda at Rome, dated 1653 (no month) signed jointly by Gilbert Blakhal and Robert Gall, representing the Scots College and Clermont College.[31]

3. Bishop Forbes in his introduction to Kalendars of Scottish Saints stated that Gilbert Blakhal presided over the college after George Leith from 1660–1662. Clearly he got the dates wrong, as Robert Barclay was certainly Principal in those years, but he seems to have preserved a tradition of Blakhal having been Principal.

In endeavouring to date Blakhal's period of office, account must be taken of the autobiographical details in his *Breiffe Narration* which gives his story until March 1653. The date is not given explicitly, but can be arrived at thus. Blakhal's illness, recorded near the end of the book, was after the second war of Paris[32] more commonly known as the Fronde of the Princes. Although this war did not finally end until after the treaty of 31 July 1653, the fighting in Paris ceased after Louis XIV triumphantly entered the capital on 21 October 1652. Blakhal thought that he was going to die on the seventh day of his illness 'which was Saterday, the eight of February.'[33] In N.S. calendar, 8 February was a Saturday in 1653. The illness continued for another month.

In placing this principalship after Blakhal's illness, and before Leith took charge again, we may conclude that it was very short, probably only meant to be temporary, and confined to 1653 (some time between March and September).

Gilbert Blakhal was a colourful character to have as Principal. Born in Aberdeen diocese, after having been a soldier, he was educated and ordained in Rome. In 1630 he went as a missioner to Scotland, but finding that he could not work there on account of the Jesuits, he went to Paris where he became a chaplain to Lady Isabella Hay. After a brief spell of work in England where he was chaplain to an uncle of Lord Witherington, he returned to Scotland in 1637 where he had a very fruitful ministry until 1642 when he took Lady Henrietta to Paris. These details are gleaned from his ms which is entitled *A Breiffe Narration of Services done to Three Noble Ladies* which was published by the Spalding Club in 1844. In this unusual work, Blakhal paints himself as an eccentric swashbuckling priest who on his journeys rode with sword, four pistols, and a musket or carabine. His account of his adventures has the air of exaggeration and melodrama. Nevertheless it is valuable as giving an account of how a Scottish Catholic missioner exercised his ministry in a noble household, and journeyed from there round a circuit of Mass stations. Blakhal probably wrote this manuscript in the Scots College. Certainly it remained there, where the students could read it, and later in 1671, one of them, Alexander Leslie, made a manuscript copy. Blakhal was to return to Scotland again c. 1668, and died in France on 1 July 1671.

Summary of this Period

We know the names of thirty students from this period, fifteen of whom became priests, but only five of whom were ordained in Paris while seven students went to Rome, three to Douai, three to Würzburg, and one to Madrid. This shows that the college at this time served more as a junior seminary than as a senior seminary. Eleven of the fifteen priests were seculars, two were Jesuits, one Benedictine, and one a Canon of St Genevieve. Thus the lure of the religious orders was not as strong in Paris as it was in Rome. Our records being so scanty, it is quite possible that some other priests were trained at Paris. There are, for example, two priests who came to the Scottish mission whose names are not found among the students from any other college. They are John Rollock who came to the mission in 1624, and John Riddoch who came to the mission before the end of 1637, apparently in company with Thomas Chambers. Was Thomas Algeo, who served in the household of Lady Abercorn, a disguised priest?[34] And if so, where was he educated? This possibility of other ordinations, and also the likelihood that more Roman students did preliminary studies in Paris, must be borne in mind when we compare Scots College Paris with Scots College Rome. It must be admitted that the Scots College Rome produced more priests than the Scots College Paris. From 1602 until 1655, seventy-eight students of the Scots College Rome reached the priesthood (but not all for the secular clergy; twenty-six became Jesuits, and a further twenty-six joined other religious orders). We are not, however, comparing colleges in identical situations. Paris was not exclusively a seminary, and it took very young students, while Rome was almost completely a senior seminary. Also the missionary oath which Roman students had to take, usually six months after entering, meant that Scots College Rome was accepting only those who were fully determined to become priests, whereas Paris was able to receive those who had not so definitely made up their minds. It was good to have a college that provided for the latter category.

Despite the fact that the Scots College Paris had provided far fewer priests than the Scots College Rome in the first half of the seventeenth century, it had an advantageous position within the University of Paris, affording an opportunity of producing a very learned clergy, able not only to debate if opportunity arose, but to produce Catholic literature which was so much needed in Scotland.

NOTES

1. Felibien, M., *Histoire de la ville de Paris* (Paris 1725), Vol I, p.562.
2. SCA/CA 1/7, Necrology of the Scots College Paris.
    Geddes MS collection (1793) fol.64, quoted by Hay, M.V., *The Blairs Papers (1603–1660)* (London & Edinburgh 1929), p.105n.
3. Fraser, A., *The Frasers of Philorth* (Edinburgh 1879), Vol II, p.147.
4. SCA/CA 1/7, Necrology of the Scots College, Paris, 8 February 1661.
5. 'Robert Philip', *Dictionary of Scottish Church History & Theology*, Ed. N.M. de S. Cameron, (Edinburgh 1993).
6. Vatican Library, Rome, Barb Lat 8614, f.85.
7. SCA/GC 13/1, Avery, f.72.

8. *Records of the Scots Colleges I*, (Aberdeen 1906), p.101.

9. Panzani, G., *The Memoirs of Gregorio Panzani*, (Birmingham 1793), p.165.

10. Hay, M.V., op. cit., pp.106f..

11. Ibid. p.75 n.1.
    Anson, P.F., *Underground Catholicism in Scotland 1622–1878* (Montrose 1970), p.49.

12. SCA/GC 13/1 Avery f.80.

13. Hay, M.V., op. cit. p.111.

14. Vatican Library, Rome, Barb Lat 8614 fol.57, G. Strachan to Card. Maffeo Barbarini (Rome) 13 June 1609.

15. Vatican Library, Rome, Barb Lat 8614, fol,56, W. Creitton to Card. Maffeo Barbarini (Rome) 28 Sept 1609.

16. *Original Letters,* Vol II (Edinburgh 1851), p.447.

17. Dellavida, G.L., *George Strachan* (Aberdeen 1956), p.25.

18. Hay, M.V., op. cit. p.111.

19. SCA/GC 13/1 (Avery) ff.85, 88, 91.

20. Ibid. f.92.

21. Durkan, J., 'Grisy Burses at Scots College Paris', *Innes Review* 22 (1971), p.51.

22. SRO Edinburgh GD 18/2364/6, John Clerk (Paris) to William Forrester.

23. Halloran, B.M., 'Spirited Scottish Students: the Scots College Paris in 1639', *Innes Review* 45 (1994), pp.171–177.

24. SRO Edinburgh GD 18/2364/6, John Clerk to William Forrester, 10 Feb 1639.

25. Ibid.

26. Vatican Library, Rome, Barb Lat. 8628, f.28.

27. *Records of Scots Colleges I*, p.110. (No.122).

28. SCA/GC 13/1 (Avery), f.113.

29. W. Christie to A. Leslie, 14 Sept 1649, cited in Hay, M.V., op. cit. p.124.

30. Hay, M.V., op. cit. pp.75–77, p.129.

31. Ibid. p.108.

32. Blakhal, G., Breiffe Narration (Aberdeen 1844), p.213.

33. Ibid. p.214.

34. Lees, J.C., The Abbey of Paisley (Paisley 1878), p.267.

CHAPTER 4

The College under Robert Barclay

Robert Barclay became Principal of the Scots College after George Leith. The date of the commencement of Barclay's principalship is, however, difficult to determine. His epitaph in the Scots College says that he died on 7 February 1682 in the thirtieth year of his rule,[1] and his successor Louis Innes said that he had been Principal for more than thirty years.[2] Alexander Winster, on the other hand, wrote on 10 December 1668 that he had been Principal for fourteen years,[3] which fits rather better with what appears to be a hand-over list of property from George Leith to Robert Barclay on 5 July 1655.[4] The epitaph over Barclay's tomb in the chapel of the Scots College declares that he was from a noble Scots family.[5] The word 'noble' (*nobilis*) had a wide meaning in the seventeenth century, and did not necessarily connote belonging to the peerage; nevertheless, Robert Barclay was from a distinguished family of the landed gentry who could trace their ancestry back to Theobald de Berkeley who was born in 1110, the third year of Alexander I's reign.[6] His father was David Barclay of Mathers and his mother Elizabeth Livingston, daughter of Sir John Livingston of Dunnipace.[7] He was thus a brother to Colonel David Barclay who served in Cromwell's parliaments of 1654 and 1656, and uncle to the famous Quaker apologist, Robert Barclay, whom we will have occasion to mention later.[8] Since the epitaph of Principal Robert Barclay says that he died about the age of seventy, and as he was a younger brother to David who was born in 1610, we may deduce that he was born about 1611 or 1612. He graduated with a Master's degree from Aberdeen University in 1633.[9] After his conversion to the Catholic Faith, as we are told by Alexander Winster, he studied philosophy and theology at the Scots College Paris.[10] The testimony of Louis Innes that Barclay was educated in the seminary of St Nicolas du Chardonnet[11] does not contradict this, as students were sent out to other colleges for most of their classes, and the most frequented college was that of St Nicolas. After ordination, Barclay taught for six years in the Seminary of St Nicolas du Chardonnet where he was staying in 1650.[12] By 5 September 1653, he was Prefect of Studies in the Scots College under Goerge Leith,[13] but whether or not part of his six years teaching in St Nicolas' College was concurrent with his being Prefect of Studies in the Scots College is impossible to say.

Robert Barclay had been involved in the planning stages of a momentous development for the Scottish Catholic secular priests in 1653. For the first time since the Reformation they were constituted into a missionary body, with an annual income of 500 crowns provided by Propaganda, under a leader who was appointed Prefect. Not surprisingly, the plans for this had been devised in Paris which had the only establishment that was under the control of the Scottish secular clergy, the Scots College Paris. William Ballantine, who was a former pupil of the college had spent a further two years there after his ordination to the priesthood. In 1649 he left for the Scottish mission, only to return in 1650, or even at the end of 1649, convinced of the need for some sort of organisation and a regular source of income. A number of Scottish priests were in Paris at the time including William Leslie who was staying with the priests of St Nicolas du Chardonet,[14] Robert Barclay who was teaching in St Nicolas du Chardonnet, and John Walker recently ordained in Rome. They began to discuss the situation. The first stage of achievement was that Ballantine and Walker were designated as missioners in 1650, and provided with a pension by Propaganda. They then appointed Robert Barclay as their agent in Paris, the witnesses to the document of appointment being George Leith, Principal of the Scots College, and Thomas Chambers, a Scots priest who was an almoner to Cardinal Mazarin.[15] Cardinal Barberini, papal legate to France, became very interested in helping the Scottish priests, and promised to further their case in Rome. The missioners decided that it was best to have one of their number permanently in Rome to act as their agent. The choice fell on William Leslie who, being offered a place in Cardinal Barberini's household, accompanied the Cardinal on his way back to Rome. In Rome, negotiations with Propaganda were successful, and in 1653 William Ballantine was appointed Prefect of the Mission. In that year he proceeded to Scotland with a team of four other secular priests, John Walker, Thomas Lumsden who resigned a Professorship of Divinity in Paris, John Smith and James Crighton.

The College as a Refuge for Exiles

In Scotland, penal laws against Catholics could still be invoked if zealots insisted. When it became impossible for missioners to remain in Scotland, a safe haven was found for them in the Scots College Paris. John Walker was the first to come. He had been arrested at Strathbogie Castle on Ash Wednesday 1655 along with Francis White (a Lazarist priest who had been sent to Scotland by St Vincent de Paul) and Fr William Grant, a Jesuit priest. The arrests were carried out with the authority of a decree against priests extorted from Cromwell the previous year by Covenanting ministers. The decree had remained unenforced for six months because of the general reluctance to carry it out, but certain magistrates, strangely described as Anabaptists, consented to do so under pressure from the ministers.[16]

Walker's friends thought that his life might be in danger because of his adhesion to the royal cause. Ballantine paid £100 sterling for Walker's bail (later refunded by Propaganda), and he was sent to Paris. Although he came to Paris to find a place of refuge after imprisonment, he became a member of the college staff. Frequently in Jesuit letters, he is spoken of as acting with Barclay or on behalf of Barclay. In Barclay's time, there were never more than two priests on the staff. Barclay was Principal and Procurator, and the other was usually Prefect of Studies. Although this title does not seem to have been formally applied to Walker, he was probably fulfilling this role. During his two years in Paris, Walker used his time well to finish and publish his work entitled *The Presbytery's Triall*,[17] an apologetic work he had begun in Scotland, based on theological dialogues with Mr Irvine of Drum whom Walker had received into the Catholic Church.[18]

Walker returned to Scotland in 1658, but the college soon had another 'refugee', this time the Prefect of the Mission, William Ballantine, who came in August 1658 following his release from prison. Ballantine's capture was not due to any hostility against Catholics in Scotland, but to a freak set of circumstances. He was going to France in 1656 when his boat was captured by an Ostend cruiser, and taken to that port. When it was discovered that Ballantine was a priest, he was immediately set at liberty. An English nobleman, however, seeing him so well treated, thought that he must be a spy, and reported the same to Cromwell. Orders were issued to watch for his return, and he was arrested at Rye. (Some are surprised at his return to the same port from which he had left, but it was because he had left his horse there.) To explain his release, he had to tell the authorities that he was a priest, and on this account he was imprisoned for two years. During that time, Thurloe, Cromwell's secretary had frequent conversations with him. On his release, he was banished and hence his stay in the Scots College, Paris, where he was made Prefect of Studies.[19] He too devoted some of his time to writing, and published a little book, entitled *Preparation for Death*, 'and at the same time, preserved such rules for the scholars' improvement as conduced to the qualifying of the worthy labourers that College sent home from time to time for the support of the Mission.'[20] He also advised that the College in Paris should be used as a pastoral training centre for priests ordained in Rome; it was suggested that 'they should for a year or two study in the Scots College of Paris, moral, practical and polemic divinity, to administrate the holy sacraments, to catechise the children, instruct the people and especially to assist them at their death'.[21] Hitherto the community of St Nicholas du Chardonnet in Paris had sometimes been used for this purpose, and we have already seen that William Leslie had been there for a time.

A third banished priest who found refuge in the college was Alexander Burnet, who after his imprisonment in England resided in the college for two months in 1675. A student called Thomas Strachan said that 'it was not with his [Barclay's] good lyking he come to the Colledge if the Nunce had not given orders for it',[22] and maintained that the fifty livres he paid was 'to much for his entertainment',[23] but Strachan was at that stage a very disgruntled student who was looking for anything he might say against Barclay. Apart from priest exiles, Barclay had a rule that priest boarders should not be allowed to stay in the college, even if they paid for their lodgings. The reason for this regulation was to prevent priests lingering in Paris who might otherwise be employed in the Scottish mission.

The ban on priest boarders did not preclude hospitality to visitors, and Alexander Leslie, a former student, stayed at the college in 1680 when he was on his way to Rome to report on his visitation of Scotland, undertaken for Propaganda in 1678 and 1679. Leslie left Scotland on 6 July 1680, and travelled by way of Holland. He stayed some time in Paris to buy clothes for himself, and to put his *memoranda* in order, many of his papers being written in cypher for fear of discovery. Having recovered his health and strength, which had suffered on his journeys, he left Paris on 6 October 1680.[24] This visit occasioned an unfortunate misunderstanding over finance. Alexander Dunbar, the prefect of the mission, had written to Barclay on 9 June 1680, asking him to advance to Leslie when he arrived at Paris 'a hundred livers or fortie Crowns as he shall need, and these with his recett theron shall oblige me to repay thankfully the same.'[25] Barclay complied with his wishes, but when Alexander Leslie got 165 livres from another source, probably from Propaganda, Dunbar expected the advance to be repaid, but Leslie had no idea of this. When Barclay put the account to Dunbar, Dunbar protested, not realising that Leslie had retained both sums of money. When he did realise it, he wrote to Barclay on 7 July 1681, 'As for A.L. if he has retind all I cannot help it, seur I ame he should have contented himself with les, unless he has been extrordinarly straitned',[26] and in August 1681, 'as to the munie I shall lev it to be taken up by A.L. himself.'[27] When Alexander Leslie was approached for the money, he was dumbfounded, as he had had no idea that the first advance was only a loan.[28] Both Dunbar and Leslie took umbrage at Barclay, but the misunderstanding was not his fault. The fault lay with Dunbar who did not make it clear that he expected repayment on his advance.

Quarrels with the Jesuits

The Jesuits must have been very annoyed at the appointment of a secular priest as Prefect of the Mission. They regarded Scotland as their mission, had a poor regard of the secular clergy, and they were superior in numbers. The Jesuits, however, were not popular in Rome, and Propaganda favoured the secular clergy, believing that there would be more stability of personnel with them, whereas the regulars could recall missioners at will. For many years there had been tension between seculars and Jesuits, but never before had the Jesuits been confronted with a body of seculars so determined and so well organised. This helps to explain the quarrels that Barclay had to face with the Jesuits, as we shall see presently.

Just before Barclay's appointment as Principal, his *bête noire* had arrived in Paris. This was Father James Macbrec, sent as procurator of the Jesuit seminary, known as Clermont College. Of a good Scottish family, James Macbrec had entered the Society of Jesus as early as 1615, and was on the Scottish mission by 1627, eventually becoming Jesuit superior. He probably accompanied Montrose's army as chaplain.[29] In January 1653, he was arrested, imprisoned and condemned to death. After a reprieve from Cromwell, he was released from prison early in 1654, but had to leave Scotland at once.[30]

The problem for Barclay was that Macbrec had a very firm prejudice that only Jesuits could run seminaries, and that the Scots College, Paris could do no good at all. He was particularly prejudiced against Barclay, and constantly criticised him in his letters. These letters are, however, most useful now as they reveal the names of many students in the Scots College. What is probably true is that the college had not been well managed in the time of Barclay's predecessor, since the epitaph already referred to tells us that Robert Barclay restored the almost collapsed discipline of the house. Whether *disciplina* refers to behaviour or to the general ordering of college affairs, this does seem to be an admission by the college itself that all was not well when Barclay succeeded George Leith. The numbers in the college must have been very small; despite some recruiting by William Ballantine, there were only seven students in 1657. Malcolm Hay, referring to a letter of Macbrec dated '3rd' March 1657, states that the College was overcrowded at that time,[31] but he has misread the letter (and the date, which is 8 March 1657); the letter says:

> being daly youths coming hirther to Paris, because of the great correspondens with Scotland, and refuses them allagien [alleging] to be no plaise, albyet ther rents be the double of that of Douay and not so many in ther hous as there:[32]

Two other letters of Macbrec in the same year, one in May[33] and the other in June,[34] explicitly stated that there were only seven youths in the college. This would appear to be the total number, and not just the number of ecclesiastical students, since a letter of 29 May complained that the Scots College Paris had more rents than Rome and Douay but 'only 9 persons upon that rent.'[35] This would seem to mean the seven students and two staff, Barclay and Walker.

The turning away of students shows that Barclay was selective, and not willing to take numbers indiscriminately. In at least one case, his discrimination seems to have been vindicated. A former preacher called Alexander Gordon arrived in Paris in 1657 with many testimonials (he had even been in touch with St Vincent de Paul or Monsieur Vincent as he was then known),[36] but Barclay would not have him despite great pressure from the Jesuits who complained to the Cardinals of Propaganda.[37] Alexander Gordon was received into the Scots College, Rome, but left without orders, and entered a Benedictine monastery in Germany.[38] When he left there, he made no secret that he had come only as a spy,[39] but Macbrec, who related this information, did not say for whom. It is not at all impossible that Gordon was a political spy, as it was just about this time that John Thurloe, Cromwell's famous espionage agent, had become interested in the Catholic ecclesiastical network which included colleges abroad, and was trying to use this for espionage purposes. Thus in 1656 a Jesuit priest was recruited by Lord Broghill at Aberdeen to be a spy in Spain. Lord Broghill wrote to Thurloe on 22 April 1656:

> i have engaged a papist heere, that is one of my intelligencers, to gaine me a Jesuit who is now about Aberdeen, and is a man of much fitness for such a worke, if he can be won; and of that, I shall not be able to give you an answer this 3 weekes[40]

The recruitment was successful as Broghill communicated to Thurloe on 13 May 1656:

> I have dispatched away above a week since your orders concerning the jesuit to goe to Madrid. The inclosed is the cypher he is to make use of. I have bid Sir James MacDonnell give him this further instruction, to be diligent to learn (if possibly) who are the Spanish intelligencers in England.[41]

A letter of intelligence, sent on 5 Sept 1656 by Wescomb to Mons Witterd Anglois at the College of Clermont, Rue St Jacques à Paris,[42] shows that Catholic colleges abroad could be infiltrated by Thurloe's men, and Thurloe through his weekly conversations with William Ballantine when the latter was in prison, would have been well aware of the existence of the Scots College Paris.

If Alexander Gordon was a spy for the Cromwell government, it is possible that Robert Barclay had private information about him from his brother David who found it expedient to be one of the thirty members for Scotland returned to Cromwell's parliaments in 1654 and 1656, and was well acquainted with Thurloe's spy recruiter, Lord Broghill, who, writing to Thurloe on 19 August 1656, had mentioned David Barclay as one of the first four 'stanch men' chosen for Parliament.[43] Although in different religious camps, Robert and David Barclay were still on good terms, as can be seen from their meeting in France in 1659,[44] and David, being a royalist at heart, would hardly have scrupled to make such a disclosure to his brother.

Despite Macbrec's bad judgement in this case, we find him complaining again in 1659 that Barclay will not admit two students, called John Clarke and George Mackenzie. Macbrec said that he understood the refusal of the second because he did not intend to be a church man, but he saw no reason for the refusal of John Clarke.[45]

This might suggest that Barclay was ready to admit only ecclesiastical students, but such was certainly not the case, and we find Alexander Dunbar, as prefect of the mission, writing to request that certain *convictores* be sent not only to study mathematics, architecture and geography,[46] but also to learn fencing and dancing.[47] It would appear that James Macbrec did not appreciate that the Scots College in Paris was not exclusively for ecclesiastical students, which led him to be unfairly critical as regards the number reaching the priesthood.

The biggest problem for Robert Barclay was James Macbrec's determination to win his best students for the Jesuits. With the threat to Jesuit domination of the mission that was posed by the appointment of a secular Prefect Apostolic, the Jesuit hope for the future depended on keeping their numerical supremacy. The Douai and Rome colleges were run by Jesuits, where they could use their powers of persuasion to induce students to join their order. Paris was in secular hands, and so Macbrec tried his best to get its students transferred to Scots College, Rome, in most cases, against Barclay's will.

The first two we hear of being sent are George Baillie and William Hay *alias* Collinson in March 1656. Macbrec's own words show his intentions and his attitude towards Barclay's wishes:

> Thes two I am to send to your Rvs, they are the floure and the best of this colige, and I dout not but some day they both may becomme of societe and will prove with tyme excellent operarii in vinea Domi[ni]. Mr Barklay is noweis contentet they should departet from him and therefore would not gaive them any viatic at all, alleging if he did send them he wold have given them, but not otherweis.[48]

Although Macbrec wrote to the rector of Rome that he wanted these two for the Jesuit society, he did not disclose this to the staff of the Paris College, and he was surprised when they discovered it,

> when I did tell Mr Walker, or now Mr Scot [an alias] that Collisone was to take the oath he replayet to me we thocht to have him ane Jesuit. Upon what grounde he did replay this to me, I doe not know: so I believe they have ther privat inteligens.[49]

Barclay forbade his students to visit Clermont College or to have any correspondence with it,[50] but this rule was not kept by all, and it did little to curtail the activities of Macbrec, although he was fully aware of the regulation, and indeed constantly complained about it. The next two to be sent to Rome were Gilbert Menzies and Gilbert Gray in 1657. Gilbert Menzies was gradually induced by Macbrec to desire the Jesuit habit. In June 1655, Macbrec wrote, 'I think Lady Bagonys [Balgownie's] sone Gilbert Maniese could be indoused to come to Rome and studie his devinite ther.'[51] Two years later, with his plan about to be realised, Macbrec wrote,

As concerning Gilbert Menzies…if you will allow 10 pistols of spaine for his viatik[52] I shal be more partiqulare with him, to know if he intends shortly after his ther being, to enter the societe or not.'[53]

Only a week later he could say, 'Gilbert Menzies…and much inclinaet for the societe.'[54] It would appear that the Jesuits might have won him, but Gilbert Menzies left Rome in 1662 without becoming a priest.[55]

About Gilbert Gray, MacPherson wrote, 'He was enticed by the Jesuits to go to Rome in hopes he would become of their order.'[56] This is not quite accurate. Gilbert Gray himself very much wanted to go to Rome, and Robert Barclay with whom, according to Macbrec, Gray did not get on well, asked Macbrec to send him there, offering to pay half his viatic.[57] Macbrec at first refused as he thought him 'to[o] much for the seqular clargy and micht herme others which inclinaet for us',[58] but later, he sent him, hoping that he could be won over. 'Mr Gray is the third. I tould him that your Rvs had expressly writting for him and that he was much obliged to your Rvs we must indevour to gain him.'[59] Barclay absolutely refused to pay any of the viatic, because Macbrec had refused to send him when he requested.[60] So 'Fr Talbot did allow his viatik…because he intendet to see if he could being admittet in the societe'.[61] Gilbert Gray was not in fact persuaded to join the Jesuits, but he was scarcely a credit to the seculars as he apostatised in 1770, eight years after his ordination to the priesthood.

In August 1656, James Tyrie, grand-nephew of the celebrated Jesuit Father James Tyrie, came to the Scots College in Paris. Macbrec set his sights on him at his first arrival. In October, he wrote to Rome:

Two months ago ther is one heere arryvet, who came with Mr Ballantin Mr James Tayry who now studies to Divinete in the Scots Colge agens my advise whome I wold willing send to your Rvs or to Fr Cresty to studie to philosophy and verie fit for our so—ty [society]…Mr Barclay is verie gelous with me, and hath no wish any of his scolers sould such frequent me.[62]

Again, on 4 January 1658, Macbrec wrote:

> James Tayry, ane excellent spirit, and ane that wold be fit for the societe. Mr Barclay heere is no wais content with me, because he thinks all his scolers are detournet from remaining there.[63]

Despite the wishes of Robert Barclay, again expressed by Macbrec in July 1658 ('albyet the Pryour of the Chartreous and Mr Barclay has no wish that the laike of him [James Tayry] sould go from ther collige'),[64] Macbrec proceeded in sending Tyrie to Rome in October 1659, but once again his plans were frustrated. Tyrie left Rome in October 1662 on the pretext of ill health, and afterwards 'became a Protestant and teached in St Andrews with great plause and is esteemed a great witt.'[65]

Another seduced away from the college was a near cousin of Robert Barclay, called John Strachan. In October 1659, Macbrec was talking about sending him to Rome or Madrid;[66] in the following month, he wrote, 'he frequents me now.'[67] In a short time, John Strachan joined the Jesuits at Naples.

Macbrec was not always successful in getting students to Rome. He tried very hard with Alexander Gordon, Fr Talbot's cousin, but he had no desire to go. Another he tried hard to get to Rome was the brother of William Leslie, the Scots agent in Rome. Although in five different letters, Macbrec gave his name as 'John',[68] probably this was a mistake for Alexander Leslie, William Leslie's brother who came to the Scottish mission in 1672, and who had in May 1671 written a transcript of Blackhal's *Breiffe Narration* (signed A.P.L.) in the Scots College at Paris. There was another brother, John, later married to Jane Stewart of Tannachie,[69] at whose house at Tullochalin, Alexander Leslie spent the Christmas of 1678;[70] this would not exclude the possibility of him being an ecclesiastical student in Paris, but it seems more likely that the brother was Alexander, especially as studying syntax in 1663 would be just about right for completing his studies in 1672. Macbrec wanted the rector in Rome to persuade William Leslie to write to Robert Barclay to have his brother sent to Rome.[71] Then he tried to get Mr Con, a distinguished Scot in the service of Cardinal Barberini, to write to William Leslie for the same purpose,[72] but his scheme did not materialise.

It seems truly amazing that James Macbrec, who was himself the rector of a seminary, should have persisted in his schemes to empty another superior's college, and should have been so insensitive as not to understand why Barclay was so annoyed and had to ban his students from visiting Clermont College. Barclay did not allow the threat to go unchallenged; apart from his embargo on Clermont College, he spoke personally to Macbrec as we learn from Macbrec himself who wrote in August 1659, 'what debats I have had with Mr Barclay...With my consent non of that hous shal from hens forth send thether',[73] and again in the following month:

> but God knows best what ane debaet I have had with Mr Barclay, and what complents he has mead heere, to the Pryor of the Charterous and to others special persons with whome I have frequently adou for plaising at the that comis from our country in the nou Converts hous: and this all be the mayens of the Pryor of Chartous: that I dou nothing but debauches thes of his hous, and intendins to make ane novitiat of that hous, for our colligis.[74]

The ban on going to Clermont College seems to have been largely effective by that time, as Macbrec wrote to Father Talbot, 'Your Cousin Alexr comes no more to see me, nor any of that hous, having expres discharge therof by Mr Barclay for his owne vaine apprehensions he has of me.'[75] Nevertheless, John Strachan was frequenting Macbrec in the following November,[76] and it was as late as 1663 and 1664 that Macbrec was trying to get Leslie's brother to Rome.

In fact, Macbrec's enticements were largely in vain. The only student of the Scots College to join the Jesuit order was Barclay's cousin, John Strachan. He finished his theology course with some distinction at Naples[77] in 1667, and became for a very brief period Rector of the Scots College, Rome from 30 Nov 1670 until his death on 10 Feb 1671.[78]

There were, however, several students of Paris who joined other religious orders. John Davidson, who left Paris in 1667, became a Dominican after he was dismissed from Rome in 1671, and later he died on his way to the Scottish mission.[79] George Collinson, who left Paris in 1661, and Rome in 1665, was professed in the Benedictine order in 1667. (He died in France on 22 July 1686.)[80] Two more famous were Abbot Thomas Placid Fleming, Benedictine Abbot of Ratisbon, and Richard Augustine Hay, an Augustinian canon who was prominent in the Catholic revival at Holyrood in the time of James VII. Richard Hay did not have happy memories of the Scots College; he wrote of himself, 'till att length growing wearied of some hard and humersome dealings of Mr David Burnett [Prefect of Studies at Paris]...he withdrew to Charters.'[81] This contrasts sharply with the sentiments of Abbot Fleming who wrote to Barclay:

> The educatione I had from you som years, and the great favors received dureing that tyme, makes me not only retaine a fresh and gratefull resentement [favourable feeling] of yr kindness...[82]

The problem of students joining religious orders was a serious one for all the colleges. The inducements to join a religious order were great. Not only did the orders claim a greater sanctity and a greater learning, but they could provide a home for banished priests, and for priests in sickness and old age. In Scotland, before 1650, secular missioners had no regular source of income, and secular clergy had sometimes been forced to leave the mission for lack of finance. Religious orders provided security, but the difficulty was that many who became regular clergy did not return to the mission. In pontifical colleges, a remedy was sought by means of the missionary oath, by which students vowed to become priests and to serve on the mission. In Rome, the oath was introduced by a Jesuit rector, Father Patrick Anderson in 1615, and the first record we have of students taking the oath in Scots College, Rome is in 1616.[83] This oath, however, did not prevent candidates joining religious orders; many did so, and were easily dispensed from that part of the oath which bound them to the mission. Colleges objected, the English and the Greek being the first to protest, and so Pope Urban VIII added a clause whereby misssioners bound themselves to work for three years on the mission before they could join a religious order. Even this did not prove effective. William Leslie pointed out to Propaganda that some priests just longed for their three years on the mission to be over, thereby making their missionary efforts languid and spiritless. Then they left the mission for their novitiate in a religious order, and seldom returned until they were too advanced in years to do much effective work. Propaganda resolved that the students' oath should be for permanent service on the mission, and got this approved by Pope Alexander VII in 1660. The Jesuits continued to entice students, and hoped for special confessors' faculties for the commutation of vows in a jubilee year, but a long letter to the students of Scots College Rome from William Leslie in 1674 seems to have won them over, and virtually put an end to the problem.[84]

It is commonly supposed that Scots College, Paris, had no missionary oath such as there was in the Scots College, Rome. This is not strictly correct; while it is true that the missionary oath was never compulsory at the Paris College, there was a voluntary oath, and according to the College Constitution of 1707,[85] those who had been a year in the college and took the oath acquired the status of *socius*. In practice, however, all ex-students of the college are described as *socii*, and so the title *socius* cannot safely be used to ascertain how many took the oath. The oath was in existence before the compilation of the Statutes, as a form of the oath from Barclay's time is still extant.[86] The reason for its introduction was most probably, as at Rome, the fear of priests joining religious orders and not going to the Scottish mission.

College Building

In 1662, Robert Barclay began the development of the new college building. This date is sometimes quoted as if it were the beginning of the building's functional existence, but in fact it is the date of the purchase of the site, at the cost of 27,000 livres, in the *Fossés St Victor*, today known as *Rue Cardinal Lemoine*. We learn from Felibien's *Histoire de la ville de Paris* that the new building was ready only in 1665.[87] There is one indication of exact numbers soon after the new building was opened. This was in the year 1669 when a request to Propaganda on 17 September 1669 said that, there were twelve students; this is the total number, including ecclesiastical students and *convictores*, as the report stated explicitly that the students were under no obligation to become priests or to return to Scotland after their studies.

It is surprising not to find any reference to the new building in Macbrec's letters, but it may have been one of the influencing factors in Macbrec's desire to amalgamate the Scots College, Douai with the Scots College, Paris. He writes to Fr Talbot in July 1667:

> I have wreting dayvers letters to Fr Gordon, to take this occasion to present to the King ane petion [petition] for the union of the Scots Collige of Douay with this of Paris & so make ane galland collige of them, both for his Maisty servis, and the good of pour coutry & Mission...All I feare wil be the oposition of the Charterous: yet if so be that the King wil grant to it, and declare that it is his wish, that union be performet: The Charterous...may be movet to grant willingly what the King desayris.[88]

As the Jesuits had no authority whatsoever in the Scots College Paris, one cannot but be astounded at the impertinence of Macbrec; one doubts if even his own order could have taken him seriously, and needless to say, his plan of amalgamation was not even attempted.

The purchase of the site in the *rue des fossés St Victor* was not the only one made by Barclay. On the 25 October 1661, he bought a house at Passy on *the grande route au Bois de Boulogne*, and on the 6 May 1662, he bought for 18,000 livres the remaining third of a house in the *rue des Oiseaux*, two-thirds of which had been bought by Principal George Leith on 29 December1648. On the 13 October 1673, before notaries, the whole of a small house in the *rue des fossoyeurs* or *Servandoni* was adjudged college property without contest. In Barclay's time, the college owned at least seven houses — the new college built in the *rue des fosses St Victor*, the building donated by Archbishop Beaton at *rue des Amandiers*, a house in *rue des Postes* No. 9 donated in 1636 by a Scottish priest called George Galloway, Canon of St Quentin, the three houses already referred to, at *rue des Oiseaux*, at *rue des fossoyeurs*, and at Passy,[89] and a seventh in the *rue des Deux Boules* which Louis Innes wanted Charles Whyteford to sell in December 1687.[90] The houses not used by the students were rented out to provide revenue for the college, although between a third and 40% of the rents was used on maintenance of the buildings. These rents, and the rent from the farm at Grisy, bought by David of Moray at the beginning of the college's existence would have provided some of the money for the new buildings, and Barclay was very insistent on fees being paid for the students, but it is still surprising that he could have built so lavishly. Undoubtedly, there were Scottish benefactors, and from the Necrology of the College a list of those in Barclay's time can be constructed. It includes William Fraser (*socius quondam*), Margaret Maitland of Lethington, Patrick Menteith of Salmonet, Thomas Chambers (priest and *socius*), David Archibald (canon of St Quentin), James Ramsay (priest and *socius*), Charles Fountain (priest), Alice Banks of Borlace, and Patrick Con (*socius*). Barclay also contributed from his own personal money.

In 1672, Barclay further enhanced the college by building a north wing and a fine chapel. No one could deny that Barclay provided a fine edifice, but there were those who regarded his achievement as self-aggrandisement; Thomas Strachan wrote, 'Mr Barclay does rather improve this hous to pleas his owne humors, nor to any publick good of the nation',[91] but Thomas Strachan was a disgruntled student on the point of leaving. As Barclay never filled the college, one could argue that it was too big; one could also reason that he had faith in the future, and that he believed a grand building might attract sons of the more distinguished families in Scotland.

In addition to the building programme, Barclay sought and obtained privileges to ease the burden of being obliged to have constant recourse to Rome for faculties. On 17 September 1669, a two-fold request was made to Rome. The first petition was for faculties to give the first tonsure. In 1617, Pope Paul V had issued a brief, which was confirmed by Pope Urban VIII in 1643, granting permission to promote students of the college to minor orders on testimonial letters supplied by the rector only, and to ordain students from there even though they were without benefice or patrimony, but no mention had been made of first tonsure, and so Pope Clement IX was asked to confirm the briefs and include first tonsure. The second request was for faculties to dispense students from an impediment to ordination, since the Holy Office had declared that having been heretic, or being a child of heretics was an impediment to ordination to the priesthood.[92]

For the internal government of the college, Robert Barclay set for himself firm guidelines, but he was not intransigent when special needs arose. It has already been seen that for the sake of banished priests, he made exceptions to his rule that the college would not entertain priest boarders. A similar rule was his insistence that all students should pay a pension. It is doubtful, however, whether Barclay was as inflexible with this rule as he was later claimed to be; at least Alexander Dunbar or Winster wrote to the college asking if Glastirim's son, James Gordon, could be taken free,[93] although later David Burnett's accounts show that Glastirim was paying a pension for his son. Dunbar made a similar request for his own nephew, James, especially because his father had been drowned in a fishing-boat accident,[94] and Barclay granted this request.[95]

Barclay's interest was not confined to his own college, but he was deeply concerned to do all he could for the Scottish mission, especially in the provision of priests; this was recognised by the Prefect, Alexander Dunbar, when in 1665, he recommended that Robert Barclay and Patrick Con, Barberini's secretary and an *alumnus* of the Scots College Paris, who had been of great service to the mission, should be consulted as regards the merits of priests who might be suggested for the mission by the Archbishop of Armagh who was at that time in Paris with a view to sending Irish missionaries to Scotland.[96] Two years later, in 1667, Barclay introduced two Franciscans, Francis and Mark Macdonnel to the Nuncio at Paris as willing to go on the Scottish mission. Propaganda granted money for their journey to Scotland, and the same allowance as was given to secular priests on the mission. They left for Scotland in May 1667, and though delayed by illness, they both reached the mission in January 1668.[97]

Estimate of Robert Barclay

Robert Barclay was not without his critics both in his own lifetime and after his death. We have already seen how Thomas Strachan accused him of improving the college to enhance his own prestige, and he added 'and we that are in the Colledge must all our necessaries of him be way of Chartie and not as due.'[98] These may be taken as the criticisms of a discontented student on the point of departure, but surprisingly, at the same time, we find Louis Innes, still a student, also passing censure on Barclay's actions. He tells John Irvine, who had left Paris for Rome, that he had defended Irvine against Barclay, 'I so defended you and confuted all his arguments (the most part of which are meer Calumnies).'[99] This is indeed strong language, yet one cannot help but sympathise with Barclay who had suffered much from Macbrec's sending students to Rome, and John Irvine had gone to Rome without writing to Barclay at his parting.

More seriously he was severely criticised by Alexander Dunbar, the Prefect of the Mission. Alexander Dunbar went to Paris in 1668, and was to remain there for four years; he had hoped to write for the benefit of the mission, but does not appear to have done so. One might have expected him to have resided at the Scots College, but instead he chose to stay with the Marquis of Huntly.[100] From Paris, he sent a detailed report on the Scots mission to Propaganda in December 1668. In this report, he mentioned that he had that year sent five youths to Scots College, Paris. He also complained about the defective state of all Scots Colleges, contending that all had pressing need of reform. Madrid was singled out as the worst since up to that time, it had produced only five priests. Dunbar observed that the seminaries had produced three times as many regular priests as secular priests for the Scottish mission.[101] The inclusion of Paris in this general complaint seems to have been rather harsh, considering the efforts of Ballantyne to enforce suitable rules, the new buildings erected by Barclay, the two Franciscan missionaries' arrival in Scotland on Barclay's recommendation that very year, and two ordinations to the priesthood, of John Irvine and Alexander Irvine, in the college the previous year. There is, however, a background story.

In March of this year, Dunbar had written to Propaganda, suggesting that Barclay who had been ordained for the mission but had never gone there (which was in fact inaccurate as Barclay had been ordained without the obligation of going to the mission, as Dunbar later acknowledged),[102] should be sent to Scotland, and that he, Alexander Dunbar, be made Principal of Scots College in his place, arguing that he would be more dependent on the Congregation, and that, as he had spent six years as Prefect of the Mission, he would be in a position to choose suitable candidates for the priesthood from the various provinces of Scotland, and give them the training required for missionary work at home.[103] This complaint against Barclay had been referred by Propaganda to the Nuncio at Paris[104] with the result that Barclay himself had in September requested Propaganda to initiate a visitation of the college, stating that the college was full of students, and that good results had come from a former visitation by Cardinal Roberti. The Congregation of Propaganda appointed the nuncio at Paris to do a visitation as requested.[105] Keeping this background in mind, it would be unwise to infer too much from the prefect's judgement of 'pressing need of reform'.

After Barclay's death, the same Alexander Dunbar wrote to his successor, Louis Innes, complaining of 'the hard and unjust usage I mett with from yr predecessor, wh I never expected to have mett with from any.'[106] This referred to a quarrel with Barclay in the last year of the latter's life. Barclay had Dunbar presented with a bill for 555 livres 'on ten days sight' in May 1681. Dunbar objected both to the amount 'wh is noways squeir', and to the manner of presentation, and therefore he wrote, 'I have therfor refused the bill, not being proper for me to be cited to Courts, nor expect executions this is the first I was ever put befor & I hope shall be the last.'[107] By August, it was known that Barclay was very ill and unlikely to recover; Dunbar wrote to him at the end of the month:

> I doe asseur yu tht I never intended by it [his letter] to offend yu in the lest, & if any thing has been therin wh has given yu occasione of anger or offence, I retract it freely and crave yr pardon.[108]

This may have been said merely because of the grave condition of Barclay's health, but having written this, it seems ungracious and unfair to have mentioned it again after Barclay's death. By contrast, David Burnet, who had worked with Barclay for four years, wrote to Innes in August 1681, 'I am sorry yr goodman is soo ill in his health, and am confident when it pleases god to call upon him, we will be at a losse almost irreparable.'[109]

Another who criticised after Barclay's death was William Leslie who accused him of theft, but Louis Innes staunchly defended Barclay and pointed out that he had left all his estate to the college.[110] Although Louis Innes did later find a claim against the college for 800 marks arising from 'Clastirim's transaction with Mr Lumsden', this was scarcely a case of theft.[111] What this most probably referred to was a legacy from Patrick Gordon of Glastirim which was invested at Paris; it was left to the Carthusian Prior to be given only to those who had been made priests in the college, and could be applied to viatics of the same when they went from Paris to Scotland. Innes admitted there was some substance in the claim, but, as it was not a clear-cut case, he referred it to the judgement of David Burnet who was procurator of the mission. Whereupon Alexander Dunbar 'generously remitted the whole', only desiring Innes to pay a tailor's bill for him in London which came to 104 livres.[112]

There is some evidence that Barclay was a stern disciplinarian, which may account for some students disliking him while others were full of admiration. In the college on the fourth storey between two student bedrooms there is a small room, known today as *le cachot*, which has all the appearance of a prison cell with an opening in the door through which food might have been passed. It is believed that misbehaving students were locked in this room. That such a form of discipline was used in the college in those days is not inconceivable, as Jesuit letters reveal two cases in Scotland of fathers locking their daughters in small rooms.[113] Even in the middle of the nineteenth century, Bishop Andrew Carruthers in the middle of dinner at a gentleman's house suddenly rose and left because he remembered that he had that morning locked a boy in a small closet![114]

During Barclay's principalship some hampering difficulties had arisen. The quarrel between Barclay and Macbrec was quite typical of Jesuit-versus-Secular rivalry, while the criticisms of William Leslie and Alexander Dunbar mark the beginning of tension between Rome-educated and Paris-educated clergy. These handicaps, however, are far outweighed in this period by the Barclay's positive contribution both to the college and to the Scottish mission.

Robert Barclay left a magnificent college building with a beautiful chapel, a prestige building that could compare well with that of any other nation. He further provided a good financial foundation by purchasing houses whose rents could bring in a constant revenue. His students were a credit to him. They included John Strachan who became Rector of the Scots College Rome, Robert Monro, the intrepid missionary martyr, Thomas Placid Fleming, the famous Benedictine Abbot, Alexander Leslie, the 'Visitator' of Scotland, Louis Innes who succeeded him as Principal, Charles Whyteford, also to become Principal, John Irvine (Cabrach) who built the first Catholic church in Scotland since the Reformation, the Augustinian Richard Augustine Hay, Thomas Innes, the future historian, Alexander Gordon, a great scholar of the Sorbonne, and James Gordon, the future Bishop. These were all men of great energy and great determination. In Barclay's time (1653–1682), fifteen secular priests followed the first five to the Scottish Mission. Of these, five were ordained in Paris, eight in Rome, and two in Spain. At least five, however, and probably six of those ordained in Rome had done previous studies in the Scots College Paris, while the other two had received pastoral training in Paris after their ordination, so that only the two from Spain, Charles Fountain and Sir George Innes, had received no education in Paris, and these two were far from being the most influential. Besides sending secular priests to Scotland, Principal Barclay had been influential in securing for the Scottish Mission the services of two Irish Franciscans. An assessment of Robert Barclay may be made in terms of the maxim, 'By their fruits, ye shall know them',[115] and during his lifetime, eighteen students of his college were ordained priests (though not all for the secular clergy), and after his death, four others who were students in his time. By the standards of the time, this was a splendid accomplishment.

The Scots College Paris, at which the missionary body had been planned, remained the financial agency for the mission, receiving all monies from Rome and forwarding them to the mission. The college provided a refuge for three exiled priests, and two books, one devotional and one controversial, were written by them within its walls. It is also highly probable that Gilbert Blakhal wrote his *Breiffe Narration*[116] in the college, possibly during his short spell as Principal, the work relating his ministry until that time, but not beyond it. Certainly the manuscript remained in the college, possibly with all its eccentricity providing some inspiration for the students.

The visitation of Scotland which was of great importance for further development, had been carried out by an *alumnus* of the Paris College, Alexander Leslie, ably assisted in this most arduous task by Robert Monro who had studied for two years in the college. Thus during Barclay's principalship, the Scots College Paris can be seen to have had a strong influence on the small Scottish Catholic Mission. If it is appropriate to speak of a golden age of the college, as some have done, the era of Robert Barclay should be included because the achievement and influence for good was as great at this time as at any other.

NOTES

1. Carr, J.L., *Le College des Écossais A Paris (1662–1962)* (Paris 1963), p.23.

2. SCA/Bl Lett 1/74/8, L. Innes (Paris) to Wm Leslie (Rome), 18 Sept 1682.

3. Propaganda Archives, Rome, SC (Scozia Vol I), f.670v.

4. Archives Nationales, Paris, *Étude Muret* No 91, liasse 306 (5/7/1655).

5. Carr, J.L. op. cit. p.23.

6. Barclay, R., *A Genealogical Account of the Barclays of Urie* (London 1812), p.5.

7. Ibid. pp.19f..

8. Barclay, H.F. & Wilson-Fox, A. (Eds), *A History of the Barclay Family* (London 1934), Vol III, p.168.

9. Anderson, P.J., *Roll of Alumni in Arts of the University and King's College of Aberdeen 1596–1860*, (Aberdeen: 1900), p.10.

10. Propaganda Archives, Rome, SC (Scozia Vol I), f.670v..

11. SCA, Bl Lett 1/74/7, Louis Innes to William Leslie, 7 June 1682.

12. SCA/GC 13/1, Avery, 'A collection of documentary information about the Scots College Paris collected in Paris by Fr Avery', Unpublished, f. 116.

13. Fr R. Browne to Rome, 5 Sept 1653, cited in Hay, M.V., *The Blairs Papers* (London & Edinburgh 1929), p.108.

14. Gordon, J.F.S., *The Catholic Church in Scotland* (Glasgow 1869), p.575.

15. SCA/GC 13/1, Avery, op. cit., f.116 citing Archives Nat., Étude Muret 91, l.286.

16. Bellesheim, A., *History of the Catholic Church in Scotland* (Edinburgh & London: 1887–1890) Vol IV, p.345.

17. Anderson, W.J., 'Presbyteries Triall', *Innes Review* 8, pp.86–90.

18. Gordon, J.F.S., op. cit. (Glasgow 1869), p.623.

19. Ibid. p.520.

20. Clapperton, W., 'Memoirs of Scotch Missionary Priests' Unpublished, Columba House, Edinburgh, Vol I, p.12.

21. Ibid. pp.16f.

22. SCA/Bl Lett 1/43/11, T. Strachan (Paris) to [a Jesuit in Rome?] 22 June 1675.

23. Ibid.

24. SCA, SM 2/9/1, Itinerary of Alexander Leslie, (which is a Copy from Aberdeen University, King's College, 2260 Box R.).

25. SCA/Bl Lett 1/61/6, A. Dunbar to R. Barclay 9 Jun 1680.

26. SCA/Bl Lett 1/68/7, A. Dunbar to L. Innes, 7 July 1681.

27. SCA/Bl Lett 1/68/9, A. Dunbar to L. Innes, 18 August 1681.

28. SCA/BlLett 1/70/15, A. Goodman of Convalhill [A. Leslie] to R. Barclay, 25 August 1581.

29. Hay, M.V., *Blairs Papers* (London & Edinburgh 1929), p.78.

30. Forbes Leith, W., *Memoirs of Scottish Catholics* (London, New York, Bombay & Calcutta.1909), Vol 2, pp.65–67.

31. Hay, M.V., op. cit. p.188.

32. SCA/BlLett. 1/19/2, Fr J. Macbrec to Fr. G. Talbot, 8 May 1657.

33. SCA/Bl.Lett. 1/19/4, Fr J. Macbrec to Fr G. Talbot, May 1657.

34. SCA/Bl.Lett. 1/19/7, Fr J. Macbrec to Fr G. Talbot, 15 June 1657.

35. SCA/Bl.Lett. 1/19/6, Fr J. Macbrec to Fr G. Talbot, 29 May 1657.

36. SCA/Bl.Lett. 1/19/7, Fr J. Macbrec to Fr G. Talbot, 15 June 1657.

37. SCA/Bl.Lett. 1/19/4, Fr J. Macbrec to Fr G. Talbot, May 1657.
    SCA/Bl.Lett. 1/19/6, Fr J. Macbrec to Fr G. Talbot, 29 May 1657.
    SCA/Bl.Lett. 1/19/7, Fr J. Macbrec to Fr G. Talbot, 15 June 1657.
    SCA/Bl.Lett. 1/19/9, Fr J. Macbrec to Fr G. Talbot, 17 Aug 1657.

38. *Records of the Scots Colleges I* (Aberdeen 1906), p.116, no. 182.

39. SCA/Bl.Lett. 1/23/8, Fr J. Macbrec to Fr G. Talbot, 27 June 1659.

40. Birch, T.(Ed), *A Collection of the State Papers of John Thurloe, Esq* (London 1742). Vol IV, p.726. (Lord Broghill to Secretary Thurloe, 22 April 1656.)

41. Ibid., Vol V, p.18. (Lord Broghill to Secretary Thurloe, 13 May 1656.)

42. Ibid, Vol V, p.346.

43. Barclay, H.F. & Wilson-Fox,A., *A History of the Barclay Family*, Vol III, p.54.

44. SCA/BlLett. 1/23/17, Fr J. Macbrec to Fr F. Dempster, 1659.

45. SCA/Bl.Lett. 1/23/12, Fr J. Macbrec to Fr F. Dempster, 5 Sept 1659.

46. SCA/Bl.Lett. 1/61/3, A. Dunbar to D. Burnet, 18 Mar 1680.
    SCA/Bl.Lett. 1/61/6, A. Dunbar to R. Barclay, 9 June 1680.
    SCA/Bl.Lett. 1/61/7, A. Dunbar, 29 June 1680.

47. SCA/Bl.Lett. 1/61/1, A. Dunbar to R. Barclay, 10 Feb 1680.
    SCA/Bl.Lett. 1/61/11, A. Dunbar to R. Barclay, 8 Oct 1680.

48. SCA/Bl.Lett. 1/17/6, Fr J. Macbrec to Fr G. Talbot, 24 Mar 1656.

49. SCA/Bl.Lett. 1/19/2, Fr J. Macbrec to Fr G. Talbot, 8 Mar 1657.

50. SCA/Bl.Lett. 1/17/9, Fr J. Macbrec to Fr G. Talbot, 14 May 1656.
    SCA/Bl.Lett. 1/17/7, Fr J. Macbrec to Fr G. Talbot, 14 Apr 1656.

51. SCA/Bl.Lett. 1/15/11, Fr J. Macbrec to Fr G. Talbot.

52. 'Viatic' or 'viatik' was money for a journey.

53. SCA/Bl.Lett. 1/19/7, Fr J. Macbrec to Fr G. Talbot, 15 June 1657.

54. SCA/Bl.Lett. 1/19/8, Fr J. Macbrec to Fr G. Talbot, 22 June 1657.

55. Anderson, P.J. (Ed.) *Records of Scots Colleges 1* (Aberdeen1906), p.116, no. 179.

56. Ibid. No. 178, p.115.

57. SCA/BlLett 1/19/3, Fr J. Macbrec to G. Talbot, 20 April 1657.

58. SCA/Bl.Lett. 1/17/7, Fr J. Macbrec to Fr G. Talbot, 14 April 1656.

59. SCA/Bl.Lett. 1/19/6, Fr J. Macbrec to Fr G. Talbot, 29 May 1657.

60. SCA/Bl.Lett. 1/19/8, Fr J. Macbrec to Fr G. Talbot, 22 June 1657.

61. SCA/Bl.Lett. 1/23/14, Fr J. Macbrec to Fr F. Dempster, 24 Oct 1659.

62. SCA/Bl.Lett. 1/17/15, Fr J. Macbrec to Fr G. Talbot, 29 Oct 1656.

63. SCA/Bl.Lett. 1/21/1, Fr J. Macbrec to Fr G. Talbot, 4 Jan 1658.

64. SCA/Bl.Lett. 1/21/12, Fr J. Macbrec to Fr G. Talbot, 19 July 1658.

65. SCA/Bl.Lett. 1/38/6, Fr A. Magee to Fr G. Talbot, 30 Oct 1669.

66. SCA/Bl.Lett. 1/23/14, Fr J. Macbrec to Fr F. Dempster, 24 Oct 1959.

67. SCA/Bl.Lett. 1/23/16, Fr J. Macbrec to Fr F. Dempster, 21 Nov 1659.

68. SCA/Bl.Lett. 1/27/10, Fr J. Macbrec to Fr G. Talbot, 17 Aug 1663.
    SCA/Bl.Lett. 1/27/11, Fr J. Macbrec to Fr G. Talbot, 21 Sept 1663.
    SCA/Bl.Lett. 1/27/13, Fr J. Macbrec to Fr G. Talbot, 14 Dec 1663.
    SCA/Bl.Lett. 1/28/5, Fr J. Macbrec to Fr G. Talbot, 1 Mar 1664.
    SCA/Bl.Lett. 1/28/11, Fr J. Macbrec to Fr G. Talbot, 26 Aug 1664.

69. Leslie, W.A., Laurus *Leslaeana* (Graz 1692), No. 103.
    Leslie, K.H., Historical *Records of the Family of Leslie (*Edinburgh 1869), Vol 3, p.373.

70. SCA/SM 2/9/1, Itinerary of Alexander Leslie, p.10.

71. SCA/Bl.Lett. 1/27/8, Fr J. Macbrec to Fr F. Dempster, 6 July 1663.
    SCA/Bl.Lett. 1/27/10, Fr J. Macbrec to Fr G. Talbot, 17 Aug 1663.
    SCA/Bl.Lett. 1/27/11, Fr J. Macbrec to Fr G. Talbot, 21 Sept 1663.

72. SCA/Bl.Lett. 1/27/13, Fr J. Macbrec to Fr G. Talbot,14 Dec 1663.

73. SCA/Bl.Lett. 1/23/13, Fr J. Macbrec to Fr F. Dempster, 29 Aug 1659.

74. SCA/Bl.Lett. 1/23/12, Fr J. Macbrec to Fr G. Talbot, 5 Sept.

75. SCA/Bl.Lett. 1/23/10, Fr J. Macbrec to Fr G. Talbot, 11 July 1659.

75. SCA/Bl.Lett. 1/23/16, Fr J. Macbrec to Fr F. Dempster, 21 Nov 1659.

77. SCA/Bl.Lett. 1/36/11, Fr J. Macbrec to J. Strachan, 27 Sept 1667.

78. *Records of Scots Colleges I,* p.190, no. 193.

79. Ibid. p.117.

80. Ibid. No. 188, p. 117.

81. Hay, R.A., *Genealogie of the Hayes of Tweeddale* (Edinburgh 1835), p.50.

82. SCA/Bl.Lett. 1/51/4, P. Fleming to R. Barclay, 27 Dec 1678.

83. *Records of the Scots Colleges I,* p.105, no.193.

84. Anderson, W.J., 'Abbé Paul Macpherson's History of the Scots College, Rome (1600–1792)*, 'Innes Review* 12 (1961), p.19, pp.23f, pp.40–49.

85. SCA/CA 1/10/2, Statutes of the College, Caput VII, No.3.

86. SCA/CA I/11, College Oath.

87. Felibien, *Histoire de la ville de Paris* (Paris 1725), Vol I, p.562.

88. SCA/Bl.Lett. 1/36/6, Fr J. Macbrec to Fr G. Talbot, July 1667.

89. SCA/CA 1/29, Farquharson, J., 'History of Scots College Paris' (unpub.), pp.12–14.

90. SCA/BlLett 1/113/3, L. Innes to C. Whyteford, 29 Dec 1687.

91. SCA/BlLett 1/43/11, T. Strachan to [a Jesuit in Rome], 22 June 1675.

92. Giblin, C. ' The "Acta" of Propaganda Archives and the Scottish Mission, 1623–1670', *Innes Review* Vol 5 (1954), p.73, n.127.

93. SCA/Bl.Lett. 1/50/14, A. Dunbar to R. Barclay, Jan 1678.

94. SCA/Bl.Lett. 1/47/8, A. Dunbar to R. Barclay, 2 Nov 1677.

95. SCA/Bl.Lett. 1/50/14, A. Dunbar to R. Barclay, Jan 1678.
96. Giblin, C., op. cit. p.65, n.93.
97. Ibid. p.67, n.102, p.71, n.120.
98. SCA/BlLett 1/43/11, T. Strachan to [a Jesuit in Rome], 22 June 1675.
99. SCA/Bl.Lett. 1/42/10, L. Innes to J. Irvine, 4 Sept 1675.
100. Propaganda Archives, SC (Scozia Vol I) f.671.
101. Bellesheim, A., op. cit., Vol IV, pp116–121.
102. Propaganda Archives, Rome, SC (Scozia Vol I), f.670v.
103. Giblin, C., op. cit., p.70,n.113.
104. Propaganda Archives, Rome, SC Scozia 1 (1623–1700), 13 Mar 1668, n.36, f.34.
105. Giblin, C., op. cit., p.70, n.117.
106. SCA/Bl.Letts. 1/76/15, A. Dunbar to L. Innes, 31 Jan 1683.
107. SCA/Bl.Lett. 1/68/6, A. Dunbar, 5 May 1681.
108. SCA/Bl.Lett. 1/68/9, A. Dunbar to R. Barclay, 28 Aug 1681.
109. SCA/Bl.Lett 1/68/9, D.L. (D. Burnet) to L. Innes, 18 Aug 1681.
110. SCA/Bl.Lett. 1/74/8, L. Innes to W. Leslie, 18 Sept 1682.
111. SCA/Bl.Lett. 1/113/14, L. Innes to C. Whyteford, 5 Mar 1688.
112. Ibid.
113. Forbes Leith, W., op. cit., Vol II, p.106.
114. Gordon, J.F.S., op. cit., p.647.
115. Mt 7:16.
116. Blakhal, G., *A Breiffe Narration* (Aberdeen 1844).

CHAPTER 5

The College under Louis Innes

Part 1: 1682 Until the Revolution

Louis Innes was born in 1651 of the Drumgask family which gave ten priests to the Church. From the diocese of Aberdeen, he pursued all his ecclesiastical studies at the Scots College Paris where he was Prefect of Studies from 1680 until 1682 when he succeeded to the principalship on the death of Robert Barclay. At the age of 31, he was young for the job, and others gave him a turbulent start. Very shortly after his appointment, he found that William Leslie, the Scottish agent in Rome, had written *Memoires* to the Superior of the Carthusians at Grenoble in an attempt to bar his appointment by saying that he was too young and too inexperienced. Leslie had also made charges of theft against his predecessor, Robert Barclay. Innes vigorously refuted the charges, and proved that he was not to be overawed or dominated by those older than himself.[1] His first correspondence with the other William Leslie, the Rector of the Scots College in that city, also began with a complaint. Louis Innes had written to his brother Walter, who was a student at Rome, mentioning the apostasy of a priest called Abercrombie and reflecting upon it. The Roman rector having censored the letter in accordance with the rules of the college, withheld it, and wrote rebuking Innes.[2] Innes accepted this rebuke, and in reply, desired that his first letter be burned.[3] Despite this stormy start, future correspondence with the Leslies is amicable enough.

In his early years as Principal, Louis Innes made three journeys to Britain, mainly to recruit students and raise funds, but before these visits, he travelled to Bourguinons, a village on the River Seine, 28 kilometres south-east of Troyes, in an attempt to get a legacy for the College. He set out in March 1684 to visit James Ramsay, the Curé of Bourguinons, who had studied at the Scots College Paris before 1643, and who had recently been very ill. It would be pleasant to think that concern for an *alumnus* of the college was the main reason for the visit, but three letters sent to Charles Whyteford, who in 1682 had been appointed Prefect of Studies in Scots College Paris, seem to show that Innes' chief concern was to get Ramsay to found a burse for the College which he thought would cost about four thousand livres.[4] Although Ramsay was very willing to do this, it would appear that the plan did not materialise because Ramsay had put his money (about ten thousand livres) into the hands of two curés for safe keeping, without receipt, and the Curé of Virey sur Bar, a village about four kilometres west of Bourguinons on the opposite bank of the Seine, who had received the major part, showed a great reluctance to return the money. This circumstance, together with the necessity of supplying for Ramsay, especially during Holy Week and Easter, kept Innes at Bourguinons until the middle of April. James Ramsay died later in the year on 6 July 1684, and although recorded as a benefactor in the College Necrology, it seems highly unlikely that the college got any benefit from his good intentions.

In May 1684 Louis Innes set out on the first of his three journeys to Britain. By making these journeys to Britain, Innes left the college in a precarious position with only Charles Whyteford to manage it, although he probably did not realise in those early years how inept Whyteford was. The first and the third journey are well documented by the letters of Innes to Whyteford. All we have for the second is a summary account in one letter of Innes to the Scottish agent in Rome.

First Journey to Britain

The first visit lasted six months. Innes' own purpose in going to Scotland seems to have been recruitment, but William Leslie gave him another task by asking him to persuade the missionary priests to assemble for a meeting. The missioners were most reluctant to do this, but Propaganda having demanded a yearly meeting of the clergy, William Leslie was afraid that the annual subsidy for the priests might be stopped if they did not conform. Innes was at least partially successful by having a meeting in Edinburgh in June at which there were five priests, four seculars and one Jesuit, who gave him their remit to represent them at a second meeting with their more northern colleagues at Gordon Castle later that month. He also recruited six scholars — John Byers, son of Byers of Coates, two sons of Gordon of Auchintoul (Alexander who became a Major-General in the Russian army and wrote a biography of *Peter the Great*, and George whose son John was to become Principal of the College), a brother of Leslie of Fetternear, and Alexander St Clair, son of Lady Roslin; the name of the sixth is not known.[5] In addition, the principal persuaded the Marquis of Huntly to increase a bursary for the education of a student from 1500 livres to 2000 livres, and he prevailed upon James Cahassy and James Devoir, Irish priests who had been recruited for the Highlands by Alexander Leslie in 1681, to stay another winter in Scotland.[6] What was to be of great significance for the future was that he met for the first time James Duke of York, the future King James VII, having been introduced by the Earl of Melfort. The Duke had not so much as heard of the Scots

College before this meeting[7] which took place in September 1684 in the south of England, but he was most impressed, and after several other meetings with Innes between then and October, promised his patronage. Innes could well be pleased with a successful journey.

Second Journey

When Louis Innes began his second journey at the beginning of 1686, the scene in Scotland had changed dramatically, albeit temporarily, in favour of Catholics. James VII was now on the throne, and the Earl of Perth who had become a Catholic was Lord Chancellor of Scotland. With conditions so favourable, it is not surprising to find that Innes was well pleased with his second journey. He wrote to Leslie, 'I found more & better freinds than I had reason to expect & the King himself was exceiding kynd & granted all my requests.'[8] This time he recruited nine new scholars, one of whom was Lord Drummond, the Lord Chancellor's eldest son.

It was on this second visit to Britain that Louis Innes began to be very involved in the canvassing for a bishop. England had been granted a Vicar Apostolic in 1685; he was John Leyburn who was consecrated in Rome on 9 September.[9] This made the Scots Catholics more pressing in their demand for a similar appointment. With a Catholic sovereign on the throne, the Pope would not appoint a bishop without the approval of the King. The King was believed to favour having a Jesuit, but this was unacceptable to the secular clergy. Hence arose the intrigues of presenting names of candidates to King James and to his Scottish ministers, especially the Earl of Perth and his brother, the Earl of Melfort.

When Innes got back to Paris at the end of September 1686, he wrote to tell William Leslie in Rome how busy he had been in the affair over the last three or four months:

> I need not tell you what shares I had in that affaire…& had I not gon over & acted as vigorously as ever I did in any business their had as yet bin no word of a Bishop for Scotland anywhere but in D. Gul[iel]mo's [Wm Leslie's] letters.[10]

In a letter three months later (29 Dec 1686),[11] Innes summarised the deliberations. There had been four candidates, William Leslie, the Scots agent in Rome, David Burnett (a secular priest strongly backed by the secular clergy of Scotland), Alexander Dunbar, the Prefect of the mission, and the Benedictine Abbot, Thomas Placid Fleming. Both Burnett and Leslie had been dropped from the list because they were not known at court, then Alexander Dunbar had been dropped for several reasons, one of which almost certainly was his illegitimacy. Thus Abbot Fleming would have been named, except that he had written, positively declining the post. The saga was to continue.

Third Journey

On Innes' third journey which began in April 1687, the discussions about a bishop for Scotland were resumed when Innes was residing in Holyrood Palace in the personal apartments of the Earl of Perth, the Lord Chancellor. Innes' letters reveal how the principal candidate kept changing on account of objections and wrangling. In June 1687, he wrote from Holyrood house:

> I believe D. Gulmo [agent, William Leslie] shall be Bishop & that shortly, tell him so much from me that I am doing his business for him here.[12]

but in August, he wrote from the same place:

> my service to Dr Nicolson who is now on the list to be Bp & it is possible he may, I have done my best faithfully & you may tell him so much secretly.[13]

Thomas Nicolson had been ordained in Douai in 1685, and was at the time of this letter residing in the Scots College Paris. He was a convert to the Catholic faith, and had been for fourteen years Regent in the University of Glasgow. He was eventually to be the first Vicar Apostolic. In September, Innes was at Drummond Castle, the Lord Chancellor's seat, and he wrote:

> you writ nothing of Mr Jameson, ther is more likely he will be B. then Mr Nicolson, my service to both.[14]

John Paul Jameson had been ordained priest in Rome in 1685, and was at the time of this letter residing in the Scots College Paris. He was a convert, and had gained his D.D. in Rome. When Innes got to London, he tried to speed things up. He wrote in Feb 1688:

> I have applyed myself to the best of my power to promote the interest of the Mission as our Missioners weall know. And as I did not think any one thing could contribute so much to their reall good as the having of a Bishop to unite & govern them, I have bin as active as it was possible for me to procure one for them.

The same letter reveals that he had been pressing the matter with the king:

> The King whom God preserve has said to my self severall tymes when I had the honor to speak to his Maty of the necessity of our having a Bp That he knew it was necessary & that wee should certainly have One.

Having heard of England getting three bishops, Innes continued:

> Upon this I have made new application & shown that the Delayes wee have still met with are now become openly scandalous & do not only open a door to divisions, & plainly hinder the propagation of the Faith, but makes our Nation ridiculous & the object of downright laughter & mockery to our neighbours. In a word I have said so much that I think all are now serious to let us have one...if non of our own can be acceptable Let us have Dr Bethan, ane Englishman but who would make a Bp beyond all exception.

His own choice, however, would be different, 'I hope it will be Dr Jameson.'[15] In the same month Innes wrote to Whyteford:

for newes know that now E. Melfort & others are very pressing wt Cromar to be Bp, but that by Gods assistance shall never be.[16]

This looks like intrigue against someone, but in fact 'Cromar' was an *alias* for Innes himself. This appears to have been the first time that Innes realised that he himself was being considered as a candidate, but he had been recommended by Thomas Placid Fleming when the abbot had renounced his own candidature. Innes wanted the job no more than Fleming did. In March, he wrote to Whyteford:

as to what you writ of a Bp I know not what may becom of that matter, but for me I can not yet think I either will or ought to consent to it, I pray God direct me: my Ld will be heir in 10 days, & then ther will be something concluded to that affair[17]

In April, Innes reported:

I think wee shall have 2 Bps, Dr Nicolson will be one & for the other I can not yet say anything but have hitherto refused & done all my endeavours to make the lot fall on some other, the matter is now referred to Bp Gifford & Dr Bethans determination.[18]

This in fact was the King's final decision. He recommended two to be bishops, Louis Innes and Thomas Nicolson. Cardinal Howard wrote to Innes on 30 August 1688:

That no time be lost, I desire you to send us word which part of Scotland is to be your district, and which that of the other, your brother bishop.[19]

Had it not been for the Revolution, Louis Innes would have been bishop along with Thomas Nicolson, but the political upheaval at the end of 1688 cancelled these plans. Had they taken effect, there may well have been a strong protest from the Episcopalians against the royal appointment of Catholic bishops. The Revolution postponed deliberations about a Catholic bishop for a further six years when Thomas Nicolson was appointed Vicar Apostolic for Scotland.

One of the reasons for Innes' third journey was to obtain funds for the college because he had contracted considerable debts and yet wanted to improve the college, and buy the house next door to it. In this quest for finance, he was eminently successful. From King James VII he got a grant of £50 sterling for the college (recorded in the Treasury Register under the date 3 June 1687)[20] and a further £1100 made out to himself (recorded in the Treasury Register under the date 21 June 1687),[21] and from the Earl of Perth, he got £300 sterling for the college. Less creditably, he pursued Alexander Brodie for money he was obliged to pay for a fine, and successfully recovered the same. Alexander Brodie of Lethin had in

February 1685 been fined forty thousand pounds Scots money for staying away from the Kirk, entertaining vagrant preachers, and holding nine house conventicles.[22] This fine was by letter of His Majesty (Whitehall 12 May 1686) assigned to Richard Viscount Preston.[23] From Lord Preston, Louis Innes had a bond for 30,000 livres to be collected on account of the fine. This had probably been given at the request of King James, since Louis Innes, when he was soliciting for funds on 24 April 1687. told His Majesty that Lethin's fine was not likely to be be paid hastily.[24]

It is sad and disappointing to find that Louis Innes went after this fine which had been imposed for the following of conscience, especially as the Covenanters' non-conformity was in legal terms so similar to that of Catholics. Had a Catholic been pursued in this fashion for a similar fine, Louis Innes would have viewed it as persecution. Innes' actions here seem inconsistent with other instances in which he appears unbigoted, and a true respecter of conscience different from his own. Thus at the beginning of his first journey, he wrote that he had enjoyed the company of a Protestant couple, Mr and Mrs Dixon, on the coach from Paris to Calais.[25] Then there is a delightful phrase at the end of one of his letters, 'we shall have...a bishop, & the Presbyterians ane Indulgence, & the Catholiks the Abbaye Church.'[26] Clearly he thought all three were blessings, and rejoiced that all would be happy.

In the Lethin case, however, Louis Innes chased the fine with the tenacity of a bull-dog, not fearing to make bitter enemies of all the Brodies who would rather have thrown their money into the sea than give it to Innes. Lethin had made a disposition claiming that he was only a liferenter, and therefore the estate could not be affected by his fine, but Innes undertook a legal reduction and improbation of this disposition.[27] With the King's Act of Indulgence against the forcing of conscience, public opinion thought it odious to be punished for what the King now declared to be no fault[28], but still Innes pursued his case, even confronting the Brodies on their own territory in Moray, until he finally got his 30,000 livres[29] which was the equivalent of £2,500 sterling, and after expenses was able to forward 26,666 livres to Charles Whyteford in Paris.[30] Perth, the Lord Chancellor, without whose backing this would not have been possible, was surely not exaggerating when he wrote to Whyteford that Innes was 'laboring for Lethin's fyne tooth & nail'.[31]

During Louis Innes' third journey to Britain, another drama was being enacted which was the turning of Holyrood into a bastion of Catholicism. King James had turned the Council Chamber in the palace into a private chapel, and had allowed the setting-up of a Catholic printing press and a school run by the Jesuits. There were also plans to refound the Abbey and install a religious order, and Innes got involved with these. At first it was intended that the Benedictines should come, and Abbot Fleming was preparing a team, for whose journey the French King gave a financial grant in February 1687.[32] The Abbey had, however, belonged to the Augustinians before the Reformation, and Richard Augustine Hay, a Scottish Augustinian, had arrived in Edinburgh in November 1686 with a commission from his prior to re-establish the Augustinian order in Scotland and England. He began talks about the Abbey with the Earl of Perth on 29 May 1687. On the 16 June, Louis Innes, who had arrived in Edinburgh on 12 June, told him that the King was under the impression that the Abbey had belonged to the Benedictines.[33] That Innes communicated this information in order to be supportive of Hay is clear from a letter that Innes wrote to Whyteford in November in which he said, 'I have some reasons to wish rather they [the Augustinians] than any had the Church'. He then advised that the monks should write directly to Lord Melfort or to Innes himself, but asking that his preferring them to the Benedictines should not be mentioned in their letter.[34] By May 1688, however, the scheme had fallen through, although Richard Hay may still have been optimistic. Innes wrote, 'What Dik Hay has writt of his Chan. reg. [canons regular] is all stories, in all likely they will not be employed.'[35]

The reign of a Catholic monarch made yet another drama possible in the North of Scotland during the time of Innes' third visit. This was the building of a Catholic Church on the ruins of an older chapel at Tynet, near Buckie in Banffshire, by John Irvine, Alexander Leslie coming to help him in 1688. It is very surprising that Louis Innes said nothing about this when in August 1687 he wrote to Whyteford from Preshome[36] which was only two miles away from the building operation.

Forebodings

Despite the euphoria amongst Catholics, with good prospects of getting a bishop, with the Holyrood developments, and the building of a church at Tynet, Louis Innes apprehended danger ahead; he could not have predicted the Revolution, but he did have forebodings about the future. By the end of the July 1687, he wrote:

> but all things heir are in a staggering condition, & I fear the presbyterians will shortly cutt out new work enough their was 10 conventicles last Sundai in Edr & the country is full of them.[37]

By November, he wrote from London,

> the Presbyterians in Scotl are not only encouraged of late by the K. but really preferred to all others wch is so far from gaining them that they begin to insult already & to give out everywher openly that Papists are Idolaters, that Idolatry is against the law of God, & that nothing lesse than the blood of the guilty can expiate the cryme of the

tollerating of it & c. God allone knows wher all this will end, but most things have a dreadful aspect to reflecting persons, wee have all great reason to redouble our prayers & I desyre that in every Masse you add a Collect expressly for peace & unity in this poor land.[38]

In January 1688, his alarm was even greater as he wrote from London:

Things go as ill as the ennemie of the K. & of the Cath Relig. could wish, & are growing dayly worse.[39]

As all know, his fears for the King were realised with the Revolution, and as for the Catholic Religion, many Scottish priests, including two brothers of Innes, were imprisoned.

Affairs in Scots College Paris

Louis Innes' stay in Britain lasted fourteen months, and one must wonder how the college fared without him. He certainly did not forget the College, and wrote to Charles Whyteford, who was deputising in his absence, many detailed instructions about both the college building and the students. As regards the building, an infirmary and chambers above the stairs were being prepared, as also a terrace.[40] Innes instructed that the terrace be 'not elevated very high but very strong'[41] and that the wood of the terrace be bound with strong bands of iron to withstand strong winds.[42] He directed that a jube or gallery be made in the chapel, 'strong & handsome tho not of the fynest kynd of work', and it is to serve also as a passage to the infirmary.[43] Orders were given to clear the ground in front of the college for recreation purposes,[44] to buy the house next door,[45] to sell the house in *Rue des Deux Boules* and the other old house near St. Sulpice,[46] and to look for a country villa such as other colleges had.[47] Difficulties arose concerning their foundation documents and recognition by the French Parliament. Innes advised Whyteford to consult lawyers and told Whyteford which documents should be produced and which should not.[48] He himself obtained a letter from James VII to the French king asking for Ratification of the College and its privileges.[49] After Innes returned, French Parliamentary ratification was given in 1688.

As regards the students, directives were sent by Innes both for the student body at large and for individual students. Rules were to be exactly kept,[50] French or Latin always spoken,[51] and recreation was to be taken.[52] There was even a command for the scholars to 'keep their chambers clean & neat' for he had heard a complaint in Scotland that 'our boys beds & chambers are extremely nasty'.[53] Having heard one of his students, Patrick Dixon, saying in London that he knew nothing of the rosary and that the only student he had seen with beads was Lord Drummond, Charles Whyteford was told to remedy the situation.[54]

For individuals, Earl Wigton's servant was to have a draw-bed; the earl and his brother were to have a special table prepared for them in the refectory;[55] Thomas Innes, Louis' brother was to look after them in place of a governor.[56] For Thomas Innes himself, he was to be more neat in his clothes,[57] and later he was to be sent to a seminary for three or four months.[58] James Donaldson, a newly ordained priest from Rome, was to be sent to Notre Dame des Vertus.[59] Alexander Clerk was to be sent to Rome, if he could be persuaded to go;[60] in fact he chose to leave. Thomas Irvine was to be put above James Brown at table to satisfy Dr Irvine and his wife who were complaining.[61] Lord Drummond was to have prizes, as also 'little James Urquhart'.[62] James Gordon was to take care of the younger ones with help from Thomas Innes.[63] John Irvine was not to be told of his father's death until he had engaged to prosecute his studies.[64]

During the fourteen months of Louis Innes's absence, quite a number of student problems arose. Alex. Clerk left at a bad time, as his father was just about to pay his fees, and there did not seem to be much chance of receiving them after his departure.[65] Thomas Irvine gave some great dissatisfaction, and Innes directed Whyteford to write to his father immediately to take him out of the college.[66] There is a reference to theft in the college in the following month (Oct 1687);[67] although there is no evidence to connect this with the preceding, it may also be noted that there is no mention of any other expulsion at this time. Innes rightly directed that the name of the supposed culprit be not disclosed. Patrick Dixon who had been visiting London gave offence by parting without so much as taking his leave of Innes.[68] Adam Strachan, whom Innes had thought very promising,[69] wrote an impertinent letter to his father before leaving.[70] John Byers, Coates' son, and a student called Ballentin were also unsatisfactory, and Innes desired that they should leave.[71] There was some crisis with the Earl of Wigton who threatened to leave, but, Innes was able to resolve the crisis so that he stayed in the college until 1690. Innes attributed the problems to getting boys too young; he wrote:

> if wee could have bigg boys of 16 or 17 years fitt for us, it wold save us much trouble, & be lesse burthensome to the house, for we would much sooner know what could be expected from them, but our Missrs [Missioners] do not take this to hart tho it be more theirs then anybodies interest.[72]

It is likely, however, that the absence of the Principal contributed greatly to the breakdown of discipline. It was soon to come to light that Charles Whyteford did not have a good way with the students, and that he got too involved with work outside the college. He did have some help from the senior members of the student community. Alexander Gordon was already ordained, John Wallace, who later became bishop, was at this time a gentleman boarder in the college and was always ready to help, and we have already seen that James Gordon, the future bishop, and Thomas Innes were deputed to help with younger students. Nevertheless, with only two of a staff, and the vice-principal not too competent, a fourteen month absence of the Principal was detrimental to the college.

During the first period of Louis Innes principalship before the Revolution, the proportion of Paris-educated priests coming to the Scottish mission dropped. Out of eight new priests in Scotland, only one, Angus McDonald, had been ordained in Paris, and one other, John Irvine, had studied for five and a half years in Paris. Only one of the other six, James Donaldson, had received post-ordination pastoral training in Paris. Nevertheless, the contribution of the Paris-ordained priests to the main events in the Scottish mission was very high at this time. We have seen that Louis Innes had great influence with King James VII, with the Earl of Perth, with the Earl of Melfort, and with the Marquis of Huntly. The chief *dramatis personae* of the drama in Scotland were connected with Paris, as Abbot Fleming and Richard Augustine Hay were both *alumni* of the Scots College Paris, as were John Irvine and Alexander Leslie who were the first since the Reformation to build a Catholic church in Scotland. These were all strong characters who had studied under Robert Barclay.

The return of Louis Innes to Paris in June 1688 coincided with the birth of James Edward. This event was celebrated the following month by a great fireworks display in the college gardens on 8 July. Innes must have felt great satisfaction; his recruiting campaigns had filled the college, building improvements had taken place, financial negotiations had proved successful, and now there was a Catholic heir to the throne of Britain. Innes triumphantly published an account of his festivities. Alas, how short-lived this success. Before the end of the year, the King had fled to France, and the severe measures were taken against Catholics in Scotland.

Part 2: From the Revolution until 1713

The consequence of the Revolution for Scottish Catholics was persecution, and it was particularly directed against priests. Although there were never more than twenty-five secular priests at any one time, fourteen of these were imprisoned between 1689 and 1704, as well as several Jesuits and members of other religious orders.[73] In this crisis, the Scots College Paris became a refuge for priests who were banished from Scotland. When he accepted these, Louis Innes wrote to William Leslie, the Scots agent at Rome, that he was departing from a strict rule made in the time of his predecessor, Robert Barclay, not to receive priest lodgers even if they paid full board. We have already seen, however, that Barclay had made exceptions to his rule in the case of banished priests, and had received John Walker, William Ballantine and Alexander Burnet in their time of exile. Innes must have been unaware of this and he was afraid that the ordinary policy of the college might prevent him getting money from Propaganda for the maintenance of the exiles. Propaganda, however, made no difficulty in making provision for them.

The first banished priest to arrive at the college was James Nicol. After some months in jail in Scotland, he was exiled in October 1692. He was in the college until spring 1694, and returned again in 1696 after a second imprisonment in Scotland.[74] Being in a poor state of health when he arrived for the second time, he died in the College some months later. Three more exiles came in June 1693, Alexander Crichton, Robert Davidson and George Gordon. Alex Crichton had been arrested at Strathbogie in 1689 and imprisoned at Aberdeen. His health was so impaired that he was deemed unfit to return to the mission, and so after some time in the college, he became chaplain to a convent of English nuns at Dunkirk. Robert Davidson had also been arrested in 1689, probably when he was on his way north to Edinburgh, and he was imprisoned in that city. He was supported by the college until 1695 when he returned to Scotland where he was to be arrested again at Leith in the persecution of 1704, and after several months in prison, he was banished to Ireland. Undaunted he came back the following year, and laboured on the mission till his death in 1711. George Gordon, a stalwart recruiter for the college in Innes' early days, had been arrested with the Countess of Errol in her Castle of Frendraught, eleven miles north-east of Huntly, in February 1690. He was too ill to go back to Scotland, and died at Dunkirk on 29 May 1695.

When Robert Monro was imprisoned in Ghent for taking sides against the Prince of Orange, Louis Innes first got some Jesuits to provide for his needs, and then was successful in procuring his release, receiving him into the college in November 1696.[75] Innes persuaded Monro to write an account of his sufferings for Propaganda, and obtained a chalice and vestments for his return to Scotland. He left for that land in June 1697, but was arrested aboard ship, and imprisoned for a year in London,[76] during which time Innes provided for his needs. He was then banished again, but only went as far as Dunkirk whence he sailed again for Scotland. Here he laboured until 1704, but in the persecution of that year, when he lay sick of a fever, he was arrested at Glengarry, thrown across a horse like a sack, and taken to Glengarry Castle. He was lain on the floor with not even straw for a bed, and given neither food nor drink, not even a glass of water, and he died within two days.[77]

On account of the persecution, all the colleges abroad experienced a dearth of students and a reduction of revenue as the fathers of students found it harder to meet the fees. Louis Innes wrote to William Leslie in Rome in April 1693, 'our College is almost ruined & will most certainly be undone if these unhappy tymes last.'[78] This was echoing what Whyteford had written to Leslie's brother in the previous month, 'if things doe not change, we will be in a very low condition.'[79] It would be wrong, however, to conclude from these statements that the Scots College Paris was immediately emptied by the Revolution. In 1689, there were at least twelve students, and there were at least seven new recruits in the next seven years. Nevertheless numbers dwindled, dropping to four in 1697.[80]

In addition to the baneful effects of the Revolution, equally serious for the college were the staff problems. Louis Innes, the Principal, made his residence with the Jacobite court at St Germain where he was one of the advisers to King James VII. Judging from comparatively small matters communicated to him by letters from other members of staff, his visits to the college could not have been very frequent. It was quite extraordinary that for twenty-five years from the Revolution until 1713, Louis Innes was an absentee from the college.

What made matters worse was that Charles Whyteford (Prefect of Studies from 1682 until 1696, and Procurator from 1696 until 1713) who deputised for Innes, was not very good at his job. Over the years, there had been several student grumblings about Charles Whyteford, but nothing had been said by anyone in authority. Towards the end of 1694, however, William Leslie wrote to Innes suggesting the removal of Charles Whyteford, claiming that 'the college needs a better leader of men to reside therein.'[81] (In this remark, there may have been a subtle hint to Innes to leave St Germain and return to the college.) Innes partly defended Whyteford, and deemed his removal impolitic. He replied:

> he [Whyteford] has to my certain knowledge bin much wronged by false reports spread against him & too asily beleeved by our friends in Scotland: I doe not say this to justify every thing he has done, I wish hartily & it had bin for our advantage some things had bin otherways managed than they have, but I truly think he has done the best he could....at this present I doe not think it proper to move any thing in these matters...the lesse noyse wee make of our condition it is the better, for noyse wold expose our weaknes, & worse our affairs, but could never better them.[82]

One is immediately curious about the nature of Whyteford's faults. Innes told Leslie that the main complaint against Whyteford 'is his being taken up dayly in other peoples temporall affairs, & scarce ever being at home'.[83] (With the Principal away as well!) A report of a conversation between Whyteford and George Adamson, Prefect of Studies, reveals much more detail. This conversation took place on St Stephen's day, 1697;

Whyteford had asked Adamson why he was so unpopular, and Adamson told him frankly. Besides the meddling in other peoples' business, there was his 'talking imprudently of the Jesuits before the boys in time of recreation', his quick change of moods, his casting aspersions on students' home backgrounds, and sending the students on too many errands. Whyteford appeared to be grateful, and promised amendment, but Adamson warned him how difficult it would be for him to recover his reputation.[84] One complaint against him has its humorous side; Adamson told Innes that Whyteford had bought two expensive shirts for himself, but when

Peter [Fraser] and 3 others wanted shirts he had cause make for them stuff fitter I doe not say [for] horse sheets but corn sacks than any thing else. I never saw the like of them befor in the house, the boys are to take the hammer to them befor they wear them. Mr Whitefurd says if they were washen once they will be soft....[Yet] he makes no difficulty to spend without reason when the fancy takes him.[85]

Although Innes was opposed to Whyteford's leaving in 1694, there is extant a draft of a letter, dated 1697, in which Innes was trying to persuade Whyteford to leave the college[86]; it is doubtful, however, whether this letter was ever sent, as Whyteford spoke highly of Innes to Adamson, saying that Innes always defended him. (The courtesy was not reciprocated as Innes was hurt by remarks Whyteford made to Robert Gordon in 1701.)[87] In 1698, Bishop Nicolson asked Whyteford to leave the college, but Whyteford refused. Such disobedience greatly surprised everyone, and Innes feared that 'it may be ane ill president [precedent] for the regulars, since our own people disobey.'[88] Whyteford was able to get away with this because he got the backing of the Carthusian prior who kept him in office, and wrote to Bishop Nicolson that 'he doubted not but Mr Whiteford wold follow the good advice he promises to give him, & so become more gratefull to all & more useful & c.' This led Adamson to criticise the system of Carthusian supervision, as he wrote to Innes:

the priours of the Carthusians att present are right negligent in overseeing the Colledge affairs, wittness the Great confidence & attache this present man has for Mr Whitefurd.[89]

By 1699, Innes found himself under attack, and William Leslie gradually emerged as the complainant. Innes complained about Leslie 'procuring any orders to the Nuncio here [at Paris] to meddle wt our College.'[90] By October, Innes knew that the Nuncio had received a letter and instructions concerning the College. 'I hope', he wrote, 'by God's assistance this storme will blow over.'[91] He desired Leslie to get him a copy of the letter, saying that he wondered that it was so hard to get, adding:

but it may be you had no mynd I should know that the ground of this letter was your complaint of disorders introduced into our College to the notable prejudice of the Mission.

Leslie tried to wriggle out, alleging to Innes 'that these disorders are meant only of the College of Douay', but Innes replied:

> that is a commentary which plainly contradicts the text of the Cardinals letter which wtout any the least shaddow of distinction or difference says the disorders are crept into both the College of Paris & Douay.[92]

Leslie replied that it was Douay that was levelled at, but Innes was not satisfied, and told the agent:

> wheras ther never has as yet, nor is like to be one word said to the College of Douai, & wee have been 3 months vexed with that continuance, & not yet at ane end tho I hope wee shall now…Cardl Nuncio will be satisfied wt what wee can do.[93]

Louis Innes appears to have survived the examination without censure. Whyteford, however, was incorrigible. A partial solution to the problem was found by making Peter Fraser a kind of assistant procurator; he was a student whom the staff deemed incapable of pursuing the requisite studies for priesthood, but kept on as one of the domestic staff, and since the college was allowed to have only two servants, he was designated 'tailor'. Whyteford worked well with him for a time, but in 1703, he was again warned to stop meddling in other peoples' affairs; he promised reform,[94] but later in the year, was described as worse than ever.[95] The following year, both John Irvine and Louis Innes spoke to him again.[96] In 1707, Bishop Gordon was distressed but not surprised that he had contracted debts.[97] Although references to this problem fade from the letters, it is doubtful whether Whiteford was ever cured. He became Principal of the college in 1713 and remained so until his death at almost ninety years of age, but was said to have behaved like a great overlord, dispensing a lavish hospitality that the college could ill afford.

From 1696, there was a third member of staff, with the position of Prefect of Studies. The first of these was Alexander Drummond, an *alumnus* of the college ordained in Paris, probably in 1696, who held the post until he left for the Scottish Mission in September 1697. Not much is known about his short time in office except his failure to discipline a tonsured student called John Dunbar. The Prefect wrote to Innes that he could not get Dunbar to do his studies or show him his work, and that the only time he went straight to study after classes was when he was told to go and clean the chapel.[98] Clearly the college was lacking a firm controlling hand.

Alexander Drummond was succeeded by George Adamson who had been ordained in Rome, but had previously been a student at Paris. Arriving at the college in April 1697, he was received most kindly by Whyteford, but thought it unlikely that he would be allowed to stay, considering the state of the college finances. Innes, however, after receiving him at St

Germain, decided on his remaining in the college.[99] He appears to have been a very good and conscientious Prefect of Studies, and it was only because of his great desire to serve on the Scottish mission that he left the college in 1703. He was even named as a possible coadjutor bishop, and although Innes wrote to James Gordon, 'you know he is the most helpless man' and he 'cannot travel by foot',[100] this was said considering him as a potential bishop; there were never any complaints of him as prefect of studies.

The same could not be said of his successor, James Paplay. He had been ordained in Rome in 1702, and had come to Paris for his pastoral training. He was only eighteen months as Prefect when Innes found him unsatisfactory, and he left for the mission which he reached in September 1704. After a few months, he disappeared, and there was great concern for his safety as it was some time before the truth came out; he had eloped and married and was running a school in Northumberland. Innes was furious, and described him as:

> the most corrupted dissembled monster that ever was heard of, going about his ordinary functions every day for severall months befor he went off wtout appearance of any scruple whilst he past the nights in the height of debauchery, & now married to a slut in the north of Engd makes use of the chalice for her drinking cup.[101]

He was years later seen in a red coat, doing sentry duty at the gates of Holyrood Palace.

After this, Thomas Innes, the brother of Louis, became Prefect of Studies. Having studied at the college, he had been ordained in March 1691, and had gone to the mission in June 1698,[102] but was sent back by Bishop Nicolson to help in the college in summer 1701. Undoubtedly a great scholar and most competent, he was later to be rebuked by Bishop Gordon for allowing his historical interests and archival work to lead to the neglect of student formation. The prescriptions for the Prefect of Studies in the Statutes of the College, drawn up in 1707, strongly suggest that this was already a problem at the time of their formulation.

Towards the end of Louis Innes' principalship, Robert Gordon was made Prefect of Studies in 1712 and held the post until 1718. Another priest who spent some time in the college was John Irvine. He was not intended for the staff of the college; after leaving Rome where he had been assistant agent, he was anxious to get back to the mission, and did in fact leave for Scotland in the spring of 1704. Louis Innes, however, having received reports of the persecution in Scotland, sent an urgent letter to Brussels to stop him there. John Irvine showed the letter to the papal nuncio at Brussels who commanded him to return to Paris[103] where he arrived on 8 June, and stayed for a year until the persecution abated. It is most likely that he helped the staff, especially as he had already undertaken staff duties in the college in the first half of 1684.

The defects of the staff are the likeliest reason for the formulation of the Statutes of the College in 1707. It has been pointed out in the chapter on the organisation of the college how they prescribed against the Principal staying away from the college, against the Procurator being involved with outside business, and against the Prefect of Studies being distracted by other tasks, even studies. For this reason it seems more probable that the drawing up of the Statutes was instigated by the Prior rather than by the staff of the college. The Statutes may have been suggested by the Statutes for the Scottish Mission drawn up by Bishop Nicolson in 1706, but such formulations were quite in vogue in the Church at this time. The Carthusians who were superiors of the Scots College Paris had a second edition of their Statutes confirmed by a Brief of Pope Innocent XI in 1682,[104] the year of Innes' appointment as Principal. Whatever the motive, the codification of the Statutes was an important development, and the Statutes remain as our best indication of the organisation of the college.

College Contribution to the Scottish Mission

Despite the defects of the staff, it is a surprising fact that in the twenty-five years after the Revolution the manpower contribution of the Scots College Paris to the Scottish Misssion compared favourably with that of the Scots College Rome. While twelve priests ordained in Rome came to the mission, as against only seven ordained in Paris, it must be taken into consideration that three of the four ordained in Scotland (Peter Fraser, John Wallace, and Alexander Smith) had undertaken practically all their studies in Paris. Another factor in the comparison is that two of the Roman ordained priests did not serve the mission for long; James Paplay apostatised, while James Thomson had to be removed on account of a drink problem. When we also consider that three of the Paris trained priests became bishops, we realise the great influence that the Scots College Paris had at this time. James Gordon was to be bishop for forty years (from 1706 to 1746), John Wallace was co-adjutor from 1720 to 1733, and Alexander Smith was bishop for thirty-one years (from 1735 to 1766). Another student who did not become a priest nevertheless made a sizeable contribution to the mission. He was Gregory Farquharson who until the 'forty-five' ran a Catholic school in Strathdown which provided many students for the Scots colleges.

The post-ordination pastoral training for Roman-trained priests was continued throughout this period, most of those ordained in Rome coming to the Scots College, Paris. The normal stay was for a year, but there were exceptions; James Kennedy only stayed six months whereas William Stuart was kept for two years because of persecution in Scotland at the time. The full list for this period includes Walter Innes, William Stuart, James Carnegie, James Kennedy, Alexander More, Robert Gordon, and Andrew Deans. Peter Reid was also there for a short time from the end of May 1709 before leaving for Scotland in September that year. Andrew Hacket appears to have gone straight to the mission in 1708; he was the only priest to do so.

Louis Innes also played a part in securing the services of two English Recollects for the mission, Fr Peter Gordon and Fr Clement Hyslop, and he got financial help from Queen Mary for Fr Peter Gordon.

In 1700, the college sent psalters to Scotland. These contained an English version of the Psalms, published anonymously by Lord Caryll in 1700, probably for the use of the Royal Household at St Germain. Bishop Nicolson acknowledged them in a letter of 5 May, 1707:

> Pray god & give my humble duty to my Lord Caryl to whom I have (?) great obligations of gratitude. Thenk him for the psalters & if any more be offered assure him that they doo good heer & many pray for him.[105]

In Paris itself, the College was playing its part in Scottish affairs. The two members of the staff, Louis Innes and Charles Whyteford, along with Thomas Innes, now ordained but still studying at the college, were amongst the very few present at the episcopal ordination of Thomas Nicolson on 27 February 1695.[106] To keep it as secret as possible, it had been decided to have the ordination ceremony in the private chapel of the Archbishop of Paris. Afterwards, Louis Innes disclosed all the affairs of the college to the new bishop. He told William Leslie:

> I thought it necessary both for my own discharge & his information to lay before him the present state & condition of the College, & therefore I lett him sie our accompts, rentes & debts, that he might be thoroughly informed of all our concerns, both of our fort & our foible, for my humour never was nor shall be to make a mistery or a secret of our affairs to those that should know them, as I think the Bishop should in the first place, & when I had laid all before him I told him plainly what I will stand to, that he knowing particularly the condition of the house, I wold refer entirely to his determination all that concernd the number & the choice of the schollars, & wold take them from his hand & upon his recommendation & not otherwise.[107]

The Bishop, on his part, made Louis Innes, not only his procurator, but also his Grand Vicar in all concerns in Paris.

Innes was the first to realise that provision had to be made for a successor to Bishop Nicolson or Scotland might again have to wait for years without a bishop after Nicolson's death. His suggestion was the establishment of a chapter who might be given the right to elect a new bishop, but at least would be able to appoint a Vicar Capitular in an interrgnum. Instead Rome decided to provide a co-adjutor,[108] i. e. an assistant bishop with the right of succession. James Gordon, an *alumnus* of the Scots College Paris, was the unanimous choice of the missioners, of Bishop Nicolson and of the court at St Germain. The only one to disagree was William Leslie, the agent at Rome, which led to an abundance of correspondence and considerable delay, but eventually James Gordon was appointed. For reasons of secrecy, he was consecrated bishop at Montefiascone by Cardinal Barberigo on Low Sunday, 11 April 1706. He then made his way to Scotland in the company of Fr Peter Mulligan, an Irish Augustinian (who later became a bishop in Ireland) whom he had recruited for work in the Highlands. They stopped at the Paris College on the way, and arrived safely in Aberdeen by the end of July to the great joy of Bishop Nicolson. After the appointment of James Gordon, Innes' next concern was to secure for him a suitable pension from Propaganda, and after much pressure, this was achieved.

The Scots College Paris had also an influence on Scottish affairs in Rome. A proposal had been made to merge the English, Irish and Scots colleges in Rome. It was made at the instigation of the Jesuits who tried to get Propaganda Fide and the Stuart Court at St Germain to support it. This led Queen Mary, queen to James VII, to desire, and no doubt she was guided by her Chaplain Louis Innes in asking for this, the English, Irish and Scots Colleges in Paris to give answer to the Memorial sent down by the Pope's order. All agreed that the three nations could never live in peace in one college. The Scots put in an addendum:

> But in our Answer wee also add that if the number of our students can bee augmented, viaticks for going up & returning home settled, & some years of humanity allowed by being united to any other College except the English or Irish, wee are for it.[109]

Louis Innes was also instrumental in a Memorial being sent to Rome, backed by letters from Queen Mary, strongly beseeching that the Roman College be put into the hands of national rectors, that viatics for journeys be settled and that all vagabonds and those not recommended by Bishops and clergy be excluded. This was occasioned by the defection of James Paplay, already referred to, but Innes also referred to the defection of James Thomson in 1700 (who, however, died penitent in 1718) and that of James Canaries in 1681. In all three cases, he claimed, the students had been received into the Roman college without the approval of the clergy.[110] (An interesting side-light on the times is that letters from Bishop Nicolson to the same purpose had to be tossed into the sea when the ship carrying them was seized by privateers.[111]) Rome granted the request, making the approval of bishop or clergy a necessary condition of acceptance for an ecclesiastical student entering any Scottish college.

Assessment of Louis Innes

Louis is probably the best known of the Principals of the Scots College Paris, much of his fame deriving from his role as a Jacobite diplomat. Undoubtedly he was a very able man who, in both Church and State, served in high offices, Principal of the Scots College Paris, Secretary of State for Scotland (under the exiled James VII), Almoner to his Queen, and Almoner to the Old Chevalier. As one would expect of a court politician, he was shrewd in judgement, and diplomatic and circumspect in all that he said or wrote, as will be instanced in our discussion of the Jansenist problems. With all his diplomacy, however, Innes put conscience before power. Louis Innes was honest and forthright, and not guilty of duplicity when he disagreed with others. In this he could be contrasted with William Leslie, the Scottish priest-agent in Rome, who congratulated Louis Innes on his appointment as Principal while writing against him to the Carthusian Superior, and although William Leslie was right to seek a Visitation of the Scots College Paris in 1699, he tried to dissemble when Innes charged him with its instigation. By contrast, Innes was not afraid to voice his disagreement. Another point of contrast with William Leslie is that he was not fanatically opposed to the Jesuits whatever his disagreements, nor would we expect him to be as Innes had two brothers who were Jesuit priests, although one of his brothers, Father John, was described as 'amongst the bitterest opponents of the secular clergy.'

Loyalty was his strongest suit. Innes was loyal to the Jacobite King after he lost his throne, and never tired of trying to restore it. Even when dismissed from office, he pledged his faithful allegiance. He was loyal to the Scottish bishops even although he suspected, maybe even knew, that the letters they had sent to Rome were the chief cause of suspicion against the Scots College Paris. He was loyal to Whyteford even though ill-served by his bungling, and hurt by remarks that Whyteford made to Robert Gordon in 1701. This loyalty in the face of adversity sprang from a true humility, and it was quite in character that he asked to be buried in a pauper's grave.

As Principal, Louis Innes did much good for the college. In his early years, he obtained considerable financial help, recruited a good number of students, and secured legal ratification of the college by the French Parliament. The Statutes of the College were formulated in his principalship, although the impetus for this development may have come from the

Carthusian Prior. Although in the Bourguinon and Lethin affairs Innes appeared to be grasping in seeking finances for the college, he was later exceedingly generous with his personal money, both to the college and to the Scottish Mission. He often paid students' fees in Paris, and the seminary at Scalan in Glenlivet could scarcely have been founded without his aid.

Innes also had a tremendous sympathy for the underdog, and often gave students a second chance when few others would have done so. His forbearance was vindicated in the ordinations of George Dalgleish (1707), John Gordon (1708), Gregor MacGregor (for the Benedictines), and James Stevens (for the Vincentians).

It would be unfair to deny the ability or magnanimity of Louis Innes, but his continued absence from the college can scarcely be justified. Even in his early years, his journeys to Britain occupied twenty-nine months out of a period of forty-nine months, and they had started after a month spent at Bourguinon. After the Revolution, he was scarcely in the college at all, so convinced was he of the priority of a political solution for the welfare of the Scottish Mission. By today's standards, this would not be regarded as a fitting task for an ecclesiastic, and even in those days when there were still ecclesiastical politicians, there were many who were critical. It has to be presumed that Innes followed his conscience in devoting his energies to the Jacobite cause, but surely he should have resigned from the college earlier than he did. No doubt at first he thought that his absence would be temporary, but there must have come a time when he realised that St Germain was taking up all his time, especially when he accepted the position as Queen's almoner. While it is true that the college was at its most influential stage during his principalship, this was partly due to the good foundations laid by Robert Barclay, and partly to the fact that the Scots College Rome produced few priests at this time. Credit must also be given to the good judgement of Louis Innes who was consulted on many issues, and took the initiative on others. The college, however, could have done much better had Innes been in residence. Out of ten priests educated at Paris who embarked on missionary work in Scotland between 1688 and 1713 (seven ordained in Paris and three in Scotland), only six had begun their studies after the Revolution. This was hardly a big harvest for twenty-five years, considering the advantages of a very ample building, and incorporation into the University of Paris. The anomaly of this period is that we must admit the benefit to the Scottish Mission derived from the Scots College Paris, particularly because three of its *alumni* became bishops, but also hold that Louis Innes' dedication to the Stuart cause deflected him from his main duty of producing priests for the Scottish Mission.

NOTES

1. SCA/BlLett 1/74/7. L. Innes (Paris) to W. Leslie (Rome), 7 June 1682.
   SCA/BlLett 1/74/8. L. Innes (Paris) to W. Leslie (Rome), 18 Sept 1682.
2. SCA/BlLett 1/79/22, W. L. Leslie (Rome) to L. Innes (Paris), 6 Jan 1683.
3. SCA/BlLett 1/79/23, W. L. Leslie (Rome) to L. Innes (Paris), 9 March 1683.
4. SCA/BlLett 1/84/2, L. Innes (Bourguinons) to C. Whyteford, 26 March 1684.
   SCA/BlLett 1/84/3, L. Innes (Bourguinons) to C. Whyteford, 31 March 1684.
   SCA/BlLett 1/84/4, L. Innes (Bourguinons) to C. Whyteford, 9 April 1684.
5. SCA/BlLett 1/84/11, L. Innes (Castle Gordon) to C. Whyteford, 1 July 1684.
6. SCA/BlLett 1/84/11, L. Innes (Castle Gordon) to C. Whyteford, 1 July 1684.
7. SCA/BlLett 1/84/17, L. Innes (London) to C. Whyteford, 19 Sept 1684.
8. SCA/BlLett 1/94/10, L. Innes (Paris) to W. Lestie (Rome), 30 Sept 1686.
9. Hemphill, B., *The Early Vicars Apostolic of England 1685–1750* (London 1954), p.10. (The date is sometimes given as 13 September.)
10. SCA/BlLett 1/94/10, L. Innes (Paris) to W. Leslie (Rome), 30 Sept 1686.
11. SCA/BlLett 1/94/1, L. Innes (Paris) to W. Leslie (Rome), 29 Dec 1686.
12. SCA/BlLett 1/94/11, L. Innes (Holyrood H.) to C. Whyteford, 29 Dec 1686.
    SCA/BlLett 1/102/10, L. Innes (Holyrood H.) to C. Whyteford, 21 June 1687.
13. SCA/BlLett 1/102/19, L. Innes (Holyrood H.) to C. Whyteford, 1 Aug 1687.
14. SCA/BlLett 1/103/1, L. Innes (Drummond C) to C. Whyteford, 12 Sept 1687.
15. SCA/BlLett 1/113/10, L. Innes (London) to C. Whyteford, 8/18 Feb 1688 (87 O.S.).
16. SCA/BlLett 1/113/13, L. Innes (London) to C. Whyteford, 27 Feb 1688
17. SCA/BlLett 1/113/17, L. Innes (London) to C. Whyteford, 26 March 1688.
18. SCA/BlLett 1/113/20, L. Innes (London) to C. Whyteford, 26 April 1688.
19. Anson, P.F., *Underground Catholicism in Scotland 1622–1878* (Montrose 1970), p.87.
20. The Register of the Privy Council of Scotland (ed. Paton), Third Series, Vol XIII 1686–1689, (Edinburgh 1932), p. xxxv.
21. Ibid. p. xxxvi.
22. *The Register of the Privy Council of Scotland* (ed. Paton), Third Series, Vol X 1684–1685 (Edinburgh 1927), p.413, p.166.
23. *The Register of the Privy Council of Scotland* (ed. Paton), Third Series, Vol XIII 1686–1689, (Edinburgh 1932), p.xxx.
24. SCA/BlLett 1/102/4, L. Innes (London) to C. Whyteford, 25 April 1687.
25. SCA/BlLett 1/84/5, L. Innes (Calais) to C. Whyteford, 4 May 1684.
26. SCA/BlLett 1/102/11, L. Innes (Holyrood H) to C. Whyteford, 28 June 1687.
27. SCA/BlLett 1/102/16, L. Innes (Holyrood H) to C. Whyteford, 19 July 1687.
28. SCA/BlLett 1/102/18, L. Innes (Holyrood H) to C. Whyteford, 28 July 1687.
29. SCA/BlLett 1/102/20, L. Innes (Preshome) to C. Whyteford, 25 Aug 1687.
30. SCA/BlLett 1/106/15, L. Innes (London) to C. Whyteford, 26 Dec 1687.
31. SCA/BlLett 1/106/15, Earl of Perth (Edinburgh) to C. Whyteford, 12 July 1687.
32. Dilworth, M., *The Scots in Franconia* (Edinburgh & London 1974), p.201.
33. Hay, R.A., *Genealogie of the Hayes of Tweeddale* (Edinburgh 1835), pp.54–56.

34. SCA/BlLett 1/103/7, L. Innes (London) to C. Whyteford, 9 November 1687.

35. SCA/BlLett 1/113/22, L. Innes (London) to C. Whyteford, 3 May 1688.

36. SCA/BlLett 1/102/20, L. Innes (Preshome) to C. Whyteford, 25 Aug 1687.

37. SCA/BlLett 1/102/18, L. Innes (Holyrood) to C. Whyteford, 28 July 1687.

38. SCA/BlLett 1/103/7, L. Innes (London) to C. Whyteford, 9 Nov 1687.

39. SCA/BlLett 1/113/7. L. Innes (London) to C. Whyteford, 26 Jan 1688 (87O.S.).

40. SCA/BlLett 1/102/10, L. Innes (Holyrood H) to C. Whyteford, 21 June 1687.
     SCA/BlLett 1/102/11, L. Innes (Holyrood H) to C. Whyteford, 28 June 1687.

41. SCA/BlLett, 1/102/11, L. Innes (Holyrood H.) to C. Whyteford, 28 June 1687.

42. SCA/BlLett 1/102/10, L. Innes (Holyrood H) to C. Whyteford, 21 June 1687.

43. SCA/BlLett 1/102/11, L. Innes (Holyrood H) to C. Whyteford, 28 June 1687.

44. SCA/BlLett 1/102/10, L. Innes (Holyrood H) to C. Whyteford, 21 June 1687.
     SCA/BlLett 1/102/17.L. Innes (Holyrood H.) to C. Whyteford, 21 July 1687.

45. SCA/BlLett 1/03/16, L. Innes (London) to C. Whyteford, 19 Dec 1687.

46. SCA/BlLett 1/113/3, L. Innes (London) to C. Whyteford, 29 Dec 1687.
     SCA/BlLett 1/113/14, L. Innes (London) to C. Whyteford, 5/15 March 1688.

47. SCA/BlLett 1/103/4, L. Innes (London)to C. Whyteford, October 1687.

48. SCA/BlLett 1/103/11, L. Innes (London) to C. Whyteford, 17 Nov 1687.
     SCA/BlLett 1/103/16, L. Innes (London) to C. Whyteford, 19 Dec 1687.

49. SCA/BlLett 1/113/16, L. Innes (London) to C. Whyteford, 22 March 1688.
     SCA/BlLett 1/113/20, L. Innes (London) to C. Whyteford, 26 April 1688.

50. SCA/BlLett 1/102/10, L. Innes (Holyrood H) to C. Whyteford, 21 June 1687.

51. SCA/BlLett 1/102/10, L. Innes (Holyrood H) to C. Whyteford, 21 June 1687.
     SCA/BlLett 1/102/14, L. Innes (Holyrood H) to C. Whyteford, 5 July 1687.

52. SCA/BlLett 1/102/14, L. Innes (Holyrood H) to C. Whyteford, 5 July 1687.

53. SCA/BlLett 1/102/19, L. Innes (Holyrood H) to C. Whyteford, 1 Aug 1687.

54. SCA/BlLett 1/113/19, L. Innes (London) to C. Whyteford, 17 Feb 1687.

55. SCA/BlLett 1/102/5, L. Innes (London) to C. Whyteford, 28 April 1687.

56. SCA/BlLett 1/102/5, L. Innes (London) to C. Whyteford, 28 April 1687.

57. SCA/BlLett 1/102/6, L. Innes (London) to C. Whyteford, 12 May 1687.

58. SCA/BlLett 1/113/7, L. Innes (London) to C. Whyteford, 26 Jan 1688 (87 O.S.).

59. SCA/BlLett 1/102/10, L. Innes (Holyrood H) to C. Whyteford, 21 June 1687.

60. SCA/BlLett 1/102/10, L. Innes (Holyrood H) to C. Whyteford, 21 June 1687.

61. SCA/BlLett 1/102/12, L. Innes (Holyrood H) to C. Whyteford, 30 June 1687.

62. SCA/BlLett 1/102/17, L. Innes (Holyrood H.) to C. Whyteford, 21 July 1687.

63. SCA/BlLett 1/102/19, L. Innes (Holyrood H) to C. Whyteford, 1 Aug 1687.

64. SCA/BlLett 1/113/11, L. Innes (London) to C. Whyteford, 17 Feb 1688 (87 O.S.).

65. SCA/BlLett 1/102/19, L. Innes (Holyrood H) to C. Whyteford, 1 Aug 1687.

66. SCA/BlLett 1/103/1, L. Innes (Drummond) to C. Whyteford, 12 Sept 1687.

67. SCA/BlLett 1/103/4, L. Innes (London) to C. Whyteford, Oct 1687.

68. SCA/BlLett 1/113/17, L. Innes (London) to C. Whyteford, 26 March 1688.

69. SCA/BlLett 1/113/14, L. Innes (London) to C. Whyteford, 5/15 March 1688.

70. SCA/BlLett 1/113/17, L. Innes (London) to C. Whyteford, 26 March 1688.

71. SCA/BlLett 1/113/17, L. Innes (London) to C. Whyteford, 26 March 1688.

72. SCA/BlLett 1/113/17, L. Innes (London) to C. Whyteford, 26 March 1688.

73. Dilworth, M., 'The Scottish Mission in 1688–1689.', *Innes Review* 20 (1968), pp.68–79.

74. SCA/BlLett 2/17/2, L. Innes (St Germain) to W. Leslie (Rome), 13 Feb 1696.

75. SCA/BlLett 2/17/7, L. Innes (St Germain) to W. Leslie (Rome), 19 Nov 1696.

76. SCA/BlLett 2/23/12, L. Innes (St Germain) to W. Leslie (Rome), 7 Oct 1697.

77. SCA/BlLett 2/100/8, L. Innes (St Germain) to J. Gordon, 7 Apr 1704.

78. SCA/BlLett 1/159/16, L. Innes (St Germain) to W. Leslie (Rome), 15 June 1693.

79. SCA/BlLett 1/168/11, C. Whyteford to W. Leslie (Rome), 11 May 1693.

80. SCA/BlLett 2/20/2, G. Adamson (Paris) to Rome, 1 July 1697.

81. SCA/BlLett 1/179/12, Wm Leslie (Rome) to L. Innes (St Germain), 30 Nov 1694.

82. SCA/BlLett 2/3/1, L. Innes (St Germain) to W. Leslie (Rome), 3 Jan 1695.

83. SCA/BlLett 2/51/1, L. Innes (St Germain) to W. Leslie (Rome), 19 Jan 1699.

84. SCA/BlLett 2/20/5, G. Adamson (Paris), 29 Dec 1697.

85. SCA/BlLett 2/43/3, G. Adamson (Paris) to L. Innes (St Germain), 2 Jan 1699.

86. SCA/BlLett 2/23/17, L. Innes (St Germain) to C. Whyteford, 26 Dec 1697.

87. SCA/BlLett 2/23/17., Innes (Bourbon) to G. Adamson (Paris), 23 April 1701.

88. SCA/BlLett 2/37/9, L. Innes (St Germain) to W. Leslie (Rome), 1 Dec 1698.

89. SCA/BlLett 2/44/7, G. Adamson (Paris) to L. Innes (St Germain), 16 Nov 1699.

90. SCA/BlLett 2/51/19, L. Innes (St Germain) to J. Irvine (Rome), Sept 1699.

91. SCA/BlLett 2/51/20, L. Innes (St Germain) to W. Leslie (Rome), 13 Oct 1699.

92. SCA/BlLett 2/51/24, L. Innes (St Germain) to W. Leslie (Rome), 15 Dec 1699.

93. SCA/BlLett 2/51/25, L. Innes (St Germain) to W. Leslie (Rome), 22 Dec 1699.

94. SCA/BlLett 2/87/4, L. Innes (St Germain) to J. Gordon (Rome), 8 Jan 1703.

95. SCA/BlLett 2/87/21, L. Innes (St Germain) to J. Gordon (Rome), 25 Nov 1703.

96. SCA/BlLett 2/100/3, L. Innes (St Germain) to J. Gordon (Rome), 11 Feb 1704.

97. SCA/BlLett 2/145/4, T. Nicolson to T. Innes (Paris), 5 May 1707.

98. SCA/BlLett., A. Drummond (Paris) to L. Innes (St Germain), 1697,

99. SCA/BlLett 2/20/2, G. Adamson (Paris) to Rome, 1 July 1697.

100. SCA/BlLett 2/116/12, L. Innes (St Germain) to J. Gordon (Rome), 10 May 1705.

101. SCA/BlLett 2/116/21, L. Innes (St Germain) to J. Gordon (Rome), 20 Dec 1705.

102. SCA/BlLett 2/37/4, L. Innes (St Germain) to W. Leslie (Rome), 21 April 1698.

103. SCA/BlLett 2/100/11, L. Innes (St Germain) to J. Gordon (Rome), 1 June 1704.

104. Helyot, P., *Histoire des Ordres Monastiques, Religieux et Militaires et des Congregations seculieres* (Paris 1718), Vol VII p.393.

105. SCA/BlLett. 2/145/4, T. Nicolson to T. Innes (Paris), 5 May 1707.

106. SCA/BlLett 2/3/4, L. Innes (Paris) to W. Leslie (Rome), 28 Feb 1695.

107. SCA/BlLett 2/3/8, L. Innes (Paris) to W. Leslie (Rome), 2 May 1695.

108. SCA/BlLett 2/116/ 15, L. Innes (Paris) to W. Leslie (Rome), 15 June 1705.

109. SCA/BlLett 2/101/5, L. Innes (St Germain) to J. Gordon (Rome), 3 Nov 1704.

110. SCA/BlLett 2/116/21, L. Innes (St Germain) to J. Gordon (Rome), 20 Dec 1705.

111. SCA/BlLett 2/116/21, L. Innes (St Germain) to J. Gordon (Rome), 20 Dec 1705.

CHAPTER 6

The College and the Jacobite Cause

When James VII took up residence in St Germain, a new element was introduced into the agenda of the Scots College Paris. From then on, an important objective was the restoration of the Stuart Monarchy. The devotion of the college to the Scottish royal house predated the Revolution. Mary Queen of Scots had saved the first foundation from financial ruin, and was venerated as a great benefactor. David Chambers who was Principal of the College from 1637 to 1641, had dedicated *De fortitudine Scotorum*[1] to Charles I, even although that monarch had not been Catholic. Ties with the monarchy, however, became very much deeper when Louis Innes, Principal from 1682, struck up a personal relationship with James VII in 1684. After the King fled to France, the members of the Scots College Paris were amongst his most steadfast supporters. This was partly because of loyalty and gratitude, but there was also a firm belief in a political solution for Catholic problems in Scotland. A Catholic sovereign would end persecution and enable the Catholic church to develop and evangelise without restraint, and indeed during the short reign of James VII, Catholics had enjoyed freedom to worship and the benefits of royal patronage, although the secular priests would have preferred less ostentation than the regular clergy displayed under James' indulgence, the catastrophe at Holyrood proving the folly of such extravagance.

In the Scots College today, there can still be seen the large portrait of James Edward Stewart, close to the chapel door; it is a symbol dominating the staircase as the Stuart cause dominated the minds of the college members. The Principal, Louis Innes, devoted his life to the Stuart cause. The letters of Charles Whyteford speak of little else. More *alumni* fought for the Jacobite cause than became priests.

When King James came to Paris, Louis Innes became one of his advisers and left the college to make his residence with the court at St Germain. He was made Secretary of State for Scotland in 1689,[2] and appears to have been one of the five who acted as a Cabinet Council to James VII at St Germain on his return from Ireland in 1690.[3] Later he became almoner to the Queen in 1701,[4] and was admitted almoner to the Chevalier St. George in 1713,[5] confirmed by warrant of appointment in 1714.[6]

Alumni of the Scots College, Paris were involved in all the attempts to regain the throne for the Stuarts. In the Irish campaign of 1689, James Drummond, the second titular Duke of Perth, whom Louis Innes had recruited for the college in 1686, attended King James VII when he embarked at Brest for Ireland. The Duke fought for the exiled King at the siege of Londonderry, at the Battle of the Boyne, at the last retreat at Limerick and the Pass of Athlone.[7] Later, as we shall see, he fought in the Fifteen.

At the Battle of the Boyne, a distinguished *alumnus* of the Scots College was killed. He was James St. Clair, eldest son of James St Clair of Roslin, Commissary of Shetland. The younger James was Page of Honour to Queen Marie, and Cornett of her Guards in Parker's Company. Perhaps a quatrain in the 'Orange Song' shows his military importance:

St Clair is dead',
And all his men are from the battle fled,
As he rode down the hill he met his fall,
He died a victim to a cannon-ball.[8]

Also on this expedition was a priest-*alumnus*, Robert Monro who had joined the Jacobite army, against the explicit orders of James Dunbar, Prefect of the Mission. (It is doubtful whether or not this was disobedience, as a prefect of the mission had far less authority than a bishop, and could not insist on a missioner moving from one station to another.) Monro was not heard of for some time, and it was presumed that he had been killed, but in February 1693 a letter of Charles Whyteford to William Leslie in Rome revealed to him that 'Mr Monroe is risen again from the deade, and hath been at the Boyne'.[9] It was for this that Monro was arrested in 1696, imprisoned in Edinburgh for a short time, before being banished to Flanders where he had the misfortune to be imprisoned again at Ghent as mentioned in the previous chapter.

Another *alumnus* in this campaign, though not in any way eminent, was a Mr Rigge, a convert minister who had studied some time at the college. He had been designated to go to Rome in 1688, but had been prevented by bad health.[10] He was to proceed to Rome in 1689,[11] but decided instead to become a soldier, and Charles Whyteford wrote to William Leslie in March 1689 that he had gone to Ireland with the King.[12]

Ties between the College and the Stuart King were greatly strengthened when Thomas Innes discovered a charter of the reign of Robert II which established the legitimacy of Robert III. It was in the spring of that same year that James VII asked James Nicol, one of the exiled priests who had found refuge in the Scots College, to go as a military chaplain to the Jacobites on the Bass Rock. By the time he arrived, however, the garrison had capitulated, and Nicol returned to Paris.[13]

In April 1695, King James visited the Scots College, staying for a few days, and he continued his patronage of the college, despite his own financial shortage. Thus in 1698, he gave a grant of one thousand livres to relieve the needs of the college, which Louis Innes considered very generous 'considering the bad circumstances of our Court at present.'[14] On 24 March 1701, King James VII continued to show his favour when he deposited in the Scots College his memoirs and papers. This led other Jacobites to follow suite, and thus the college became not only the official home of the royal documents, but also the foremost Jacobite archive.

The services of Louis Innes were acknowledged by James VII on his death-bed in September 1701. As Louis Innes and the Duke of Perth with many others knelt round the bedside, the King said aloud, 'M. Inese I have had great confidence in you, & you have served me well.'[15]

Franco-Jacobite invasion of 1708

Alumni continued to play prominent roles in the Jacobite rebellions. Charles Fleming, brother to the Earl of Wigton and later Earl himself, was probably the most involved Scotsman in the Franco-Jacobite invasion of 1708. He was in the plot from the beginning acting as Nathaniel Hooke's emissary in contacting the Scottish nobles in 1705. We find him leading Hooke to the Duchess of Gordon at her house on the Castlehill, then bringing the Countess Marischal to Hooke at Comiston, and conducting Hooke back to Edinburgh to meet the Earl of Home and the Earl of Panmure.

Although it was agreed that four Scottish representatives should cross to France in October, only Charles Fleming made the voyage, arriving in France as the solitary envoy. Despite his ship being intercepted by a privateer, and some difficulty with the Dutch authorities at Ostend, Charles Fleming had been able to conceal the purpose of his visit from his adversaries.

When the time for the invasion came in 1708, Charles Fleming left France ahead of the fleet in order to alert the Scottish nobles. At nightfall on 25 February, he shipped out of Dunkirk aboard a light frigate named the *Cigalle*; six days later he transferred to a fishing boat and landed on Scottish soil. Then began his impetuous rides round the country to alert the Scots that the invading fleet was almost here. He contacted the Countess of Errol, and then the Marquis of Huntly at Gordon Castle. On 5 March, he was at Lord Strathmore's in Angus, and that same evening at the house of Lord Nairne near Dunkeld. From there he rode up Strathtay to the Castle of Alloch to alert the old Earl of Breadalbane, and thence to Drummond Castle. The next day (6 March) he was on his way to Stirlingshire to Viscount Kilsyth, and to his own brother the Earl of Wigton who was also an *alumnus* of the Scots College. By 11 March, he finished this part of his task by going to Cochrane of Kilmarnock who was in Dumbartonshire. He then instructed James Malcolm of Grange to meet the French ships when they reached the Forth, while he himself waited patiently for news of James Edward. When he heard that James had landed somewhere north of Tay, he set out by a circuitous route through Perthshire to meet his lord, still hopeful that James Edward's cause would prevail. The failure of the Franco-Jacobite invasion of 1708 could certainly not be attributed to the gallant efforts of Charles Fleming.[16]

1713–1714

When James Edward decided to leave St Germain for Bar-le-Duc in Lorraine in 1713, he insisted on Louis Innes accompanying him. Innes himself was most reluctant, and tried hard to resist going; as his brother Thomas wrote:

> he [the King] will absolutely have Mr Simple [L. Innes] to goe along wt him, notwithstanding his infirmities which render [him] most unfitt for voyaging, and more yet by the want wee'l have of his presence here, & tho he hath done all that's possible for a subject to doe W[ith]out formall dissobedience, M. Arthur [the King] will not alter his resolution.[17]

There were some diplomats who disapproved of the King's decision, but the Marquis de Torcy, the French minister for Foreign Affairs, expressed the view that the King could not do better than have Louis Innes with him.[18] Accordingly Innes resigned as Principal of the Scots College in February 1713, and left for Bar-le-Duc on 8 March.[19] Before the King left St Germain, Louis Innes managed to get him to sit for a copper plate engraving which was gifted to the college.[20]

Already Almoner to Queen Mary, Louis Innes was admitted also as Almoner to King James on 30 November 1713.[21] Thereafter he was in all the secrets of James' court,[22] and was in a position to give advice directly to the King. Thus in 1714 Innes was heavily involved in the diplomacy which tried to secure James' succession to Queen Anne. On 8 April 1714, the Duke of Berwick reported to the King that Innes had had a long conversation with the Marquis de Torcy, French minister of Foreign Affairs.[23] The Duke planned further consultations with De Torcy, Pralin and Innes on what to do on the death of Queen Anne.[24] Innes sent the King an account of deliberations he had with De Torcy on 16 April,[25] and also told His Majesty what Louis XIV was willing to consent to.[26] Later in the same month, Berwick and Innes discussed the religious issues involved in a restoration.[27] Berwick, believing that the religious issue was quite secondary to that of the succession, thought that the Jacobite Court would do best to ignore religious questions asked by the English.[28] This was probably his reason for disagreeing with the answer that Innes proposed to be sent by the Duke of Lorraine to Queen Anne in May 1714,[29] since Berwick advised King James that 'Queen Anne would be much perplexed and Harley might take occasion to have vote against James in both houses.'[30] Despite some disagreements on matters like this, Innes and Berwick worked closely together, as we can see from the frequent references to Innes in Berwick's letters to King James. For example, when Innes returned to St Germain in November 1714 after a short stay in Paris, Berwick wrote to the King, 'I am glad Innes is here, for his advice will be very useful to me.'[31] It was therefore very sad that when the King dismissed Berwick from having any part in his affairs in November 1715, it was Louis Innes who got the unpleasant task of taking the King's letter to Berwick.[32]

Preparations for the Fifteen

After the death of Queen Anne and the succession of George I, Louis Innes was a leading figure in plotting the Stuart restoration by force of arms. He was no pacifist. Indeed when King James approved of Bolingbroke's suggestion of sending Innes to Sweden, he wrote, 'his [Innes'] pretentions in warlike affairs run so high that he might be disgusted and embarass'd should he remain hereabouts.'[33] Several initiatives were taken by Innes in the preparations for invasion. In December 1714, when he realised that the brother of Arbuthnot was going to Port Mahon, he took the opportunity of urging Berwick to write to see if the English fleet could be won over to the Stuart cause.[34] In April 1715, he wrote to King James about the necessity of sending someone to the Duke of Ormonde,[35] and when Ormonde arrived in France in August 1715, Innes met him preparatory to his rendezvous with King James who told Innes that he was very glad that Ormonde had made such favourable impressions.[36] In May, Innes advocated 'making up what Castelblanco proposed to the number of 10,000 arms.' The King approved, but his difficulty was finding the money.[37]

In his preparations for the rising in Scotland, Louis Innes involved his brother Thomas and the Scots College, Paris. In a letter to his brother Thomas on 13 November 1715, he repeated instructions 'to pay four baggs of the Kings gold to Ld Bollingbrokes order.' Clearly the College had been holding the king's money, and the letter continues:

> I believe you have but one left & the broken one. These last 4 are to be sent to Scotland wt the ship that has 1300 stand of armes & a good quantity of powder wh[ich] is to part immed[iate]ly. I have been long working to get th[i]s done & have enabled it at last.[38]

By the date (13 November) it may seem at first that these arms were too late for Sheriffmuir which was fought on 13 November, but Innes writing in France used new style dates, as can be confirmed from the instances where he put the day of the week as well as the date. By new style dating, the Battle of Sheriffmuir was on 24 November 1715, and there is every chance that these arms were in time.

The Fifteen

Many are of the opinion that Louis Innes was in Scotland during the Fifteen, but close consideration of the evidence does not bear this out. In *The Jacobites and the Union,* Charles Terry, at least from an index reference, presupposed that a Lewis Innes on the battlefield of Sheriffmuir was the same person as the King's almoner who had been Principal of the Scots College, but that scarcely seems possible.[39] Our Louis Innes wrote letters from St Germain on 16 November[40] and 28 November N.S.,[41] and a letter written on the night of 24 November N.S. (the day of the battle) has no indication that it came from Scotland and no hint of battle news.[42] The first news of the battle that Louis Innes received was from Tannachy Tulloch's son who arrived at St Germain on 12 December, having left the Duke of Mar eight days previously.[43]

The author of an article about the Inneses of Balnacraig stated that Father Louis Innes accompanied the Chevalier St Georges to Scotland and officiated in the chapels of Glamis and Scone,[44] the source of his information being the Innes Family Prayer Book, but that does not seem possible either. King James wrote Innes twice from Normandy, giving details of the King going to Scotland, but there is no mention of Innes going with him.[45] Thomas Innes said that when the King arrived in Scotland on 2 January N.S., Captain Cameron was the only Scotsman with him.[46] On 19 January,[47] 24 January[48] and 26 January,[49] Louis Innes wrote to his brother that there was as yet no news from the King. Innes' letters of 6 February,[50] 15 February and 18 February[51] were written from France as can be deduced from their contents, and a letter of 25 February[52] gave news of the King being back in France. There does not seem to have been time between these letters for Innes to have journeyed to and from Scotland.

Although Louis Innes was not in Scotland for the Fifteen, several of his pupils took part in the campaign. James, second Duke of Perth who had served in Ireland in 1689–1690, joined the Earl of Mar, and played a prominent role. After an unsuccessful attempt to surprise Edinburgh Castle on 8 September, he commanded the cavalry at the Battle of Sheriffmuir, and throughout the insurrection was one of the ablest leaders.[53]

The most distinguished *alumnus* on the field of battle in the '15 was General Alexander Gordon of Auchintoul. The eldest son of Lord Alexander Gordon of Auchintoul, a 'law lord', he with his brother George were among the six who had been recruited for the college by Louis Innes on his visit to Scotland in 1684.[54] After his studies at the Scots College, Alexander Gordon had a most distinguished career, beginning as 'a cadet in one of the companies raised at the desire of King James VII to assist in the wars he then had in Catalonia.' He joined the Russian army of Peter the Great in 1695, where shortly afterwards he was summoned to appear personally before the Czar for having physically beaten six men at a wedding in defence of the honour of Scotland. The Czar was so impressed that he immediately gave him a Major's commission,[55] from which he rose to become Major-General, continuing in the Czar's service until his return to Scotland in 1711. Later he wrote *The History of Peter the Great, Emperor of Russia*, published posthumously at Aberdeen in 1755.

General Alexander Gordon's part in the rebellion was prominent. He was present at the meeting at Aboyne on 9 September when it was decided that the time was ripe to take up arms, after which Gordon proceeded to recruit 4,000 men in the Highlands and Islands. After an unsuccessful attempt to take Fort William, Gordon advanced to Inverary where he prevented the Earl of Islay from taking action. A compromise was reached whereby Gordon withdrew and agreed to compensate the poor people for their losses, on condition that the Hanoverian troops would not molest the clans. Arriving at Drummond Castle at the beginning of November, General Gordon joined the Earl of Mar's army on 10 November. Three days later at Sheriffmuir, he commanded the centre of the first line which proved victorious against the enemy. When the Chevalier's army reached Montrose on 3 February 1716, Gordon was put in command and led the troops back to Aberdeen and thence to Badenoch, commanding so well that, though hotly pursued, he lost very few men. Thereafter he hid in the Highlands until he escaped to France in 1717.[56]

George Gordon, brother of General Alexander Gordon, who had gone to the Scots College with his brother in 1684,[57] also took part in the rising though in a much lesser capacity. Afterwards he perished at sea, while escaping to Holland.[58]

Two older *alumni* of the college, friends of Innes in his student days under Robert Barclay were also active in the Fifteen. John Stewart of Boggs, who was described as 'Chamberlain of the Enzie' i.e. to the Duke of Gordon, was out for the Jacobites, although Lord Findlater had previously predicted to the contrary. Writing to William Lorimer, his Chamberlain, on 10 August 1715, Findlater had said, 'Letterfury, Bogs and Tanachie will also be friendly.' He was wrong about all three. In September 1715 orders were issued by the Marquis of Huntly to John Stewart of Boggs and Colonel James Innes, whom he had appointed commander of that district, to raise all his vassals in Strathbogie. Stewart did not ignore the command;

his zeal in fulfilling it can be seen in the plea of Alexander Hay of Arbroath that he had been forced out by Stewart of Boggs.[59]

James Gordon of Letterfourie, whom Findlater had also expected to be friendly to the Hanoverians, was present on the Jacobite side at Sheriffmuir where he is said to have killed six men. According to the *Chiefs of Grant,* he surrendered himself after the Rising and a recommendation was forwarded to the Government that the measures taken against him might be lenient. In spite of his adherence to the Stuart cause in 1715, he was on the Hanoverian side in 1745 (although he had to pay Cess to the Jacobites), receiving also from the ministers of Cullen, Deskford and Rathven on 26 April 1746 a 'Testimony and Recommendation' in which the three divines declared that 'James Gordon of Letterfoury during the time of this unnatural Rebellion has behaved himself at home discreetly and civily to all persons concerned in the present happy establishment.'[60]

One notable *alumnus* of the college was prevented from taking part in the rebellion by imprisonment. He was John Fleming, the sixth Earl of Wigton, whose brother Charles had made such strenuous efforts in 1708. At the outbreak of the Jacobite rising, he was imprisoned in Edinburgh Castle as a suspect by warrant of Major-General Williams on 20 August 1715.[61]

1715–1718

The bitter disappointment of 1715 in no way diminished college fervour for the cause of James Edward. Louis Innes, continuing in the service of the Jacobite King, played a prominent part in drafting the King's defence of the campaign that was published in April 1716,[62] and in the care of expatriots who had suffered for the Jacobite cause.[63] Not only did he advise the King about the legitimacy of his protecting and maintaining the Church of England,[64] but he was inviolved in the King's marriage plans,[65] and in the diplomacy surrounding the King's move from Avignon.[66] He was a most staunch promoter of the plans to persuade the King of Sweden to invade Britain.[67]

The college itself was still a bastion of support. Lord Nithsdale who made the now famous escape from the Tower of London disguised as his wife, found refuge within its walls on his arrival in Paris. His nephew, Charles, Lord Linton, wrote to his mother, Lady Traquair, (25 March 1716):

> He [his uncle, Lord Nithsdale] came to town yesterday, and stays at present in the same lodging with us, he does not design to stay long here, but has a mind to go somewhere elsewhere more wholesome to breath in, for fear he should relapse into his late sickness.[68]

Lord Linton and his brother were at this time both students of the Scots College, Paris. No doubt Lord Nithsdale found life in the college too restrictive, as Lord Linton wrote to his mother on 6 May 1716:

not knowing that he [Lord Nithsdale] had any other friends here, came straight to us, where he stayed some few days, but not finding all convenienceys that he might have elsewhere, he took an apartment of his own, and remain'd for some time there.[69]

In August 1716, King James asked Thomas Innes to write a complete history of Scotland up to the Union of the Crowns. Thomas Innes, though pleading lack of ability and the demands of his vocation, accepted the challenge as a command from the King. When his *Critical Essay* was published in 1729, he sent a copy to the King explaining that beyond the motives of writing set out in the preface of his work, he had the intention of vindicating the hereditary monarchy by showing that the story of the first forty kings, of whom about a third are punished by their subjects, was no more than a forgery popularised by Boece and Buchanan. Thomas Innes demonstrated that primogeniture was the ancient law in Scotland, and although Scots had been forced to give the command to a near relation when there was a minor in time of war, Kenneth III who came to the throne in 971 AD had with the consent of his nobles restored the primitive law of primogeniture.[70]

In February 1718, Louis Innes was dismissed from his post of Almoner to the King and forbidden to meddle any more in the King's affairs. No reason was expressed in the order, and Innes who at first had no idea what had occasioned the King's displeasure, thought that it might have been on account of the frankness he was accustomed to express to his majesty. The King, however, disclaimed this, but gave many different reasons to different people. The first reason given was that Innes in making a French translation of a letter of King James had missed out some words, thereby giving a false interpretation injurious to the King's reputation in England. To Father Gaillard, however, King James alleged that Innes was setting James and Queen Mary at variance one against the other. To the Duke of Ormonde, the King wrote that Innes was causing jealousies and mistakes, that by diminishing the confidence people have in Mar, he might have more share in business, and that he was leading General Dillon to believe that Mar was jealous of Dillon. The King went as far as to call Innes 'the chief author of misunderstanding'. Innes later believed that the real reason was one that does not appear in the Stuart correspondence of the time, namely that Mar had complained to King James that Louis Innes had received into the Scots College Colin Campbell who had brought out Campbells against the Stuart King at Sheriffmuir. Innes argued Colin Campbell's complete change of side:

it was wt much ado Debrie [Louis Innes] could except himself by showing that M. Col. was now quite another man & most sensible of his former fault, but that fault was insisted on & exaggerated by Allan Cameron and Ld Mar, but especially by the last who was present & pretended that the misfortune that happened proceeded from thence, that it made a deep impression on Sr John [King James] which I have reason to believe remains still [14 August 1733].[71]

History was to vindicate Louis Innes, as Campbell fought on the Jacobite side in the '45 in which he gave his life for King James on the battlefield of Culloden.

The importance of Louis Innes in the Jacobite circle can be appreciated by the fact that King James personally sent intimation of the dismissal to Lord Oxford,[72] to the Bishop of Rochester,[73] to General Dillon who was given the unpleasant task of handing the King's order to Innes, to the Earl of Panmure, to Cardinal Noailles,[74] to the Earl Marischal,[75] to the Duke of Ormonde[76] and to Cardinal Gualterio.[77]

A letter from Captain John Ogilvie to the Duke of Mar expresses how stunning was the news of Innes' dismissal:

when they saw that Inese was laid aside, it entirely struck a terror into the whole party, for when they found that strong tower was levelled, it made them all think there was no kicking against pricks.[78]

Queen Mary who was required to dismiss Innes as her almoner was most distressed and very reluctantly complied with the order. She told Innes that the King's displeasure was grounded on misinformation and mistakes which she hoped to set right, but she died on 7 May 1718, leaving to Innes vestments and other effects from her chapel and some of her books.[79]

Some rejoiced in Innes' downfall, but General Dillon had the courage to express his good opinion of Innes to King James. The Earl of Panmure declined to comment, even after he heard that the King had expected him to do so. He wrote to James:

I was very concerned to find by a letter from the Duke of Mar that I had incurred your displeasure by not showing my approbation of Mr Inese's being laid aside... it never entered into my thoughts that you expected any approbation from me.[80]

Innes himself was glad to be relieved of a job that he had been reluctant to accept in the first place, but the manner of his going undoubtedly hurt. Nevertheless in thanking the King for the vestments and books that he had received from Queen Mary's will, tells him that he is about to offer prayers [Mass] for the King, and that his loyalty to the Stuart cause had never wavered.[81] King James, who did regret the manner in which he had dismissed Innes,[82] later gave Innes and Dr Ingleton a present of Mass vestments which had been brought from England at the time of the Revolution. Innes in his acknowledgement, thanked the King also for 'the fine manuscript old Church books which shall be kept in our archives together with the royal papers.'[83] Although writing from St Germain, Innes is undoubtedly referring to the Scots College archives, since that was the repository of the royal papers.

After dismissal as almoner, Innes remained at St Germain, and was soon involved again in Jacobite affairs, but not at as high a level as he had been as almoner.

1719

Prior to the 1719 rising which ended in the defeat at Glenshiel on 10 June 1719, General Alexander Gordon who had distinguished himself in the '15 was amongst those at Bordeaux planning invasion. Being too sick to board any of the Spanish ships which sailed in March, he left Bordeaux with forty other officers in two Swedish ships.[84]

The Forty-five

The rebellion of 1745 was one in which *aluumni* of the Scots College Paris played a most distinguished role. Prince Charles himself was to have been a guest at the college in 1745, but excused himself on account of pressing business (how pressing was soon to be seen). The College had to be content with a visit from his brother, Henry, Duke of York, who was entertained in the College on St Andrew's day 1745[85] when the Prince's campaign was still doing well, the Jacobite army having reached Manchester,[86] and the Duke at that time hoped to lead some troops to Britain in support of his brother.

Several *alumni* of the College were involved at every stage of the rising. Right at the start of the campaign, one of the seven men of Moidart was Aeneas or Angus Macdonald, the son of Kinlochmoidart, an *alumnus* of the Scots College, Paris, who had at first intended to become a priest before he became troublesome, and finally left on 17 March 1727.[87]

He later became a banker in Paris where he remained a great friend of the college. Prince Charles stayed at his house in the capital, and it seems likely that Aeneas Macdonald was a prime influence on the prince in the decision to campaign in Scotland, as well as a provider of much of the finance needed for such an expedition. He was with the prince throughout the campaign, after which he surrendered to General Campbell in the north-west of Scotland on 13 May 1746 upon terms which were not fulfilled. Imprisoned first in Dumbarton Castle, he was conducted to Edinburgh Castle at the end of August 1746. Thence he was taken to the Duke of Newcastle's office at Whitehall, London, where he was committed into the custody of a messenger. One day when he was on a jaunt to Windsor with Miss Flora MacDonald, he was taken out of the messenger's hands and imprisoned first at Newgate and then in Southwark. On 28 May 1747 an indictment for high treason was found against him. On 2 July, however, Aeneas Macdonald escaped from Newgate by throwing snuff in the turnkey's eyes, but being shod with loose slippers, he was recaptured while running down Warwick Lane. At his trial on 10 December 1747, several witnesses testified that they had seen him in the rebel army at different places in Scotland and at Carlisle, armed, and in highland dress. He was condemned to death, 15 January being the date set for his execution, but he received a conditional pardon involving perpetual banishment, and was eventually released from prison on 11 December 1749. He returned to France where, in his very old age, he was killed during the French revolution.[88]

On Prince Charles' arrival in Scotland, he was dressed in the garb of a student of the Scots College Paris[89], and when *alumni* of the college came to his aid in the early stages of the campaign, they had something of the air of an 'Old Boys' Club' making sure that they would not let the side down. After the disappointment of Macdonald of Borrodale's refusal to join the prince, it was Aeneas Macdonald who suggested that they sail to Moidart. Amongst those he brought aboard the Prince's ship there, was another *alumnus*, young Clanranald. He was despatched to Skye to summon Sir Alexander MacDonald and MacLeod of MacLeod. Despite the disappointment of being unable to secure their help, young Clanranald joined the Prince with all the men he had on the mainland.[90] He then suggested to the Prince that Kinlochmoidart, Aeneas' brother, be sent to inform the Duke of Perth who had also been a student at the Scots College Paris. The royal standard was blessed at Glenfinnan by Bishop Hugh Macdonald who as a priest had studied in the Scots College Paris from July 1730 until September 1731, while the Prince's chaplain throughout the campaign was Alan Macdonald who had also studied for a short time at the college from February to June 1727. While it is not suggested that these were the only important characters of the early campaign (the allegiance of Cameron of Lochiel was crucial), they did make a significant contribution.

When the Prince arrived at Holyrood in the autumn of 1745, there took place a touching though inconsequential incident that shows how close the Paris *alumni* were to the person of the Prince. Margaret Frances Smyth, wife to John Gordon of Beldorny who had been in the college in the 1730s, offered to embroider a waistcoat for the Prince, and borrowed two of his satin vests as patterns. Mrs Gordon began work on a crimson one, but owing to the circumstances of the time was never able to finish it. Her husband was with the Prince throughout the campaign, and was one of the few who escaped capture afterwards as is recounted in *Jacobites of Aberdeen and Banffshire in the Forty-five*:

John Gordon of Beldorney fought at Culloden, and on his return home was hidden by his wife in a secret chamber at Beldorney. Another version of the story is that his widowed mother occupied Beldorney Castle, and, shortly after Culloden, a man was employed to build a dry-stone dyke on the estate. This workman must have been employed for some time, for the number of dykes erected by him was considerable; he was also inexperienced for the dykes were not very well built. One day he disappeared as suddenly as he came, and it subsequently turned out that he was none other than John Gordon of Beldorney whose hurried departure was probably due to his identity becoming known to the authorities.[91]

John Gordon's brother George who had also been at the college in Paris was sent round gentlemen's houses in East Lothian to gather arms and horses. A. & H. Tayler comment that he must have been a careless person since near Tranent he dropped his pocketbook which was subsequently found by the authorities. Had they known of his outbursts of madness at the Scots College, they might have marvelled that nothing worse befell him on this venture. After Culloden he intended to surrender himself, but before he did so, he was arrested at Huntly on 15 September 1746 on suspicion of being an officer in the rebel army, and was imprisoned. He was still in prison on 14 December 1746.[92]

Another *alumnus* who joined the Prince at Edinburgh in October 1745 was James Gordon of Glastirim, nephew to Bishop Gordon. He was described as 'a captain and very active in recruiting men for the Rebels.' After the rising, he surrendered at Fochabers in the summer of 1746, was excepted from the Indemnity, and despite the powerful advocacy of the Earl of Findlater to whom he had written a rather cringing letter, he was put on trial in Edinburgh on 12 October 1748, a verdict of '*Ignoramus*' being returned for lack of evidence.[93]

A relative of James Gordon of Glastirim who was also an *alumnus* of the college was Alexander Gordon of Letterfourie whose father, James Gordon, was said to have killed six men at Sheriffmuir. He was described as 'a volunteer in Pretender's son's Life-guards.' After the rising, he joined his brother James in Madeira, but later succeeded to Letterfourie.[94]

Another Gordon *alumnus* of the college in the forty-five was Alexander Gordon of Dorlaithers whose father George and uncle General Alexander Gordon had both fought in the Fifteen. It could not have been long since he left the college, as he only went there in 1742. Described in Rosebury's List as 'an Officer in the rebel army', he was never captured although Mr Sharpe, Solicitor to the Treasury, had evidence against him.[95]

The most eminent *alumnus* in the rising was the Duke of Perth who joined the insurrection at Perth on 4 September when he and Lord George Murray were appointed Lieutenant-Generals. At Brampton, he strongly urged the Prince to capture Carlisle. In the disputes which followed, he nobly resigned his lieutenant-generalship in the interests of unity, and reverted to the command of his own regiment. At Culloden, Lord James commanded the left wing. The Duke's soldiers consisted largely of Macdonalds who were aggrieved at being deprived of their place of honour on the right. Lord James was bold and resolute, and did his best to restore morale; standing with his back to the enemy, he doffed his hat and declared, 'If you fight with your usual bravery, you will make the left wing a right wing', and he promised that if they did well, he would ever afterwards assume the honourable name of Macdonald. Even when his wing was broken, he desperately tried to rally his men with the cry of 'Claymore'.[96]

Lord John Drummond, the Duke's brother and also an *alumnus* of the College, was in France at the beginning of the rising, but arrived in Scotland on 22 November with about eight hundred French troops, and issued a declaration in the name of the French King in favour of Charles Edward. He was present at the battle of Falkirk, and commanded the centre at Culloden. Before the action at the latter, he walked far to the front of his command in an effort to tempt Cumberland into an advance. Unfortunately, when his regiment was surrounded, his nerve broke, and he shouted on John Daniel to flee with him.[97]

Another *alumnus* who tried to come with troops from France was young Glengarry, Alastair Ruadh Macdonnell. He had been sent to France in 1745 by some Highland chiefs to try and dissuade Prince Charles from coming until he had French troops with him. Having missed the Prince in France, he was coming back to Scotland at the close of 1745 with a detachment of the Royal Scots in French service and a piquet of the Irish brigade, when he was captured at sea. He was imprisoned in the Tower of London for twenty-two months, until his release in July 1747.

The Earl of Traquair was also imprisoned in the Tower of London, although this *alumnus* of the College had played but a small part in the rising. As Lord Linton, he had been one of the seven 'Associators' who had put his signature to the famous letter sent to Cardinal Fleury in March 1741 in which some Scottish nobles had announced their readiness to rise, and asked for French help. Though at first reluctant, the Earl had been prevailed upon to go to London to sound out the English Jacobites. He took no active part in the campaign, but according to tradition, he received Prince Charles Edward at Traquair on the march to England in November 1745, and closed the gates behind him not to be opened until the restoration of the Stuart monarchy. According to Blaikie's itinerary, the Prince slept at Lauder on his way south, but it is possible that he visited Traquair.[98] Lord Traquair was arrested at Great Stoughton, Huntingdon, on 29 July 1746, and was not 'at full freedom' until 12 March 1749.[99]

Colin Campbell, the priest who had caused much difficulty for his *Alma Mater* in the Jansenist disputes, as will be fully discussed in the next chapter, was one of at least five Catholic priests, including his fellow conspirator in the aforesaid controversies, John Tyrie, on the battlefield of Culloden. It is almost certain that he was killed at the battle, while John Tyrie suffered two sword wounds to the head.

After the tragedy of Culloden, yet another *alumnus*, Neil MacEachan played an important role in the Prince's escape. A short article in the *Innes Review*[100] by the present writer demonstrated how the craftiness required for such a task was already manifest in his student days. Accompanying Prince Charles in his island wanderings during the months of May and June 1746, he it was who took the Prince to Flora Macdonald,[101] and accompanied them both to Skye when the Prince was disguised as Betty Burke. Neil parted company with the Prince at Portree, but rejoined him aboard *L'Heureux* on 20 September, and became a personal servant to the Prince in France where he shared his imprisonment in the Chateau de Vincennes in 1748.[102] Neil visited Scotland again in 1747, possibly as a Jacobite spy planning a fresh invasion for the following spring.[103]

The letters of George Innes, Principal of the Scots College during the forty-five, show an avid interest in the early stages of the rising, but there is a gap in his letters between 26 December 1745 and 2 September 1746, probably due to the difficulty of communication at the time. After the rising, priests in Scotland were not safe. Several were imprisoned, while others had to go into hiding. Among those imprisoned was Alexander Gordon, a Jesuit and a brother of John Gordon of Glencat. Alexander Gordon had been present at Culloden. After his arrest, he was sent to the jail at Inverness where he died about three weeks later.[104] The Paris College now became a place of refuge. First to arrive was Bishop Hugh Macdonald who had blessed Prince Charles' standard at Glenfinnan at the beginning of the rebellion, although he had advised the Prince that the time was unfavourable.

Bishop Macdonald had made his escape from Scotland on a French ship in August 1746, and arrived in Paris 'without one farthing of mon[ey], or so much as cloths upon his back to appear in'. George Innes, knowing that the College was still suspect in Rome on account of the Jansenist controversies, was afraid of what the Cardinals would think of the Bishop's presence in the College, but explained that he had had no choice.[105] Bishop Macdonald was to stay in France until 1749. After his return to Scotland, Bishop Macdonald was arrested on 19 July 1754. A sentence of banishment was pronounced on 1 May 1755, but the government authorities connived at his escape, and the sentence was never enforced.

Other two missionaries to find refuge at the College were Alexander
Forrester and Alan MacDonald, the Prince's chaplain who had enlisted in
the army as 'Captain Graham', wearing a sword. Both priests were arrested
in 1746,[106] brought to London, and imprisoned, first aboard a man-of-war
and then in Newgate prison. It was feared that they would be sent to the
plantations,[107] but they were finally banished for life,[108] and arrived
penniless at the College in the autumn of 1747, where they remained until
the beginning of August 1748. Forrester returned to Scotland, and resumed
his charge at Uist, though for a time he had to take refuge in Ireland. Alan
MacDonald went to Rome where he was appointed superior of the New
Converts' House, with a pension of ten crowns a month obtained through
the intercession of the Cardinal Duke of York. George Innes encouraged
him to write an account of the Prince's adventures in Scotland, which he
did, although the manuscript seems to have been lost.[109] In August 1768,
Alan Macdonald eventually returned to Scotland at the instance of the
Bishops. He was, however, somewhat restless after his return to Scotland,
serving the mission in Traquair, Edinburgh and Drummond, and for a time
back in Uist. He retained some of the craftiness of his old fugitive days
with the Prince as the following anecdote shows. It was written by
Alexander Geddes after the anti-Catholic riots in Edinburgh in 1779:

> Mr Ranaldson [Alan MacDonald] was the only man who remained in his own
> lodgings. He artfully enough sent for his landlord: told him he was going out of town
> for a few days: called a coach in the gloom of the evening: gave the driver ten pence
> to drive it a mile or so, and then locked himself an[d] his maid in till all the hurry was
> over. [110]

Did Prince Charles himself find refuge in the Scots College? It would
appear that sometimes he did. Intelligence was sent from Paris to the
English government in London that when the Prince was in Paris, the
Scots College was one of his residences.

> Paris, October 5, 1750.

> It is supposed that the Pretender's Son keeps at Mountl'hery, six leagues from Paris,
> at Mr Lumisden's, or at Villeneuf St Georges, at a small distance from Town, at Lord
> Nairn's; Sometimes at Sens, at Madme la Princesse de Talmont's, or the Scotch
> Seminary; nobody travels with him but Mr Goring, and a Biscayan recommended to
> him by Marshal Saxe: the young Pretender is disguised in an Abbé's dress, with a
> black patch upon his eye, and his eye-brows black'd.'[111]

One dressed as a priest would cause little surprise in the college. The
question arises as to how the Prince's presence in the college came to be
known. The most probable explanation is that the information was sent or
came from young Glengarry, *alias* Pickle the Spy, the only *alumnus* to
betray the Stuart cause. The Principal of the college, George Innes, believing

him still to be 'truly a good subject' was sending letters to Rome for Glengarry in May 1750,[112] and could easily have sent a coded letter telling him that the Prince was in the college. In the light of Glengarry's double-dealing, he would hardly have scrupled to pass this information to the British government.

Alastair Ruadh Macdonnell, young Glengarry, whom Andrew Lang has identified as Pickle the Spy, had entered the Scots College Paris as a student on 6 January 1741. As will be recorded in chapter seven,[113] his conduct had left much to be desired, and the Principal's way of dealing with this did not prepare him well for his future career. Having left the College in 1744, one year later he was acting as a messenger in the preparations for the 'forty-five'. His espionage activities must have begun very soon afterwards.

This perfidy led to accusations against a Scottish priest called James Leslie who had been forced to escape from Scotland after the battle of Prestonpans. The Jacobites knowing that there was a spy in their camp, charged James Leslie with treachery. After Leslie protested his innocence, it was the Scots College, Paris which was appointed to determine the case. Mr Kelly who had received the complaint from Scotland wrote to Leslie on 11 October 1748:

> Mr Sandison [Bishop Macdonald] and the people of Grisy house [Scots College Paris] have a copy of the accusation sent against you from Scotland. If you can clear your conduct to them it will be sufficient.

It was at this time that young Glengarry wrote to James Leslie on 19 October 1748 the sentence that is quoted by Andrew Lang, 'One needs not be a wizard to see that mentioning you was only a feint, and the whole was aimed at me.'[114] Writing this was sheer bluff; the Jacobites did not suspect Glengarry, although they should have done so, but it was no doubt the close association of the priest with the young chieftain that brought suspicion on Leslie. Leslie had brought young Glengarry to Paris in January 1741, and during the latter's three years at the College had liaison with Old Glengarry to collect the fees and pocket-money for his son. Young Glengarry had brought James Leslie into Jacobite intrigues on 1 May 1745 when he entrusted some papers to his custody, thereby leading the priest to act as a messenger for the plotters. Leslie had saved young Glengarry's life by warning him of plans to arrest him, had stayed in the same hotel with Glengarry in Paris, and spent four months doing Glengarry's business in London. The Jacobites were close to their quarry, but picked on the wrong man.

The verdict at the College hearing on 15 December 1748, cleared Leslie's name with the declaration:

Whereas Mr Kelly lodged with us in October last ane accusation against N.N. [James Leslie] alleging that he had kept close correspondence with the Ministry at London during the years 1745 and 1746, and likeways he had been sent to France by Mr Murray of Br[ough]ton, had gone back again to Great Britain and returned a second time for further Intelligence, the said Mr Kly by his R.H. s orders requiring of us to examin N.N.'s conduct leaving the final determination to our judgement we here declare that we are intirely satisfied with the accounts NN gives of himself and conduct, and are convinced of his innocence by the undeniable proofs he had given us and that the most of the articles alleged against him are notoriously false according to our own certain knowledge. Given at Paris the fifteenth day of December 1748. Signed by Sandison [Bishop Macdonald who had fled to the College after Culloden].'[115]

It is sad to reflect that there was even one alumnus who betrayed the Stuart cause, but the appointment of Grisy to judge James Leslie's case is evidence of how highly the College was esteemed by the Jacobites.

Estimate of College Involvement

The part played by the *alumni* of the Scots College in the Jacobite risings is impressive. Numbers from such a small college could not be great. Yet *alumni* held positions of command at the Battle of the Boyne, in the Fifteen and in the Forty-five, while the chief Scottish actor in 1708 and one of the planners of the 1719 attempt were also from the College, and Louis Innes, both *alumnus* and principal, was in the highest councils both of James VII and Chevalier St Georges. Bruce Lenman has minimised the Catholic influence in the Jacobite risings, pointing out how small were the numbers of that faith.[116] Is it not surprising then that a tiny college with an average of about eight students at a time should have played such a strong role? The Catholic import is not to be gauged by numbers alone.

The involvement does raise serious questions both about the propriety and the value of such dealings. It must of course be remembered, and it is so often forgotten, that the Scots College Paris was not simply a seminary for the training of priests, but a college for the education of Scottish Catholics. Non-ecclesiastical students had every right to play the fullest part in party politics. Yet two factors go beyond this. The first is that the priests of the college staff were deeply involved, and the second is that the ethos and atmosphere of the college was a formative force producing the most fervent Jacobitism. Subjectively the college staff considered this to be justifiable as they believed that the restoration of the Stuarts would be the best thing for Scottish Catholicism. Objectively their other work suffered.

At the end of the day, the Jacobite cause did not succeed, and the college found itself on the losing side. Scottish Catholicism, exhorted to armed rebellion by the Scots College, was in fact disadvantaged, and it was extremely difficult for Catholics to play an influential part in the affairs of the country.

Today, however, the unsuccessful Jacobite rebellions are romanticised, and are celebrated in song, to the extent that they play a significant part in expressing the character of the Scots people. In the episodes that became symbolic the Scots College Paris contributed not a little.

NOTES

1. Chambers, D., *De Fortitudine Scotorum* (Paris 1631).
2. Ararat, R. *The Jacobite Peerage*, (London & Edinburgh 1974), p.214.
3. Innes, T., 'The Inneses of Balnagraig. A Family of Deeside Jacobites', *The Deeside Field*, fifth number, 1931, p.78.
4. *Miscellany of the Spalding Club*, Vol II, p.376.
5. Ibid. p.377.
6. Ibid. p.377.
7. Paul, J.B.(Ed.), *The Scots Peerage* (Edinburgh: 1904–1911), Vol VII, p. 53.
8. Saint-Clair, R.W., *The Saint-Clairs of the Isles etc* (Auckland, N.Z. 1898), p. 292.
9. SCA/BlLett 1/168/3, C. Whyteford (Paris) to W. Leslie (Rome), 15 Feb 1693.
10. SCA/Bl. Lett 1/126/9, C, Whyteford (Paris) to W. Leslie (Rome), 22 Feb1689.
11. SCA/Bl. Lett 1/126/8, C, Whyteford (Paris) to W. Leslie (Rome), undated.
12. SCA/Bl. Lett 1/126/15(2), C, Whyteford (Paris) to W. Leslie (Rome),28 March 1689.
13. SCA/BlLett 1/172/6, L. Innes (St Germain) to W. Leslie (Rome), 12 March 1694
14. SCA/Bl Lett 2/37/7, L. Innes to J. Irvine, 1698.
15. SCA/Bl. Lett 2/69/4, L. Innes (St Germain) to ?, 4 Sept 1701.
16. J.S. Gibson, *Playing the Scottish Card* (Edinburgh 1988), pp. 42, 46, 56, 60, 69, 112, 113, 115, 121, 139, 143, 164.
17. SCA/BlLett, T. Innes (Paris) to W. Stuart (Rome), 30 May 1712.
18. Duke of Berwick to James VIII, 24 Feb1713, *Calendar of the Stuart Papers* (London 1902–1912), (Henceforth referred to as *'Stuart Papers'*), Vol I p.256
19. SCA/BlLett 2/184/3, T.Innes (Paris) to W. Stuart (Rome), 27 March 1713.
20. SCA/BlLett, T.Innes (Paris) to W. Stuart (Rome),13 Feb1713.
21. James VIII to D. Sheldon, 29 Nov 1713.
22. *Stuart Papers* I p.xxxvi
23. Duke of Berwick to James VIII, 8 April 1714, *Stuart Papers I* p.314
24. Duke of Berwick to James VIII, 11 April 1714, *Stuart Papers I*, p.315
25. Duke of Berwick to James VIII, 15 April 1714, *Stuart Papers I*. p.316.
26. Duke of Berwick to James VIII, 20 April 1714, *Stuart Papers I*, p.317
27. Duke of Berwick to James VIII, 22 April 1714, *Stuart Papers I* p.318
28. Duke of Berwick to James VIII, 1 March 1714, *Stuart Papers I*, p.304
 Duke of Berwick to James VIII, 13 March 1714, *Stuart Papers I*, p.307

Duke of Berwick to James VIII, 22 March 1714, *Stuart Papers I*, p.309
Duke of Berwick to James VIII, 28 March 1714, *Stuart Papers I*, p.310
Duke of Berwick to James VIII, 6 April 1714, *Stuart Papers I*, p.314
Duke of Berwick to James VIII, 11 April 1714, *Stuart Papers I*, p.315
Duke of Berwick to James VIII, 22 April 1714, Stuart Papers I, p.318

29. Duke of Berwick to James VIII, 6 May 1714, *Stuart Papers I,* p.320

30. Duke of Berwick to James VIII, 7 May 1714, *Stuart Papers I*, p.321

31. Duke of Berwick to James VIII, 25 Nov 1714, *Stuart Papers I*, p.336

32. James VIII to Lord Bolingbroke, 15 Nov 1715, *Stuart Papers I*. p.459

33. James VIII to Lord Bolingbroke, 23 Aug 1715, *Stuart Papers I*, p.400

34. Duke of Berwick to James VIII, 23 Dec 1714, *Stuart Papers I*, p.339

35. Duke of Berwick to James VIII, 26 April 1715, *Stuart Papers I*, p.360

36. James VIII to L. Innes, 23 Aug 1715, *Stuart Papers I*, p.399

37. James VIII to Duke of Berwick, 9 May 1715, *Stuart Papers I*, p.369ff

38. SCA/Bl. Lett 2/197/4, L. Innes to T. Innes, 13 Nov 1715.

39. Terry, C.S.(Ed.), *The Jacobites and the Union* (Cambridge 1922), p.269 and p.128

40. SCA/Bl. Lett 2/197/5, L. Innes to T. Innes, 16 Nov1715.

41. SCA/Bl. Lett 2/197/7, L. Innes to T. Innes, 28 Nov 1715.

42. SCA/Bl. Lett 2/197/6, L. Innes to T. Innes, 24 Nov 1715.

43. SCA/Bl. Lett 2/197/10, L. Innes to T. Innes, 12 Dec 1715.

44. Innes, T., 'The Inneses of Balnacraig', *The Deeside Field*, fifth number, 1931, pp. 76–83

45. James VIII to L. Innes, 9 Nov 1715, *Stuart Papers I*, p.455
James VIII to L. Innes, 11 Nov 1715, *Stuart Papers I*, p.456f

46. SCA/Bl. Lett 2/209/1, T.Innes to W. Stuart, 1716.

47. SCA/Bl. Lett 2/203/4, L. Innes to T. Innes, 19 Jan 1716.

48. SCA/Bl. Lett 2/207/5, L. Innes to T. Innes, 24 Jan1716.

49. SCA/Bl. Lett 2/207/6, L. Innes to T. Innes, 26 Jan 1716.

50. SCA/Bl. Lett 2/207/7, L. Innes to T. Innes, 6 Feb1716.

51. SCA/Bl. Lett 2/207/9, L. Innes to T. Innes, 18 Feb1716.

52. SCA/Bl. Lett 2/207/10, L. Innes to T. Innes, 25 Feb!716.

53. *The Scots Peerage*, Vol VII, pp.53f..

54. SCA/Bl. Lett 1/84/11, L. Innes to C. Whyteford, 1 July 1684.

55. Gordon, A., *History of Peter the Great* (Aberdeen 1755), Vol I, pp.vif

56. Bulloch, *The House of Gordon*, Vol I, pp.138f

57. SCA/Bl Lett 1/84/11, L. Innes to C. Whyteford, 1 July 1684.

58. Tayler, A. & H., *Jacobites of Aberdeenshire & Banffshire in te Rising of 1715* (Edinburgh & London 1934), pp.104f.

59. Ibid. p.192.

60. Ibid. pp. 108f.

61. *The Scots Peerage*, Vol VIII, p.554.

62. L. Innes to Duke of Mar, 30 March 1716, *Stuart Papers II*, pp.46f

Duke of Mar to L. Innes, 20 April 1716, *Stuart Papers II*, pp.99f
L. Innes to Duke of Mar,13 May 1716, *Stuart Papers II*, p.148

63. L. Innes to Duke of Mar, 18 Aug 1716, *Stuart Papers II*, p.351
Duke of Mar to L. Innes, 25 Aug 1716, *Stuart Papers II*, pp.369
L. Innes to Duke of Mar, 17 Sept 1716, *Stuart Papers II*, pp.442f
L. Innes to Duke of Mar, 29 Sept 1716, *Stuart Papers II*, p.488

64. L. Innes to Dr J. Ingleton, 26 May 1716, *Stuart Papers II*, p187

65. Duke of Mar to L. Innes, 1 Jan 1717, *Stuart Papers* III p.382

66. L. Innes to James VIII, 11 Dec 1716, *Stuart Papers* III p.574

67. 'Memoir prepared by Louis Innes and sent out by Lt General Dillon to James VIII', 12 Sept 1716. *Stuart Papers* II, pp.429.
Duke of Mar to James VIII, 7 June 1717, *Stuart Papers* IV p.324.

68. Taylor, H., *Lady Nithsdale & her Family* (London 1939), p.64

69. Ibid. p.66

70. Innes, T., *A Critical Essay on the Ancient Inhabitants of the Northern Parts of Britain or Scotland (*London 1729).

71. SCA/Bl Lett 3/4/15, L. Innes to Bp Gordon, 14 Aug 1733.

72. James VIII to Earl of Oxford, 8 Mar 1718, *Stuart Papers* VI, p.107f

73. James VIII to Bp of Rochester, 8 Mar1718, *Stuart Papers* VI, pp.108f.

74. James VIII to Card. de Noailles, 15 Mar 1718, *Stuart Papers* VI, pp.150f.

75. James VIII to the Earl Marischal, 1 April 1718, *Stuart Papers* VI, p.243.

76. James VIII to Duke of Ormonde, 7 Mar 1718, *Stuart Papers* VI. pp.102–4

77. James VIII to Card Gualterio, 11 Mar 1718, *Stuart Papers* VI, p.133

78. Capt J. Ogilvie to Duke of Mar, 12 May 1718, *Stuart Papers* VI.

79. L. Innes to James VIII, 21 June 1718, *Stuart Papers* VI, p.560

80. Earl of Panmure to James VIII, 13 June 1718, *Stuart Papers* VI.

81. L. Innes to James VIII, 21 June 1718, *Stuart Papers* VI, p.560

82. Lt Gen Sheldon to James VIII, 18 April 1718, pp.322f.
James VIII to Lt Gen Dillon, 9 Mar 1718, *Stuart Papers* VI, p.117

83. *Stuart Papers* VII p.194f

84. *The House of Gordon*, Vol I, p.139

85. G. Innes to P. Grant, 5 Dec 1745, SCA/Bl Lett 3/84/17

86. Blaikie, W.B., *Itinerary of Prince Charles Edward Stuart* (Edinburgh: 1975), p.29.

87. SCA/Bl Lett, T. Innes to W. Stuart, 19 Aug 1726.
SCA/BlLett 2/305/10, D. McDonald to A. McDonald, 11 Jan 1727

88. SCA/BlLett 2/305/10, D. McDonald to A. McDonald, 11 Jan 1727

89. *The Lyon in Mourning,* p.198.

90. Blaikie, *Itinerary*, pp.3–5

91. Tayler, A. & H., *Jacobites of Aberdeenshire & Banffshire in the Forty-five*, (Aberdeen, 1928), pp.246f..

92. Ibid. pp.247f..

93. Ibid. pp.234–238.

94. Ibid. pp.203f.

95. Ibid. p.202.

96. Prebble, J., *Culloden.* (London 1961), p.110.

97. Ibid., p.109.

98. Taylor, H., *Lady Nithsdale & her Family* (London 1939), pp.63f.

99. Ibid p.257

100. Halloran,B.M., 'Neil MacEachan at Scots College Paris' *Innes Review* 43 (1992), pp.176–81

101. MacEachain, N., 'The Young Pretender' *New Monthly Magazine*, 1840, Part 3rd, p.335

102. MacLean, A., *A Macdonald for the Prince* (Stornoway 1982), p.68

103. Ibid. p.61

104. Bellesheim, A., *History of the Catholic Church of Scotland* (Edinburgh & London1887–1890), Vol IV, p.400.

105. SCA/Bl Lett 3/88/2, G. Innes to P. Grant, 21 Jan 1747.

106. SCA/Bl Lett 3/86/11, G. Innes to P. Grant, 7 Oct 1746.

107. SCA/Bl Lett 3/88/6, G. Innes to P. Grant, 5 June 1747.

108. SCA/Bl Lett 3/88/8, G. Innes to P. Grant, 7 July 1747.

109. SCA/Bl Lett 3/91/7, G. Innes to P. Grant, 23 June 1748.

110. SCA/BlLett 3/311/4, A. Geddes (Edinburgh), 8 March 1779.

111. Lang, A., *Pickle the Spy* (London, New York & Bombay: 1897), p.109.

112. SCA/Bl Lett 3/100/9, G. Innes to P. Grant, 18 May 1750.

113. Chapter 7, pp.318f.

114. Lang, A., op. cit., p.152 Lang supposed that this was written in 1752, as Leslie had quoted it in a letter of 27 May that year when accusations against Leslie were renewed, but in another letter of 15 May 1752 Leslie quoted the same passage and gives the date of 19 ctober 1748. (SCA/Bl Lett 3/109/11, J. Leslie (under alias Johnson), 15 May1752.)

115. SCA/Bl Lett 3/109/11, J. Leslie (under alias Johnson), to Bp Smith, 15 May1752.

116. Lenman, B., 'The Scottish Episcopal Clergy and the Ideology of Jacobitism' in Cruickshanks, E., *Ideology and Conspiracy; Aspects of Jacobitism, 1689-1759*, pp.36-48.

CHAPTER 7

The College and the Jansenist Controversy

Part 1: Events leading to the Propaganda Decision of 1736

In the Principalship of Charles Whyteford (1713–1738), the Scots College Paris got caught in a vortex of Jansenist controversy which profoundly affected the college and its reputation.

Jansenism was a religious movement concerning the problem of reconciling divine grace with free will. Before the Reformation, the Catholic solutions had been the Augustinian and the Thomist, both systems being similar to each other. Since Calvinism had developed these into an extreme form of predestination, Luis de Molina reacted by holding that God gives to everyone sufficient grace which becomes efficacious when we co-operate, in contradistinction to the Thomist view which said that God, with fore-knowledge of how each will act, gives efficacious grace to the elect, but sufficient grace to all. Cornelius Otto Jansen reacted against Molinism in a work entitled *Augustinus* which was published posthumously in 1640. Jansen virtually denied free will, and his work was condemned several times. The first condemnation was by the Inquisition in August 1641, followed by the bull *In eminenti* of Urban VIII in June 1643. In May 1653, five propositions attributed to Jansen were condemned in the bull *Cum occasione*, and because it was claimed that these propositions were not in Jansen's work, the bull *Ad sanctam beati Petri sedem* in October 1656 affirmed that the propositions were contained in *Augustinus*. In February 1665, Alexander VII in the bull *Regiminus apostolici* ordered the signing of a formulary condemning the five propositions and recognising that they stemmed from Jansen. Yet another bull *Vineam Domini* in July 1705 condemned those who advocated observance of a 'respectful silence' as to the fact (*fait*) of whether or not the condemned propositions were in Augustinus.

A new phase in the controversy came with the condemnation of 101 propositions taken from *Réflexions morales* of Pasquier Quesnel in the bull *Unigenitus Dei Filius* of Clement XI in September 1713. The bull immediately occasioned difficulties. After the past experience of many denying that the five condemned propositions were in Jansen's book, the Church had this time decided to condemn exact quotations from Quesnel's book; this method had its own problem, viz. in themselves and apart from the context of the book, some of the propositions seemed to have an orthodox sense. This was the chief cause of the reluctance of many to subscribe to the bull. Nevertheless, the general tendency of Quesnel was to see fallen human nature as totally corrupt, to underestimate free will, and to limit the distribution of divine grace. Later, the condemnation of one of the propositions was seen as a milestone in the development of Catholic doctrine. This was the twenty-ninth proposition which said, 'Outside the Church, no grace is given.'[1] In one sense, this proposition might be considered a legitimate conclusion from the doctrine, *'Extra ecclesia nulla salus'*, but if, as Quesnel seems to imply, *'ecclesia'* is limited to the visible Catholic Church, then the proposition is abhorrent. Its condemnation leads on to *Mystici Corporis Christi*, an encyclical letter of Pius XII issued in 1943, in which the pope speaks of those outside the visible Catholic Church who are 'related to the mystical Body of the Redeemer by some unconscious yearning and desire.'[2] This in turn is developed by the Second Vatican Council, which stated, 'This Church [i.e. the unique Church of Christ], constituted and organised in the world as a society, subsists in the Catholic Church',[3] thereby excluding an absolute identification of the Church of Christ with the Catholic Church. This brief account of the development of doctrine may help to show the importance of *Unigenitus*, though this was scarcely noted at the time, and even today, many critics of the bull fail to see its significance. This seriously calls in question the view that opposition to *Unigenitus* 'can be acknowledged as a principled, far-sighted and courageous stand against what many historians now agree to be one of the most misguided of all Roman decrees.'[4] Although the presentation of the Constitution was in many ways unfortunate, and even flawed, it did contain vital elements of Catholic truth, and hence was reiterated by several successive popes.

On 5 Mar 1717, four French bishops placed on record at the Sorbonne a notarised act by which they appealed against the bull *Unigenitus* to a General Council of the Church. They gathered a support of twelve bishops and three thousand priests. These became known as Appellants, and they were excommunicated by Clement XI in August 1718. Despite this, the four bishops renewed their appeal in September 1720. The Regent of France regrettably retaliated with political measures of prison and exile which were intensified from 1722 onwards.

Another stage in the Jansenist movement was reached in 1732 with the extraordinary manifestations and claims of miraculous cures at the tomb of the Deacon, François Pâris, in the cemetery beside the Church of St Médard in Paris. The cures were claimed to justify the position of the Appellants who objected to *Unigenitus*. However bizarre this may appear to be nowadays, this played an important part in the controversies at the time.[5]

Scotland was brought into these controversies which bitterly divided the missioners. There can be little doubt that the controversies arose in Scotland on account of the Scots College in Paris. The college and its staff were the main objects of attack, and after them, the bishops, James Gordon and Alexander Smith, both *alumni* of the college. The chief assailant was Colin Campbell, a highland priest who had pursued all his ecclesiastical studies in Scots College, Paris, and amongst other attackers was Killian or Gregor MacGregor, a Benedictine priest who had at one stage also been a student in the college.

The Scots College was situated in the Latin Quarter of Paris, surrounded by the great bastions of the Jansenist movement; within easy walking distance were the Sorbonne where the Appellants' notarised act was placed on record, the Convent of Port Royal which might be considered the cradle of Jansenism, the Church of St Jacques-du-Haut-Pas which was a fervid centre of Jansenism, and the Church and cemetery of St Médard which was the scene of manifestations and 'miracles' around the tomb of Deacon Pâris. Within a stone's throw of the College was the Church of St Étienne du Mont where the militant Jansenist Bishop of Montpellier, Charles Joachim Colbert, had once been Curé; as relationships between the parish church and the college had always been excellent, it is probable that he was a personal friend of the staff, and was certainly greatly admired by Thomas Innes. It was therefore inevitable that the college personnel would hear the great debates, and highly probable that they would be suspected of sharing the views of their close neighbours. Such accusations of Jansenism were indeed made, but for many years these were trivial and inconsequential, and it was not until the 1730s that there were lodged serious complaints that soon affected the whole Scottish Mission.

Jansenism was born in 1640, but no accusation of Jansenism was made before or during Robert Barclay's time (1655–1682), and indeed one of Barclay's most distinguished students, Alexander Leslie, was a Molinist, as was David Burnett who was Prefect of Studies from 1676 until 1680.[6]

The first time that Jansenism was mentioned in the time of Louis Innes, it was done so with revulsion and repudiation. In 1687, Louis Innes wrote from Scotland to Charles Whyteford in Paris:

> I pray let not the very name of Jansenism be mentioned among us, nor any of the religions be named but honourably by our people & c. & take occasion in the recreation and publicly to notify this to our scholars frequently, & to punish such as contreveen.[7]

This shows clearly that Louis Innes was utterly opposed to that type of Jansenism which narrowed the grace of God to the visible Catholic church, maintaining that Protestants could not be saved. He was for his time more than usually well disposed and friendly to those who were not Catholic. The same was true of Thomas Innes, and instances can be seen in his intimate acquaintance with the Epicopalian Bishop, Robert Keith, and in his great joy when correspondence was resumed with Glasgow University. In their ecumenism, the Inneses were the very opposite to being Jansenists.

The first accusation of Jansenism, which was made in September 1699, was both petty and ludicrous, but a good illustration of how the word 'Jansenism' could be bandied about and flung at one's adversaries. After a dinner party at the college, at which Lord Perth and his son were guests, Charles Whyteford was walking in the garden with a Jesuit priest called Père Bigné when the latter asked Whyteford why the college chapel had no opening onto the street. Whyteford replied that there was no need for a street entrance, and mentioned the obligation of going to one's parish church for the fulfilment of the Sunday obligation, to which the Jesuit replied that this was Lutheranism. Then he turned to Jansenism, predestination and grace, defining a Jansenist as *'un Calviniste qui dit la Messe.'* Whyteford replied that he had never heard that Calvivists said Mass, but that this had nothing to do with the obligation of going to one's parish church. The argument then became heated, and would have been of no consequence, had not Whyteford gone that very night to tell the local Curé, who took the names of those involved, and said that he would go to the archbishop. In reporting all this to Louis Innes, George Adamson, the Prefect of Studies, who tended to be alarmist, added, 'if we be brought upon the stage, God knows what ill it may doe to the house.'[8] In fact, it was unlikely that the Archbishop of Paris would pay any attention; about the same time, he largely ignored another Jesuit complaint from Père Beniers which suggested that the college was 'engaged in dangerous principles and enemy of the Society', and Louis Innes was at the time much more concerned about William Leslie's complaints to Rome, about general lack of discipline, complaints that led to a Visitation of the college. There is no evidence of a substantial complaint of the Scots College Paris professing Jansenism prior to *Unigenitus*.

In Scotland, in 1702, there were complaints of Jansenism levied against some of the Secular clergy by the Jesuits. Four of the secular priests subscribed to an appeal to Bishop Nicolson demanding redress from the Jesuits. The four were Robert Strachan, Robert Monro, James Carnegie, and Alexander Drummond.[9] All four had Paris connections. Robert Strachan had studied for the priesthood in Scots College Rome, but had spent a year (1685–1686) in Paris, but not at the Scots College there. Robert Munro had been a student at the Scots College Paris for two years. James Carnegie had been trained in Scots College Rome, but afterwards spent about eighteen months in Paris (1696–1697). Alexander Drummond who wrote the letter had done all his studies in Scots College Paris. All except Robert Munro who died in 1704, were to appear in later disputes about Jansenism.

Despite such complaints, when *Unigenitus* was published in September 1713, there did not seem to be any serious Jansenist problem in Scotland. Thomas Innes wrote from Paris on 12 Feb 1714 to William Stuart, the Scots agent in Rome:

> This is to free you of the apprehension you seem to be in that the birlies [Jesuits] may draw some odium on our Mission by the Constn agt P.Q.'s [Pasquier Quesnel's] book, but as to that I think there's nothing to be feared, for (1a) I have seen most generally all the books sent to Scotld these 20 years or upwards & I am persuaded there never went 3 copies of P.Q.'s book to Scotland in any language that I could hear of it. I never knew but of one copie in the Mission & that in french to my knowledge the owner layd it up in the bottom of a chest some 14 years agoe: and our lay men have none nor ever had among them. (2a) the Constn & prohibition of the book is sufficiently notified everywhere to Miss[ioner]s & others: & you may depend that our Phisitians [Bishops] will have suppressd & taken it up whever it is to be found & forbid to all the use of it, but, as I said, their zeal will find lttle mat[t]er to work upon in our Country when the book was scarce known till the noyse the Constn hath made about it. In the next place I conceive that unless you be askd about it, it is not proper to speake a word of it…In Eng[lan]d there have been co[u]n[t]less challenges & complaints about Jansenisme (tho I have reason to think it was occasiond at the bot[t]om by base envy agt the clergy) but in our country never any, & thanks to God, great unity.[10]

Thomas Innes wrote to Bishop Nicolson in a similar vein, but this letter has not survived. A search was ordered by Bishop Nicolson and Bishop Gordon, and only three copies of the book were found in all Scotland. Bishop Nicolson then wrote back to Thomas Innes:

> that he had always made it his business to stopp all dangerous books & those relating to Jansme & keep unity & peace among laborers of all kinds, & that he wonder'd how I [Thomas Innes] could write to him of this new Constn as if it had regarded them.[11]

In January 1719, Bishop Gordon, now in charge of the mission as Bishop Nicolson had died on the 23 Oct 1718, was convinced that none of his clergy would fail to subscribe to the Constitution if asked, and declared that he would withdraw faculties from any priest who did refuse. No sooner had he said this than the first rumblings began. In February, he refuted charges made by the Jesuit rector that Robert Strachan, a secular priest in Aberdeen, had spoken against the Constitution:

> I having been now about a fortnight in the place [Aberdeen] can assure you [William Stuart, agent in Rome] 'tis a pure calumny, that privately & publickly he has declar'd that all are bound to pay a perfect & entire obedience to it, & having examin'd a great many people on the subject, I could never find by any that ever he had spoke so much as one word agt it.[12]

In October of that same year, the Bishop had to return to Aberdeen after fresh complaints against Robert Strachan. The bishop preached a sermon, part of it still preserved,[13] deploring the divisions, and publicly vindicating

Robert Strachan. Strachan had been distributing a little book entitled *The penitents regrets on the Pater*, a translation of a French work of devotion. One sentence was the cause of offence, 'Thou desirest me to serve Thee only for love' in which the word 'only' was the offender. The translator wrote to David Tyrie, second son of the laird of Dunideer in which he explained that he had not had time to revise his manuscript, in which he had meant to delete the word 'only', and that this circumstance was well known to the Jesuit, Fr Hudson. William Stuart, the agent in Rome, feared that the book would go before the Inquisition, and on learning this, Bishop Gordon wrote to the publishers asking them to delete the word 'only' in all unsold copies, and he wrote to Fr Hudson ordering him to make the correction in any copies he might see. In this year, too, there were some complaints against Thomas Innes. The death of Bishop Nicolson had made it likely that a coadjutor would be appointed to help Bishop Gordon. Some of the clergy hoped that it would be Thomas Innes, while others accused him of Jansenism.

Two Scottish catechisms, published in 1724 and 1725, were the next occasion of Jesuit complaints of Jansenism amongst the secular clergy. The first, *A catechism for those that are more advanced in years and knowledge* (1724) was compiled by James Carnegie who had sent it to Bishop Gordon for examination before publication. The second, *Catechism of abridgement of Christian doctrine* (1725), was prepared by another secular priest, Andrew Hacket, under the auspices of the Duchess of Perth who was understood to have aided in the expense of publication. Both catechisms were derived from the Montpellier Catechism which had been condemned, and for this reason, the Jesuits presumed that they must be heretical, while the seculars attributed Jesuit opposition to jealousy. Thomas Innes thus conveyed the matter to William Stuart, the Scots agent in Rome:

> Birlies [Jesuits] will never be at peace, enemies to everything thats good, & envious of everything that comes not from them. The short Montp[ellier] Cat[echism] render'd by Mrs Gray's [Duchess of Perth's] labourer [priest] is carp'd at as containing Jans[enis]m. I know not what they'll make out. However we use it meantime, & I judge their difficulties are groundless, for they have first accused before they have seen it[14]

The Jesuits were, however, in the right, and both Catechisms were eventually condemned.

The next serious accusation of Jansenism was taken as far as to Cardinal Sacripanti, the Cardinal Protector for Scotland. James Carnegie, a very distinguished secular priest, went to Rome in 1726 to see the exiled Stuart King on political business. Naturally, the reason for his visit was kept secret, and the Scots Jesuits in Paris, thinking that he wanted himself promoted to the episcopate, accused him of Jansenism to the Nuncio at

Paris who in turn forwarded the complaint to Rome. On Carnegie's arrival in Rome, however, Cardinal Sacripanti showed him the letter, and said, 'Observe the artifices of our Scots Jansenists, and mark the zeal and charity of our Scots Jesuits.'[15]

In the following year, Thomas Innes went to Scotland to see about the publication of his *Critical Essay on the Ancient Inhabitants of Scotland*. While he was at Edinburgh, his nephew, George Innes, told him, as Thomas Innes himself had feared, that several of the clergy in Scotland suspected him of being a Jansenist. He wrote on 29 Sept 1727, 'You are taken for what you expected, and no less is privately whisperd about among us.'[16] On account of these whisperings, Thomas Innes, on his return to Paris, resigned his membership of the Sorbonne. The Appeal against *Unigenitus* had been made from that Universisty, and although Innes had not joined in the appeal, he feared that his continuing as a member could bring opprobrium on the Scottish mission.

About the end of 1731, or the beginning of 1732, Fr Killian McGregor, wrote to Hon John Stuart, the son of the Countess of Bute who was staying in Rome, saying that Jansenism was rife in the Scottish mission, and that the Bishops encouraged it. Both McGregor and Stuart, who was a layman, were *alumni* of the Scots College Paris. Killian McGregor was a Benedictine priest on the Scottish mission who had a very fractious temperament, and caused Bishop Gordon much anxiety. His stay in Scots College Paris from 1705 to 1706 had been very short, having been terminated by his running away from the college without giving any notice of his intent.

The accusations which led to a serious division among the clergy began in 1732. This year some of the Highland District missioners began to demand that subscription to *Unigenitus* be made compulsory for all missioners, and they cast aspersions on the Scots College, Paris. The Highland District had been constituted as a separate Vicariate in the previous year, and Hugh Macdonald had been consecrated as its bishop on 18 Oct 1731. The missioners of this district were demanding a division of the mission funds, some maintaining that they needed twice as much as the Lowland Clergy on account of the distances they had to travel, and others demanding a *pro rata* division according to the numbers of lay people which were considerably greater in the Highlands. This feeling of grievance seems to have motivated the Highland clergy to make accusations against the Lowlanders, and against the Scots College Paris. Thomas Innes showed himself aware of the financial elements in the quarrels when he advised Bishop Gordon that there was a grave danger of contention between the College and the Missioners over the money that John Law had bequeathed, pointing out that the bequest had been absolutely annulled and cancelled, and that the amount eventually recovered was less than that intended for the college alone. Nevertheless it was Louis Innes' intention to give some of it to missioners whenever the college could afford to do so.[17] At this stage, the accusers appear to have been led by Alexander Paterson; Abbé MacPherson was later to write that Paterson was decoyed into the Colin Campbell faction, but at the start, the Inneses believed him to be the instigator, and Thomas Innes said that their information came from Bp Hugh Macdonald and from Robert Gordon who was then in Edinburgh.[18] Thomas Innes, who realised that the allegations concerning the college were mostly directed against himself, pointed out that he had resigned from his position in the Sorbonne in order to prevent the Scottish mission incurring criticism.

At the annual clergy meeting in the following year, on 26 April (9 March) 1733, at which Bishop Wallace presided, Colin Campbell declared that Bishop Macdonald, at the request of one unnamed, had asked him to put forward the proposal that all clergy be made to sign a formula against Jansenism. Bishop Wallace, however, did not think that it was expedient to discuss the matter. The decision, however prudent, merely postponed the storm.

In June of that same year, 1733, two meetings were held in Glenlivet, one at Scalan and the other at Clashinore, at which were drafted three letters to be sent to Rome. These became known as the 'Clashinore letters' which were to have such a decisive effect on the reputation of the Scots College, Paris. Two accounts of the circumstances of the meetings have come down to us. The better known is from a transcription of Bishop Gordon's letter to the Paris College. Writing to William Stuart, Scots agent in Rome, Thomas Innes quoted the letter:

> [I] shall content myself to transcribe the rest of M. Fife's [Bp Gordon's] forsd [foresaid] letter. Thus then he continues — 'I shall send you soon a fuller account of what past lately at a meeting in Scalan but must give you some touch of it now. M Fife had gone up to Scalan for his health, not dreaming of such a meeting, when on a sudden there came upon him greater number of laborers than could be expected both from Highland & Lowlands and all crying of many laborers here suspected of Janson and nothing could satisfy them till a new order was made by Nicopol [Bp Gordon] & Dianere [Bp Macdonald] that all laborers, Birlies [Jesuits] and Traders (Crows) [Benedictines] in Scotland should subscribe Constn Unigen and all other Constns which was done by nine present and I hope will be done by all the rest. Thus M. Fife.[19]

Bishop Gordon was clearly representing to the priests in Paris that an element of compulsion was brought to bear on him which led Louis Innes to tell the Bishop in his reply:

> it being evident by his [Bp Gordon's] own letter that what consent he past was by clamour and violence extorted from him, and consequently void, and null and leaves him still at full freedom.[20]

This account was widely circulated, and has become the basis of the traditional interpretation of events. It is, however, at variance with the account that the Bishop himself sent to Rome. At the beginning of the letter to the Cardinal Protector of Scotland, Bishop Gordon wrote, 'Since the Most illustrious Bishop of Diana [Bishop Macdonald] and I, along with some serious and select missioners came here to deliberate about grave matters…'[21] A later report of events written in Latin by Bishop Gordon and Bishop Smith recounted how Colin Campbell conspired to get Bishop Gordon's sanction for the meeting.[22] This is corroborated by a letter of Bishop Macdonald in which he said that Colin Campbell had told him that Bishop Gordon required his presence and that of select missioners to discuss Jansenist problems.[23] The convenient story of Bishop Gordon's convalescence being unexpectedly invaded can hardly hold water. Yet it was this version of events that has led to the presumption (explicitly stated by Clapperton)[24] that the Clashinore meeting took place first, and then the missioners, with plans and documents prepared, invaded Scalan. The so called 'Clashinore letters' are all three dated 'octavo Idus Junii' i.e. 6 June 1733, whereas the account of the Clashinore meeting is dated 8 June 1733, two days[25] after the Scalan meeting.

The Clashinore letters played such an important part in future events that it seems expedient to quote them in full, especially as they have never been printed and there appears to be little knowledge in Scotland of their exact contents. Knowledge of these letters leads to a new appreciation of why Propaganda demanded subscription to *Unigenitus* to be signed by all Scottish missioners. The first is from Bishop Gordon and Bishop Macdonald to the Pope:

> After kissing the feet of Your Holiness, we present the humble commendation of ourselves and the mission.
>
> Since we are attempting with the greatest diligence we can to give our efforts to the propagation of the Catholic faith, there is nothing more we desire than that those who are destined for the holy work, should be embued with the best form of education and most pure proofs of the faith, but we profess with great grief that we have discovered that those in charge of the Scots College in Paris do not give us this satisfaction, and although in accordance with my duty and sincerely for the flock entrusted to us we have insisted with repeated warnings, rebukes, nay rather prayers on many occasions that those in charge should most carefully give attention to the young men who are devoted to studies in their house. Indeed we have confirmed that no one should be received or accepted within this mission unless persons of unsullied doctrine and who are most humbly reverent and obedient with regard to the Holy See. Nevertheless we have been informed by the persons who are worthy of credit and have discovered by sure experience that we have had little success with them. it remains therefore that we should have recourse to the common Head of the whole Church and the sole support of this mission. May we therefore beseech Your Holiness with very humble prayers that he should deign to take in hand the reformation of this college

and see to the complete removal of those men whom we suspect to be the origin of such great evil. We think that this can most easily be done through the Prior of the Carthusians to whose charge that college has been immediately entrusted as being the first highest superior. If Your Holiness does not mind ordering that, we do not cease to beseech the Highest greatest God that he should preserve Your Holiness safe for abolishing the depravity of any heresies, and propagating the glory of His name and the solicitude of this mission as long and as happily as possible, and throwing ourselves forward to kiss the feet of Your Holiness we testify that we are, most holy and blessed father, the most humble obedient and devoted sons of Your Holiness.

James Bp of Nicopolis, Vic Ap of Lowland Scotland
Hugh Bp of Diana, V. Ap of Highland Scotland

Near River Livet
(Glenlivet),
6 June 1733.[26]

The second letter was written by both Scottish Bishops to the Cardinal Protector of Scotland. It read:

Since the Most Illustrious Bishop of Diana and I, along with some serious and select missioners came here to deliberate about grave matters, it is our duty to report to Your Eminence what was decided by us and what we think should be demanded from the Apostolic See relying on the help of Your Eminence. We shall report what other matters were decided by us in another letter shortly. We shall write now about our College in Paris. It seems necessary therefore much to our great grief to signify to your Eminence that we have discovered by sure proofs that their pupils are so educated by the superiors of that College that they furnish an excessive handle to depraved rumours about Jansenism. Since on this point all our efforts were in vain nor were we able to achieve anything by our repeated prayers and demands that a remedy should be applied to so great an evil, of necessity we repair to the Apostolic See so that by Its supreme authority there should be a very diligent inquiry into the whole matter and a very careful reformation of the College should be undertaken if matters so require. Most of all those persons should be removed whom we suspect to be the source of the whole evil. Our remarkable cleric who is here with us presses us to write to our Most Holy Lord about a business which is of greatest importance to this mission. The epistle sent to the Most Holy Lord accompanies this one which we are writing to His Eminence and at the same time we beseech you that Your Eminence may be most kindly willing to join his efforts to our pleas with His Holiness so that our wishes may be able to have the desired effect. The venerable cleric himself will write to Your Eminence about the same business so as to testify and display on this occasion in what great danger this whole mission may be eventually involved unless Your Eminence sees to the application of a most present remedy to the grave evil. The undersigned pray with fervent heart that God may keep Your Eminence safe for the Universal Church and especially for this mission.

Most Eminent and Reverend Master
Your most humble and obedient servants
James Bp of Nicopolis, V. Ap of Lowland Scotland
Hugh Bp of Diana, V. Ap of Highland Scotland

Near River Livet
[Glenlivet]
6 June 1733[27]

Bishop Gordon does not appear in a good light in these letters. Undoubtedly we can believe that he was pressurised and bullied. Besides being possessed of a meek and conciliatory temperament, he had a great love for Thomas Innes and for the College in Paris which was his *Alma mater*. In many ways, he was an excellent bishop and a credit to the Scots College Paris. Zealous, exceedingly hard working, he undertook arduous missionary journeys, happy to endure severe hardships for the sake of the mission. On this occasion, however, his desire to please everybody led to loss of integrity. In the first instance, we have already mentioned his two differing accounts of how the meeting at Scalan came about. Secondly he conveyed a false impression when he wrote:

> on this point all our efforts were in vain nor were we able to achieve anything by our repeated prayers and demands that a remedy should be applied to so great an evil.[28]

Certainly the bishop had written at least two severe letters to Thomas Innes rebuking him for lack of discipline and for not training the students well enough, but there is no evidence that he had ever rebuked Thomas Innes for 'Jansenism' (or his anti-Constitution stand). Once he had rebuked George Innes for not insisting enough on obedience to Roman authority.[29] To classify these rebukes as 'repeated prayers and demands that a remedy should be applied' to Jansenism seems exaggerated and unfair. Thirdly there was absolutely no need to get Rome to remove Thomas Innes from the Scots College. A simple request from Bishop Gordon would have been enough. As it was, as soon as Thomas Innes heard of the meeting, he made plans to leave the college without any demand from Rome and without orders from the Prior of the Cathusians. In fact, the Prior was furious, claiming that the dismissal was a usurpation of his authority, but Louis Innes urged him to let it be.[30] Fourthly Bishop Gordon gave no thought as to how Thomas Innes was to find a livelihood in the future. This Louis Innes did not fail to make clear to Bishop Gordon:

> They propose to have him turned out of the shop [College] without the least mention or concern how he shall subsist for the future. They know he has nothing of his own, and I am sure they know not whether Debrie [Louis Innes himself] is or is not in a condition to help him: however as long as Debrie has a morsell of bread for himself, Mr Flemin [Thomas Innes] may count of haveing a share of it.[31]

Fifthly, and perhaps most importantly, the college had neither been given the opportunity to speak in its own defence, or offered the chance to correct what was amiss. Another astonishing phrase in the letter to the Cardinal Protector is the description of those present at the Scalan meeting as 'some serious and select missioners'. None of the seven were especially prominent in either Highlands or Lowlands, and Louis Innes' designation of them as 'a few young unexperienced men'[32] seems nearer the mark.

The third letter was signed by seven missioners, three from the Highland district and four from the Lowland district. It is addressed to the Cardinal Protector for Scotland. It read:

Most eminent Prince,

We have long had it among the objects of our ambition to send a letter to your Eminence, in which we might not only profess the reverence that is due to your dignity but also congratulate a protector who is so kind to us and repay your kindness with most grateful sentiment. But since our expressions of devotion must needs be incapable of matching such outstanding kindness and equally outstanding dignity, we ought at least to acknowledge the duty that is not in our power to discharge. But no small hindrances have up till now stood in the way of our zealous inclination. These hindrances having been removed at this time, we gladly embrace the opportunity to do our duty to you, and also to report a very grave matter which, since it tends to the detriment of the Mission, cannot but inflict great anxiety upon us. For several years the most illustrious bishop of Nicopolis (and recently also the most illustrious bishop of Diana) has not ceased to oppose the looming peril by means of warnings, rebukes and pleas and finally with all their strength, but since the hoped-for success has not attended such numerous and great efforts, almost in desperation, in accordance with the intention of each of the two Roman vicars, we by unanimous joint decision, come running to your Eminence, as to our last place of refuge.

We know for certain that there is someone in our Paris College who while disdaining the Apostolic Constitutions nevertheless has had much power for several years now that he has to a far degree been leading the minds of the other teachers and especially of the pupils to his own point of view. Hence the man in charge of the domestic studies of the young men, although he had outwardly satisfied the Archbishop of Paris by giving homage to the apostolic decrees, nevertheless does not apply due diligence to preventing the pupils of the college from being tinged with crooked opinions, or from being freed from errors taken from elsewhere. Therefore some ignorant young men, having been taught error either by the teachers of the college themselves or by others on account of the formers' supine carelessness, have reached such a pitch of perversity that they have preferred to leave the college without holy orders rather than to receive them from the Archbishop of Paris, because they know that no one was to be ordained unless he had professed entire veneration for the apostolic constitutions. We know also that for the same reason a young man of their number was sent by the teachers to a rather careless bishop and got ordained subdeacon by a kind of theft. We say nothing of the others who were involved at this time in that course of studies: but this we cannot conceal, that they were so far from being instructed in the precepts of a fairly pure doctrine by the advice of their teachers, that the more they shrank away from the Apostolic Constitutions, the more they were prized and petted by the teachers. Finally we know that the chief instigator of this evil exerted himself to teach a noble youth, who had been brought back from heresy to the Catholic faith by very strong arguments concerning the authority of the church, to resist once more the authority of the Church and exerted himself to drag him over to his own opinion, scorning the apostolic constitutions. Since this is so, we think it will be clear to your Eminence that, so long as the affairs of the college remain thus, it is to be expected that no other missionaries will be produced by the school but those who can harm rather than help our mission. But of whatever quality they may be they send very few workers into our vineyard. For although this college is amply adequate to feed twelve students as they themselves claim but more as we are rightly persuaded, within the past twenty years it has only produced two priests. They cannot plead in mitigation that suitable young men were not sent: assuredly as many were continually sent as they wished either to summon or to admit into the College. It cannot be doubted but that your Eminence is to be aroused to seek an explanation of this from them, given Your Eminence's ardent zeal for this mission; especially since, as it is possible to see from the records of our college in Rome, flourishing under the auspices of your Eminence, 13 of its pupils within the same period of time have returned to their country and have been working as hard as possible for the salvation of souls. But we are not striving to bring these things to your notice in this way, most eminent Prince, in order to flaunt our industry and zeal before your Eminence by doing down and defaming others, or to deny that some excellent missionaries have come to us from that college. But to our great grief we are compelled to open the wounds of our brethren. We would be eager to keep them covered, were we not wholly dedicated to seeking a remedy for them. So we bring to your Eminence the humble pleas of the whole clergy that your Eminence should press for the reform of our college in Paris, and should see to the removal of those who are agreed to be the leaders of the whole evil, and should allow no one to be appointed in their place unless the selection made by the Roman vicars and the assent of the clergy has proved him to be very suitable for such a job. But we entrust the whole matter, which so nearly pertains to the success of the whole mission, to the wisdom of Your Eminence, to which we know this mission is of great concern. Bending to kiss your purple, we pray that God may long preserve you safe for his Church and this Mission,

Most eminent Prince, the most humble and devoted servants of Your Eminence

John McDonald, missionary
John Tyrie, missionary
Colin Campbell, missionary
George James Gordon, missionary
James Lesley, Scots missionary
Thomas Brockie, Scots missionary
George Duncan, Scots missionary

Near the river Livet [Glenlivet] among the mountain Scots
6 June, 1733.[33]

The main thrust of the missioners' letter was to get Thomas Innes and George Innes put out of the Paris College. Thomas Innes is that someone 'who while disdaining the Apostolic Constitution nevertheless has had much power for several years' while George Innes is 'the man in charge of domestic studies' who 'has outwardly satisfied the Archbishop of Paris.' There is however a certain amount of caution shown in the wording of their letter. They do not accuse George Innes of teaching Jansenism but say that he 'does not apply due diligence to preventing the pupils of the college from being tinged with crooked opinions, or from being freed from errors taken from elsewhere'. Yet the letter is not altogether fair. The 'ignorant young men' who preferred to leave the college without holy orders rather than to receive them from the Archbishop of Paris were John Paul Gordon, John Farquharson and his brother William Farquharson who were expelled from the college. Louis Innes' reply to this was surely justifiable:

> It seems a little odd that Grisy's [Scots College Paris] management may be charged with the loss of the 3 prentices [students] since tis notoriously known that all possible means were used to reclaim them, and that their proving obstinat and irreclaimable from these principles was the only reason why they were turned out of the shop.[34]

Perhaps odder still that Bishop Gordon who was allowing these complaints to go to Rome should ordain John Paul Gordon the following year.

The complaint about only two ordinations to the priesthood in twenty years was true (although one of the signatories to the complaint, George Duncan, had studied at Paris for two years), but the comparison with Rome was unfair because Paris was not purely a seminary but took non-ecclesiastical students as well. As Louis Innes said:

> it is well known to those who know anything of Grisy either in its first or second foundation that nowhere is there one word mentioning of the Miss[io]n or of promoting youths that are bred in it to H.[oly] Orders, but to educat youth of the Country in piety and learning.[35]

The 'noble youth' who had been exhorted to scorn the apostolic constitutions was James Campbell, brother to Colin Campbell who had been ordained in Paris. The proceedings against the Scots College appear to have been instigated by the two brothers. This was certainly the opinion of James Carnegie, then Procurator of the college. 'This whole noise is caused by two brothers of the name of Campbell and near cousines to the Duke of Argyle.'[36] Carnegie also believed that James Campbell had gone to the Scots College Paris in order to spy for the Jesuits who wanted evidence of Jansenism in the college, although this does seem a bit far-fetched. After he had left the Scots college, instead of going to the Highland district to help his bishop as had been intended, he went to Aberdeen where Carnegie believed that he had plotted with John Innes, a Jesuit brother of Thomas 'and the cunningist Birlie [Jesuit] of our Nation.'[37] It would appear that Thomas Innes had rashly explained his anti-Constitution position to James Campbell, contrary to his usual custom of not discussing these matters with students. James Campbell had resided at Scalan for ten days before the meeting of the 6 June, using his time to visit the local Lowland priests and stir them to join in the plans to get the Inneses removed from Paris.[38]

Two days after the Scalan meeting which produced the three letters, another meeting was held at Clashinore, a hamlet in Glenlivet about two miles from Scalan. The proposals of the meeting were said to be 'fully resolved & condescended upon' by Bishop Macdonald with all his own clergy with six of the Low Country' who were Alexander Grant, Thomas Brockie, James Duffus, John Godsman, William Shand and John Tyrie.[39] It seems unlikely, however, that more than three of these Lowlanders were present, since the meeting decided upon the immediate signing of subscription to *Unigenitus* and in an extant copy of these signatures[40] only John Tyrie, Alexander Grant and Thomas Brockie were amongst the first group of signatories. It is likewise virtually impossible that all the Highlands priests were there; only the Bishop and three other Highlanders had been present at the Scalan meeting two days previously. Of these, Colin Campbell and James Leslie were both present at this second meeting. There is, however, no mention of John McDonald who may have had to get back to Lochaber for his Sunday duties (the Clashinore meeting of 8 June was on a Friday). Bishop Macdonald may possibly have been present; later he was indignant when George Gordon called the meeting a 'cabal',[41] and he was no lover of the Scots College Paris. Although he had been sent there to be better prepared for the office of Bishop, and the College had offered fine hospitality, he later falsely accused the staff of not forwarding mail to Rome, alleging that he had seen the letters in the college; what he had seen were copies.[42] It is perhaps significant that James Campbell had been at the college at the same time as Bishop Macdonald, and the two had spent a holiday in the country together. Campbell had left the college at the same time as Hugh Macdonald on the understanding that Campbell would continue his studies for the priesthood under Macdonald's supervision. There seems to have been a bond of friendship between the two, and Bishop Macdonald may have been more sympathetic to the complaints of the missioners in the early days than he would have liked to admit in the later stages of the controversy.

The resolutions of this meeting at Clashinore were five in number:

1. That all should subscribe to *Unigenitus* as soon as possible.
2. That Alexander Grant be sent to Rome as Procurator, with the approval of Bishop Macdonald, whether Bishop Gordon approved or not.
3. That the whole body of Scottish clergy should be consulted before the appointment of a Vicar Apostolic or Coadjutor for either district.
4. That the Procurator at Edinburgh be changed. He was Robert Gordon, and they proposed James Campbell although he was not a priest, but only tonsured.
5. That what they called the 'Paris Club' should be excluded from holding any offices. The 'Paris Club' were named as Alexander Smith, Alexander Drummond, Andrew Hackett, George Gordon Scalanensis, George Gordon Mortlach, and Robert Gordon.[43]

These resolutions give a good indication of ulterior motives at the beginning of the controversy. One can discern the dissatisfaction of the 'cabal' with Bishop Gordon, with the Procurator Robert Gordon, with the agent in Rome William Stuart, and with the 'Paris Club' whom they suspected of heresy. The Highlanders wanted their own man as Procurator and wanted a say in the appointment of Lowland Bishops. Colin Campbell was aggrieved that he had not been chosen as Vicar Apostolic of the Highland district and now believed he could succeed John Wallace as co-adjutor to Bishop Gordon. Other highland priests were dissatisfied with financial arrangements and believed that the Scots College had used money that should have come to them. Thus it can be seen that motives at the Glenlivet meetings were not altogether altruistic.

Although James Campbell was only a tonsured cleric with no orders, the missioners were demanding that he should replace Robert Gordon as Procurator of the Mission. Bishop James Gordon thwarted this plan by appointing him as the messenger who could take the three letters to Rome. A strong argument in favour of this choice was that it spared all the priests for the mission.

James Campbell duly proceeded to Rome, but did not get the chance to place his case before Propaganda. So he left the three letters that he carried from Scotland in the safe keeping of Aeneas Gillis, a student for the priesthood in the Scots College, Rome, who was later ordained priest for the Highland vicariate.

The next move began in 1735 when several Highland clergy demanded that Bishop Hugh Macdonald should go to Propaganda in Rome to present their grievances, which were mainly financial. The bishop at first agreed to go, then changed his mind. The clergy then insisted on a delegation of two being sent, and the bishop agreed to send Colin Campbell and John Tyrie, who from then on were known as 'the pilgrims'. They received only a restricted commission, were directed to submit all their papers to Mr Stuart, agent in Rome, and were strictly charged to attack no individuals. Bishop Macdonald afterwards declared that they were only delegated to present financial matters, and had been given no remit to raise doctrinal issues. The pilgrims began their journey from the West country about 8/ 19 Aug 1735. No sooner had they gone than Bishop Macdonald seemed to regret his decision; writing to Bishop Gordon from Morar on 13/24 Aug 1735, and repeating the letter on 15/26 in case the Bishop was at Edinburgh, he declared that he disliked this method of approaching the Roman authorities, but that he had been forced into it by his missioners who would never be satisfied until this were done. He emphasised the restricted nature of the pilgrims' commission, but feared that they would go beyond it, and begged Bishop Gordon to explain his position to William Stuart, the Scots agent in Rome. Peter Grant, who had been in the mission for only a few weeks also wrote to Bishop Gordon on 8/19 Sept 1735, telling him that he had heard from James Grant, a young priest in Lochaber with John McDonald, that the pilgrims' real intention was to get the Paris College reformed, and all the Inneses turned out, and that they also intended to accuse the Bishop himself of Jansenism, one proof being that he had appointed Alexander Smith as his coadjutor. Meanwhile, Colin Campbell had the audacity to write to Bishop Macdonald, forbidding him to assist at the consecration of Bishop Smith, or else he would denounce him to the Holy See as a Jansenist. Bishop Macdonald ignored this impertinent letter, and assisted at the consecration of Bishop Smith in Edinburgh. The pilgrims on their way to Rome stayed some time at Würzburg with Gregory Killian McGregor who had already accused Bishop Gordon of Jansenism, and at Würzburg, they were joined by a partisan Benedictine, Robert Gallus Leith, who accompanied them to Rome. The three arrived at the Scots College, Rome, on 15 Feb 1736 where they appear not to have met any of the staff of the college, but distributed letters among the students.

In Rome, the pilgrims soon lost credibility when their accusations were unsubstantiated. They claimed that Thomas Innes still ruled in the Paris College, that two students had got the subdiaconate outside Paris, and that Alexander Smith had been an appellant. When all three charges were found to be false, the pilgrims were discredited. They still pressed their charges of heresy, presenting a memorial of seventy or eighty sheets to Propaganda at the beginning of August 1736, but the discredited pilgrims would never by themselves have brought an unfavourable verdict against the Scottish mission. There was, however, much more damning evidence, and this was in the three Clashinore letters. These had remained in the custody of Aeneas Gillis. Bishop Gordon had written to him demanding their surrender, but Mr Gillis said that he would not surrender them until commanded by his own bishop. Bishop Macdonald then wrote for them, but before his letter arrived, Cardinal Rivera, Cardinal Protector for Scotland demanded the letters. Gillis handed them over unsealed; whereupon the Cardinal demanded that he seal them, and took them with him without reading them. Colin Campbell, however, said that he already had exact copies. The letters were laid before Propaganda on 16 Aug 1736, and this led to the unfavourable decision of 10 Sept 1736 whereby all priests in Scotland had to sign a formulary accepting *Unigenitus* and declare their rejection of the condemned catechisms. This decree revoked the earlier privilege by which subscription to formularies need only be demanded at the discretion of the bishops. The Cardinals also directed that Monsignor Lercari should inform them on the state of the Scots College Paris. The decisive factor could not have been the pilgrims' accusations,

1. *La ferme des Ecossais* at Grisy.

2. Illustrations from the Book of Grisy (*Columba House, Edinburgh*).

IACOBVS DE BETHVNE
ARCHIEPISCOPVS
GLASGVENSIS IN SCOTIA
COLLEGII SCOTORVM
PARISIENSIS FVNDATOR 2.ᵘˢ

ANNO ÆTATIS SVÆ
86 CHRISTI 1603
24 APRIL

3. Archbishop James Beaton II, of Glasgow, the second founder of the College. From the memorial portrait in the Scots College, Paris *(Innes Review)*.

4. Façade of the College, built by Robert Barclay, 1662–65, in the Rue des-Fosses-Saint-Victor, now the Rue du-Cardinal-Lemoine (*Innes Review*).

5. (a) Interior of the College Chapel, completed in 1672 *(Innes Review)*.

5 (b) Painting behind the altar of the Scots College, Paris *(Columba House)*.

COLLEG.SCOTOR.IN.
ACAD.PARIS.

6. (a) Book-plate of the Scots College, Paris.

6. (b) Seal of the Scots College, Paris.

7. Obelisk and display of fireworks in the College garden to mark the birth of James Edward Stuart 1688. Frontispiece of *Feu d'artifice et des illuminations,* by L Innes. Paris, 1688 *(Trustees of the National Library of Scotland).*

8. (a) Sculpture of George Con (*c.* 1598–1640), from his monument in San Lorenzo in Damasco, Rome *(Innes Review).*

8 (b) (Left) Richard (Augustine) Hay (1661–*c.* 1735), Augustinian Canon;
(Right) The Hay Arms *(Columba House, Edinburgh).*

9. Abbot Thomas (Placid) Fleming of Ratisbon (1642–1720), a relative of the Earl of Wigton *(Abbot Mark Dilworth & Columba House, Edinburgh).*

10. Major-General Alexander Gordon (1669–1752) *(St Andrews University Library).*

11. James Drummond, 2nd titular Duke of Perth (1673–1720), by Sir John Baptiste de Medina *(Scottish National Portrait Gallery)*.

12. Lord John Fleming, 6th Earl of Wigton (1673–1744).

13. (a) Charles Stewart, 5th Earl of Traquair (1697–1764) *(In the collection of Traquair House).*

13. (b) John Stewart, 6th Earl of Traquair (1699–1779) *(In the collection of Traquair House).*

14. (a) James Drummond, 3rd titular Duke of Perth (1713–1746) *(In the Collection of the Drummond Castle Trust).*

14. (b) John Drummond, 4th titular Duke of Perth (1714–1747) *(The Scottish National Portrait Gallery).*

15. (a) James Gordon of Letterfourie (1660–1748).

15. (b) Alexander Gordon of Letterfourie (1714–1797).

15. (c) Alastair Ruadh Macdonnell, alias 'Pickle the Spy' (1725–1761).

16. (a) Principal Alexander Gordon, Principal of the Scots College, Paris, *c.* 1740–1818 *(The Trustees of the National Museums of Scotland).*

16. (b) Dr Alexander Geddes (1737–1802).

as is commonly claimed, because Campbell and Tyrie had lost credibility. It was the declaration in the Scottish Bishops' letters that the college in Paris was affected by Jansenism, and that it had spread the contagion to Scotland. The bishops regretted having written these letters when they realised that the accusations had little foundation, that ulterior motives were present, and that Bishop Gordon himself was accused. Little wonder they tried so hard to get the letters back from Aeneas Gillis By the brief of 10 September 1736, the whole Scottish mission was made to feel the effects of the 'Clashinore' proceedings which at first had been directed against the staff of the Scots College. The very fact of the demand to sign *Unigenitus* being imposed by Rome gave Scotland a damaging image. Even today it can take great efforts to show how little Jansenism there was in the country. The Scottish priests in Paris were surprised at Rome's decision, but they had not seen the Clashinore letters. Both Louis and Thomas Innes, though disappointed with the verdict, recommended compliance with the Roman decree.·

Ulterior motives in making accusations have already been hinted at, but before considering these in a little more detail, it would seem best to ascertain to what extent Jansenism had affected the Scots College Paris by making an examination of the theological views of the members.

Part 2: Theological Views of College Members

In reviewing the views of the staff of the Scots College Paris, it should be stressed that none of the college staff were involved as writing theologians; not as much as an article on Jansenism appeared from their pens. Their views can be partially gleaned from letters and reports, but not with the precision that might have been possible had they written treatises.

Thomas Innes

As Thomas Innes was the most controversial member of staff, and more accusations were levelled against him than against any other, it seems appropriate to start with his case. Before the publication of *Unigenitus*, there are no definite indications that he was anything but loyal to Catholic orthodoxy. It was true that he had friends at Port Royal where he had celebrated Mass, and he had attended Mass there as far back as 1695. He had a cordial relationship with Duguet and Rollin who later became Appellants, and he had developed an admiration for Abbé Colbert, Curé of St. Étienne-du-Mont who became one of the few appellant bishops.[44] There is little doubt that Thomas Innes was a great devotee of Jansenist piety, and it was probably on account of this that the Scots College Paris was a secret distribution centre for the banned Jansenist publication,

Nouvelles Ecclésiastiques. Before 1713, however, there was no accusation of Jansenism against Thomas Innes. There was just a tantalising statement made by his brother, Louis, to the effect that there was one reason why Thomas could not be made bishop. Louis Innes does not say what this reason might be, and it is possible that he was referring to a Jansenist or Gallican leaning, but this is far from being certain.

After 1713, the case is different. There is no doubt that Thomas Innes did not agree with *Unigenitus*. In 1714, he confided in Bishop Gordon that he thought that the bull was:

> the erecting of Molinme [Molinism] in dogma (as some Physitians [bishops] have here declared in their Mands [mandates] & a condemning the d[oc]trine & practice of the best & learndst Physitians & Laborers [priests] as well new as old,[45]

but he begged Bishop Gordon not to let his view be known beyond himself and Bishop Nicolson. That the bull established Molinism, as against the older Augustinian and Thomist systems, was always Thomas Innes' chief argument against it. He wrote to Bishop Wallace in 1721 that 'the whole drift of the birlies [Jesuits] in the Constn was the establishment of their novelties on the ruins of the ancient doctrine',[46] and again he wrote to Bishop Gordon and Bishop Wallace in 1732 that the bull 'set up an inquisition which had undone upon many heads the ancient doctrine in this country [France] and substituted to it Molina's novelties.'[47]

This common interpretation of *Unigenitus* was refuted by Benedict XIII on 28 June 1727 in the bull *Pretiosus* which declared that the teaching of St Thomas and the Thomist school had nothing to do with the errors of Jansen and Quesnel. This bull might have led Thomas Innes to reconsider his view had he still been in Paris, but he had left for Scotland in the middle of June, and we do not know how long the bull took to reach him. Writing ten days after its publication, his brother Louis said nothing about it, but rather communicated the impression that the Pope himself was on the side of those who opposed *Unigenitus*:

> We hear M. Cant [the pope] had privately drawn a paper confirming the 12 art[icle]s & some other parts to some purpose, but his birlified [under Jesuit influence] brethren by their spies getting notice of it, came upon him like so many hornets, & never left him till they had undon[e] all, they say the poor man cryd bitterly. Never man in his station was so used since Peter Celest[ine]. But good man knows not his own stren[g]th.[48]

In addition to the hindrances to accepting *Pretiosus* that were created by distance, Thomas Innes was at the time preoccupied with the publication of his *Critical Essay on the Early Inhabitants of Scotland*, and his health had recently suffered; while embarking on the boat from France, he had fallen into the sea, and although he was rescued, he had failed to change his soaking garments, and was ever afterwards partially paralysed on one side.[49] The combination of circumstances was not at all conducive to a change of mind, and in October, we find him in Edinburgh regretting the condemnation of Soanes, Bishop of Senez.

Only once do we find Thomas Innes commenting on an individual proposition of *Unigenitus*. Writing to Bishop Gordon in 1733, he said:

> I shall only tell you here by way of Anticipation that if the Condemnat'n of the 91 proposn of this Decree had been admitted in Scotland neither K. Rob Brus nor any one of the name of Stuart who all derive their right from him, had ever come to the Crown of Scotld, no more than Henry IV or any of the House of Bourbon come to the Crown of France.[50]

The 91st condemned proposition is:

> The fear of unjust excommunication ought never to hinder us from the fulfilling of our duty; neither are we cast out of the Church, although men by their villainy seem to excommunicate us, if we are united by love to God, to Christ, and to the Church.[51]

One can discern the lack of theological precision in condemning such a proposition without elucidations, but the general tenor of Quesnel's statement is contentious. Although this is the only instance that we can find of Thomas Innes making detailed commentary, he claimed to have examined the Constitution thoroughly, and his verdict was that it was 'a decree that cannot bear a lecture of any man that is thoroughly instructed in his religion on true principles.'[52]

In no way did Thomas Innes consider *Unigenitus* to be an *ex cathedra* pronouncement, and he was a supporter of the letter (which he calls 'a noble letter')[53] sent to the Pope on 9 June 1721 by seven French bishops asking the Pope to withdraw *Unigenitus* and declaring that it could not be regarded as *ex cathedra*. Although the Pope had this petition censured by the Holy Office, theologians would agree that *Unigenitus* was not an *ex cathedra* statement. Thomas Innes, however, did not even regard *Unigenitus* as a normal exercise of the Magisterium of the Church. This can be perceived from his letter to Bishop Gordon on 6 Sept 1734 in which he declared that he would 'yield to none in an entire submission to all _∧^{real} decrees of the Catholic Church and in recommending that submission to all others.'[54] McMillan points out that the emphasis here is on the word 'real'. What is even more significant is that the word 'real' has been added above the line with a caret underneath. In other words, at his first writing, he did not even include *Unigenitus* as a decree of the Church at all. Thomas Innes always believed that *Unigenitus* would be abrogated. Thus when Benedict XIII became Pope on 29 May 1724, he was delighted, as the new pope was a Dominican and a Thomist, and Innes claimed that he 'wd never have past *Unigenitus* had he been in place.'[55] Again in 1732, when there was a move to reconsider some decisions of Pope Clement XI on Chinese matters, Thomas Innes asked:

> What will be said of another (Only begt) which was made on a sudden, in the greatest fear of, without hearing the party concerned, tho earnestly craving Audience & c?[56]

As successive popes, however, not only failed to withdraw *Unigenitus*, but confirmed it, the original suddenness of its publication became less and less relevant, but many still failed to realise that there was a fundamental issue at stake. Time has brought a clearer perspective, especially as regards the condemnation of the twenty-ninth proposition — 'Outside the church, no grace is given.'[57] Paradoxically, it was a point that Thomas Innes would not have disputed, as he had a great regard for the worth of his separated brethren. That was the tragedy of his position.

Ruth Clark in her book *Strangers and Sojourners at Port Royal* stated that Thomas Innes joined in the Appeal against *Unigenitus*, but on the advice of friends kept his name off the lists. This was denied by Thomas Innes himself, and his nephew, George Innes emphasised the denial in a letter to Rome:

> All I need say of it is, that if your padrons considered the trouble and vexation and even upbraidings Mr Thomas [Innes] mett wt both in publick and private for refusing positively to sign the appeall, or to have any thing to do with it, they woud commend mr Whitf[ord] and him for their behaviour on that occasion insted of blaming them, nay their absolute refusal to meddle wt the appeal directly or indirectly amidst of the most pressing callin[g] citations thereto, was all the protestation they durst venture at that time, nay such was the violent heatt and ferment that then re[i]gned that it would not have been safe for them to make any further advance.[58]

Bishop Gordon also declared that none of the college ever took part in the Appeal. Thomas Innes undoubtedly accepted papal authority, but there is just a hint of Gallican tendencies in that he recommended to Patrick Leith, a priest in Scotland, a book entitled *Justification des discours et de l'histoire de M. Fleury* which attempted to refute accusations that Fleury's *Histoire Ecclésiastique* contained 'Gallican Libertis',[59] although it is generally considered that Fleury's judgements are themselves tinged with Gallicanism, especially as regards the papacy. On the other hand, in the same year, 1736, Thomas Innes was very annoyed when he was accused of perverting James Campbell, and accused of arguing with him against the infallibility of the Catholic Church. He also urged Bishop Gordon to send Bishop Smith's attested acceptance of *Unigenitus* to Rome *quam celerrime*.

One point about which Thomas Innes was always adamant was that he never taught his personal views to any of the students. Writing to Bishop Gordon, he said that 'his Maxime always hath been to keep our young people from meddling in these matters',[60] and in another letter, he declared, 'Its false that he ever excited any other young or old agt it.'[61] Again he wrote, 'However he judges of it, he leaves all others to their own conscience',[62] and more specifically with regard to his great adversary, Colin Campbell, he wrote to George Gordon, 'no body knows better than you my moderation in regard of Onlybegot when the heats were greatest against it at this place' and that Colin Campbell 'was severall years under my care in this house in the greatest heats, without having a word from me about these maters.'[63] Thomas Innes' claim never to have taught his views to students tends to be corroborated by John Gordon of Glencat who in his diatribe against the Catholic Church ridiculed the staff of the Scots College Paris for their easy acceptance of *Unigenitus*.[64]

Thomas Innes, however, seems to have broken his own rule of not discussing these matters with students in the case of James Campbell who came to Paris in July 1730 and left in September 1731. No doubt it was his mature age, and the high regard Innes had for his brother Colin, that led Thomas Innes to confide in James Campbell. This was to have the direst consequences.

There was also an *alumnus* of the Scots College Paris whom Thomas Innes encouraged in his anti-Constitution stand. This was Gilbert Wauchope, and in his correspondence with him, perhaps more than in any other, Thomas Innes can be seen as an active encourager of anti-Constitutionist views.[65]

It is also true that Thomas Innes approved of John Gordon of Birkenbush going to Troyes for the subdiaconate because it could not be received in Paris without submission to *Unigenitus*. Both he and his brother Louis tried to justify this step to Bishop Gordon, telling him that the Bishop of Troyes did not demand subscription to *Unigenitus*. This was a gross understatement. The Bishop was Jacques Bénigne Bossuet, nephew of the famous Bossuet. Rome had been so suspicious of him after his appointment to the bishopric on 7 March 1716, that she made him wait for bulls of appointment until 1718. When consecrated bishop, he had placed a Jansenist at the head of his seminary.[66] At this time (1731), Thomas Innes also regarded the miracles at the tomb of Pâris as a vindication of the anti-Constitution position, and he blamed the defection of John Gordon of Glencat on his acting against his conscience in subscribing to *Unigenitus* on the advice of Charles Whyteford. To Bishop Gordon he claimed that John Gordon of Birkenbush, and John and William Farquharson would rather give up all than be advanced to Holy Orders at the price of submission to *Unigenitus*, and further claimed that Glencat's example had confirmed them in this. Although he did not teach students to reject *Unigenitus*, Thomas Innes evidently approved of them doing so.

Thomas Innes' views were probably fairly well known in Paris, and this led to the cessation of an annual pension of 1600 livres which the college was accustomed to receive from the French clergy. When either Charles Whyteford or Thomas Innes came to claim this, the Bishop of Chalons, who was presiding at the Assembly of Clergy, asked him whether he accepted the Constitution, and on seeing the hesitation, stopped the pension.[67]

This analysis of the position of Thomas Innes, gleaned from his own letters, may at first seem very condemnatory. There is no doubt that he personally did not accept *Unigenitus*, but not strictly accurate that he refused to sign. He was simply never in the position of having his signature demanded. As he was not serving on the mission, he was not bound by the obligations placed on Scottish missioners, and although Bishop Gordon hinted that his signature would stop complaints, the bishop never made the demand. Moreover, Thomas Innes is seen in a favourable light in so far as he never made his opposition public. He did not quite keep to his original intention of confiding only in Bishop Gordon and Bishop Nicolson.[68] Confiding his thoughts to his brother Louis and to William Stuart, the priest agent in Rome, was not pernicious, as these were men in responsible posts who could be expected to keep confidences, but writing about the issues to Gilbert Wauchope was not laudable, especially as Wauchope circulated one of his communications.[69] Discussing the matter with James Campbell was even more foolish, and for this Innes paid the penalty. Even before these disclosures, however, his views had leaked out, but it does not seem to have been his intention that they should have done so, as he had no intention of causing public dissent. Whether he should have been left in a position of authority in the college is another matter, but that decision was the responsibility of others.

Louis Innes

Louis Innes, also accused by the anti-Jansenist party, though no longer officially a member of staff after 1713, nevertheless had great influence in college affairs, and so his position must be examined. Louis was far more circumspect, and much more restrained in his language than was his brother Thomas, and his views were more moderate.

We have already seen how Louis Innes repudiated Jansenism with abhorrence in 1687. At the time of the promulgation of *Unigenitus* in 1713, Louis Innes was occupied with plans for the Jacobite rebellion in Scotland, and it is not until April 1716 that we get his first comment. He wrote to his brother Thomas:

> Send us what you can learn of proceedgs of Sorbonne. I wish they wold work at a body of D[oc]trin in opposition to Consn. I wish they had chosen a deeper & more tryd man th[a]n Mr Chevr f[or] send[in]g th[a]t errand.[70]

This request shows that Louis Innes disliked *Unigenitus*, and had reservations about accepting it. In 1727, when he wrote to his brother Thomas in Scotland, in a passage we have already quoted, he showed that he was still hoping for change, and believed that the pope was being bullied by those under Jesuit influence.

In the following year, 1728, he wrote to his brother Thomas telling him that Cardinal Noailles had accepted the Constitution, but that the Cardinal's submission was still conditioned on the Pope's acceptance of the twelve articles. It would appear from his letter that Louis Innes favoured Noailles' position i.e. acceptance of the Constitution with elucidations.[71] When Louis Innes tried to justify John Gordon's subdiaconate ordination at Troyes by saying that the Paris demands were unreasonable, this does not necessarily mean that he had rejected *Unigenitus*. Rather he disliked this way of proceeding by subscriptions, and since subscriptions were not demanded in Rome, nor at that time in Scotland, it seemed to him unfair of the French hierarchy to impose them on Scottish students.

Like his brother, Louis was careful not to teach dislike of the Constitution to the students; 'we do all we can to keep anttg relatg to the unhappy subject from our prentices.'[72] Nevertheless, the students learned of the controversies at the University, and made up their own minds:

> by conversing with comerads in publick scholls they drink in opinions that are absolutely incompatible with what is requird from those who would be advanced, & consequently they cannot be advanced at this place.[73]

The college did make efforts to correct Jansenist views among the students, and as Louis Innes pointed out to Bishop Gordon, three ecclesiastical students, John Gordon, John and William Farquharson 'were turned out of the shop [college]' upon 'their proving obstinat & irreclaimable from these [Jansenist] principles.'[74]

Louis Innes' other comments after the Clashinore accusations were not intended to argue against the Constitution, but simply to show the incompetence of the missioners sitting in judgement:

> I say a few inexperienced men, who are so little acquainted with the discipline & government of the Church should take upon themselves to determine all of a sudden what 40 Bps chosen by the Ch. of Fr & the Birlies [Jesuits] as the most favourable to the Constn could not determin in 4 months sitting closely upon it, & were forced at last not to propose the receiving of it but with a great many explications and restrictions.[75]

There is no evidence to support Lercari's accusation that Louis Innes was an appellant. Lercari also reported that Louis Innes had perverted the Scots at St Germain, mentioning in particular Lord Milton and Lord Perth. Lord Perth was indeed a Jansenist, although the case is hardly proved, as

Lercari suggested, by his avoidance of a Jesuit mission, but there is no evidence that Louis Innes taught him Jansenism.

Louis Innes never rejected the Constitution. though he did not like its wording, and for a time hoped that it would be changed; his attitude was circumspect, but his loyalty to the Pope unquestionable, and the tenor of his cautious words on *Unigenitus* was that he accepted it with the proper explanations. There is no need to question the testimonial given after his death by Mgr Romigny, Vicar General of Paris, that he was sound in doctrine, and always loyal to the Church.

George Innes

George Innes was the third member of the Innes family to be accused of Jansenism. He was Prefect of Studies from 1727 until 1735, and also Procurator from 1734 until 1738, and became Principal in 1738. He had formally subscribed to *Unigenitus* at least by 1732, and he was the most adamant in denying charges of Jansenism, and defending the orthodoxy of Bishop Gordon and of the college. Thus he pointed out in 1735 that Bishop Gordon had strongly advocated acceptance of *Unigenitus* long before the Glenlivet meetings of 1733. We have seen that it was George Innes who told William Stuart in 1737 that Thomas Innes and Charles Whyteford had suffered both public and private upbraiding in the Sorbonne for their opposition to the Appeal. It was he who invoked the Vicar General of Paris to write the posthumous testimonial in favour of Louis Innes.

Nevertheless, George Innes was rebuked by Bishop Gordon for taking a neutral stance on *Unigenitus* when teaching the students, and reminded that in matters of doctrine, the authoritative teaching of the Church is paramount. This seems to indicate that although George Innes became a staunch supporter of the orthodox position, he had earlier misgivings about *Unigenitus*, and even after 1736, he used the Montpellier Catechism, albeit in corrected editions, and a theological work of Dupin, who was accused of both Jansenism and Gallicanism. Although the staff of the Scots College had warned the students of errors in Dupin's work, the use of it along with the Montpellier Catechism was very rash, and could have laid the college open to serious criticism.

Charles Whyteford

Charles Whyteford, the Principal of the college, must at first have kept his thoughts largely to himself, since Louis Innes wrote to Thomas in 1729 that he did not know what Whyteford would do if *Unigenitus* were pressed on him, for 'he seems as averse to Only [Begotten] as any',[76] but at least by 1732, Whyteford had signed the Constitution. Before that, he had persuaded John Gordon of Glencat to accept *Unigenitus* prior to his diaconate. It was most unfortunate for Charles Whyteford that his successful persuasion had such a disastrous aftermath.

Robert Gordon

Robert Gordon was Prefect of Studies 1712–1718, and Procurator 1713–1718. In 1718, he returned to Scotland, and became chaplain to the Duke of Gordon. Thus he left Paris long before the heated accusations against the college. Lercari's report listed him third amongst the most notorious Jansenists in Scotland. This echoed the unremitting accusations of Campbell and Tyrie who kept up their persecution until 1740 when Robert Gordon felt so weary of the situation that he retired to London, only to return within a year to vindicate himself against the pilgrims' charges that he had embezzled from the mission funds.

Far from being a Jansenist, Robert Gordon had immediately declared himself against the Appeal in 1717. The Appeal was recorded on 5 March 1717, and Robert Gordon wrote on 9 March, 'far from any sort of accommodation [it] will ruin all. God send peace to his Church.'[77] It would appear that the sole reason for the pilgrims' accusations was that Robert Gordon had helped to block Colin Campbell's appointment as bishop, since it was Robert Gordon who had first sown doubts about Colin Campbell in Bishop Gordon's mind by telling him that he had come from college a staunch anti-Constitutionalist.

Alexander Smith

Alexander Smith, who became bishop, was Procurator 1718–1729, and was an *alumnus* of the college, although he was ordained priest in Scotland. His ordination in his native country had nothing to do with Jansenism. His father had called him home, and although Alexander Smith had wanted to go back to Paris, Bishop Gordon had decided otherwise, ordaining him at Preshome in 1712; this was before the publication of *Unigenitus* in 1713.

Alexander Smith was described in Lercari's report of March 1737 as 'a man much suspected in these parts', and the report alleged 'that during the time of his rsidence in Paris he was regarded as a Jansenist', and added, 'were he to succeed Mgr Gordon as a vicar-apostolic, the mission would greatly suffer.'[78] When he was nominated to be bishop, Rome held up his bulls of appointment until his signed acceptance of *Unigenitus* should arrive. It was sent immediately, and his appointment as coadjutor was approved. His accusers had latched onto two enquiries he had made; he had asked that the Jansenist passages in Hacket's catechism be pointed out, and he had asked Thomas Innes to send him information about Jansenism for his private study. Rome was satisfied that his intentions were proper with no substance to the accusations. Indeed there had never been any question of Smith's orthodoxy, nor even of any personal difficulty with the Constitution.

James Carnegie

James Carnegie followed Alex Smith as Procurator 1729–1734. He had been among the first of the secular priests to be involved in Jansenist squabbles, having been one of the four who had written to Bishop Nicolson in 1702, seeking redress from the Jesuits after their accusations of Jansenism.[79]

The next complaint against Carnegie was occasioned by the publication of his Catechism in 1724. The condemnation of this Catechism indicates that Carnegie had either absorbed some Jansenist ideas or more probably that he had failed to discern the errors in the Montpellier Catechism.

The third time that accusations were made against Carnegie was when the Jesuits induced the Nuncio at Paris to complain to Rome as Carnegie was on his way to see the Stuart King. Cardinal Sacripanti's complete dismissal of the charge seems to have protected him against further accusations. He was dead two years before Lercari's report.

Dr Alexander Gordon

Dr Alexander Gordon, who died in Paris in 1724, was an *alumnus* of the Scots College, Paris who had started his studies in Robert Barclay's time. He had stayed some years in the college after his ordination, only leaving for the Scottish mission in December 1693. After a few years on the mission, his health broke down, and he returned in June 1698 to Paris where he became an eminent doctor of the Sorbonne. Though not on the college staff, and probably not residing in the college, the students found him a great help in giving advice on their studies. After his death on St Andrew's day,1724,[80] Thomas Innes declared that 'he was entirely opposite to Only beg[otten]'.[81] This would be consistent with his membership of the Sorbonne, and although Thomas Innes was biased against the Constitution, he was too precise an historian to invent something that was exactly contrary to the facts. In the list of Apellants printed in *La Constitution Unigenitus Déférée*…one twice finds the name of 'A. Gordon, Docteur de Sorbonne'.[82] This is probably Dr Alexander Gordon. It is the only case of an appellant who had studied at Scots College Paris.

Alexander Gordon (Coffurich)

Alexander Gordon of Coffurich was an *alumnus* of the college who had studied there until he received the subdiaconate, and then completed his studies at Scalan where he was ordained priest in 1734. Soon after June 1735, he was sent back to Paris where he was appointed Prefect of Studies. By a trick of fate, he was made the scape-goat. The Clashinore letters had demanded the removal of superiors from the Scots College Paris, and the missioners' letter had specified the Prefect of Studies. At the time of this letter being written (1733), the Prefect of Studies was George Innes, but at the time of the letter being read by the Cardinals in Rome (1736), the Prefect of Studies was Alexander Gordon. When the investigation of the college was undertaken, Lercari's report did nothing to redeem Alexander Gordon. In it, he said:

> It is not known that George Innes, or Alexander Gordon, the present prefect of studies, has made any act of acceptation of the bull, so that little regard should be paid to the letter subscribed by them in 1735, and sent in order to justify themselves in the eyes of the S. Congregation; and the more so, as they keep up the same correspondence as before with the Jansenists, and are entirely dependent on Thomas and Louis Innes.[83]

There is also a draft copy of a letter in Italian in the hand of John Tyrie, which may or may not have been placed before Propaganda, which reads:

> To reform the college in accordance with the wishes of the Vicars and the Missionaries of Scotland, there is no other wish than to put in place of that young priest, the said Alexander Gordon, as Prefect of Studies, a missionary of sound doctrine, and to give him absolute authority in spiritual matters as in the temporal ones of the said college...one can reform the said college solely by changing the Prefect of Studies.[84]

It is also possible that the signature of 'A. Gordon' had been found amongst the appellants, but this could not have been Alexander Gordon of Coffurich who was only a boy of ten in Scotland at the time. One can, however, see how circumstantial evidence was stacked against him, and a Propaganda meeting on 17 Dec 1737 decided on the removal of Alexander Gordon from the college. He left Paris for Scotland on 10 June 1738.

The Scottish bishops certainly did not think him guilty of Jansenism, for within a month of his return to Scotland, they made him rector of Scalan, but his denunciation by Lercari and the Propaganda decision of 1737 later barred him from the episcopate. When in 1750, a memorial was presented to Propaganda seeking his election as coadjutor, the authorities, as Peter Grant wrote, 'raked up some old stuff in the time of his being at Grisy [Scots College, Paris].'[85] Alexander Gordon was a second time recommended by Alexander Smith as coadjutor, but Cardinal Spinelli, on his own initiative, chose James Grant, probably bypassing Alexander Gordon on account of his Propaganda file. Coffurich was still appreciated in Scotland, and was made Vicar General on 3 Dec 1778.

Theological Views of College Students

A number of the students' opinions about *Unigenitus* are ascertainable, and these help to provide a thermometer of the theological climate of the college. From the foregoing survey of the staff's standpoint, it is clear that most of the superiors of the Scots College Paris were unsympathetic to *Unigenitus* although they were careful not to express formal dissent, and tried to keep their views from the students. Nevertheless in a small community, students must have been able to discern the hesitation of their superiors, and it is therefore not surprising that some of them chose not to be on the orthodox side.

John Augustine Arthur

One student who rejected *Unigenitus* was John Augustine Arthur who died in the college on 9 Jan 1729. Louis Innes described him as 'full of indiscreet zeall',[86] as he tried to get Alexander Smith to declare that he would not accept *Unigenitus* without making any headway at all, and although Louis Innes wrote ten days later that after some difficulty, 'he is now sett right',[87] after John Augustine's death, Louis Innes revealed that the student had signed with his own hand a formal declaration condemning all those who received *Unigenitus* with or without explications, declaring that he could have no confidence in anyone who was not of his opinion.[88]

John Gordon of Glencat

John Gordon of Glencat thoroughly denounced *Unigenitus* in his book, and although he had subscribed before his diaconate, Thomas Innes has told us that he had previously been opposed to the Constitution until converted by Charles Whyteford, and Glencat himself has told us that he was accused of holding Jansenist principles by a student called Alan Macdonald. Over and above his own views, Glencat may have shed a little light on Jansenist piety in the college. He is the only student, as far as we know, who has given details of penances he received for his misdeeds. As far as penitential prayers were concerned, there was little difference in the type of penances he received from Jesuit and from Secular confessors. A Jesuit in Scotland prescribed 6 Paters and 6 Aves daily for two months,[89] while a secular priest in Scotland, probably Peter Fraser who had been educated in Paris, gave him 5 Paters and 10 Aves for ten days,[90] and Alexander Smith in Paris prescribed seven Penitential Psalms daily for two weeks. The difference in Paris was (or so he claimed) that pen and ink were provided for the examination of conscience, and that in addition to the prayers, he was required to sleep in his clothes for two weeks.[91] If this was true, and it would be a strange fabrication, it might be evidence of

Jansenistic piety in the college, which of course can be present quite independently of Jansenist theology. As already said, Glencat seems to confirm that he was not taught Jansenism by his superiors.

John Gordon Birkenbush, John Farquharson, William Farquharson

Three students were expelled from the college for holding Jansenist views; they were John Gordon of Birkenbush, John Farquharson and his brother William Farquharson. In September 1731. John Gordon Birkenbush received the subdiaconate in Troyes to avoid subscribing to *Unigenitus*. The college authorities connived at this, but in 1732, he and the two Farquharsons were expelled from the college on account of Jansenist principles. John Gordon was, however, ordained priest at Scalan in 1734, and William Farquharson was ordained priest at Troyes by Jacques Bénigne Bossuet, a notorious Jansenist, in 1735. When William Farquharson, after his ordination, considered applying for the Scottish mission, George Innes told him that a prior condition would be the acceptance of *Unigenitus*, but he never actually made the formal application.

John McKenzie and William Duthie

Then there was the case of the two who received minor orders at Troyes on 5 July 1733. They are never named in college or Scottish letters, but referred to as the 'two eldest'. Jacques Bossuet's Register at Troyes, however, proves beyond doubt that they were John McKenzie and William Duthie, and that their ordination was all the more secret as it did not take place in Troyes itself, but in the chapel of the bishop's summer residence at St Lyé.[92] A full year elapsed before Bishop Gordon heard of these ordinations, and thinking that they had just taken place, he wrote a stern rebuke to Louis Innes on 24 July 1734.[93] The ordinations had, however, taken place before the college had word of the Scalan and Clashinore meetings of the previous year. John McKenzie later signed the Constitution, became Prefect of Studies in Scots College Paris in 1738, and became a stalwart defender both of the orthodox position and of the orthodoxy of the college. William Duthie also changed his mind to accept the Constitution, and insisted on being ordained in Paris to prove his orthodoxy.

Colin Campbell

Even Colin Campbell, a ringleader in making Jansenist accusations, must be listed among the *alumni* of the college who at one time held unorthodox views, because Robert Gordon told Bishop Gordon that Colin Campbell had come from the college a strong anti-constitutionalist, the strongest he had ever known.

Lord Edward Drummond

There can be little doubt about the Jansenism of Lord Edward Drummond, later sixth titular Duke of Perth, who was imprisoned in the Bastille on account of his Jansenism on 30 Oct 1739. He was an *alumnus* of Scots College, Paris, having gone there in 1698 at the early age of eight, but as he had left the college before the publication of *Unigenitus*, the college could hardly be blamed for his non-acceptance of that Constitution.

Lord Linton

If any reliance can be placed upon the letter 'pickpocketed' from Patrick Gordon, S.J., Lord Linton, son to the Earl of Traquair, and an *alumnus* of the college, might have had some leanings in the Jansenist direction, as the letter said that when Robert Gordon was asked, 'Why did you not take up the *Année Chretienne?*', he had answered, 'How could I do so since its the book of Devotion that My Ld Linton makes constantly use of at Mass.'[94]

Gilbert Wauchope

Another *alumnus* who was most adamant against the Constitution was Gilbert Wauchope, from the family of Wauchope of Niddrie near Edinburgh, who had been an ecclesiastical student at the college from 1693 until 1704, had returned to study medicine in 1706, and became a medical doctor in London. He had left the College before *Unigenitus*, but became a fervent anti-constitutionist who acted as an agent between Dutch Jansenists and a group of English non-jurors. When Thomas Innes was in London supervising the publication of his *Critical Essay*, he stayed with Gilbert Wauchope, and afterwards continued a correspondence with him. In 1733, Innes sent the doctor a paper on the Constitution which the doctor circulated in London[95], and in the following year sent him a present of a book or treatise on the subject which pleased Wauchope a great deal:

> I return'd you allready thanks for your excellent Present which I read twice with a great deal of pleasure & shall perhaps give it as many more readings. 'Tis concise & nervous & strikes the only Begotten at the very root without entering into an endless discussion of the Proposit. condemn'd.[96]

Wauchope asked Innes to obtain for him Duguet's *Principes de la Foi, Le Nécrologe de Porte Royal,* and the 1693 edition of Pasquier Quesnel's *Morales Réflexions,* but he obtained a copy of the latter before Innes had time to send one. Ruth Clark stated that Gilbert Wauchope had ventured to write to Bishop Petre, the Vicar-Apostolic of the London district on the subject.[97] There may be a little confusion here. Soon after they took place, Wauchope had heard of the Clashinore meetings in Scotland from one of the priests who had studied in Paris. Wauchope was so incensed at the attack on the Paris College and on the Innes brothers that he told Louis Innes that he intended to write to Bishop Gordon,[98] and in the following year, 1734, he told Thomas Innes that he had sent the Bishop a 'sketch' against the Constitution, Wauchope claimed that the Bishop in his reply

> shows himself surprisingly hamper'd & perplexed to get out of the noose, & other attempts failing, is forc'd to have recourse to high words of authority, cross-purposes, opprobrious language & c. the common & last resources of a weak cause.[99]

It is possible that Wauchope also wrote to Bishop Petre, but it seems more likely that Ruth Clark presumed that a letter from London to a bishop would have been sent to the Vicar-Apostolic of the London district. She does not seem to have known that Wauchope was an *alumnus* of the Scots College, Paris; otherwise, she would have discussed his views in her chapter on the college, especially as he was connected with Thomas Innes. When the Bishop's letter was sent to the Jansenist Petitpied at Utrecht, the latter sent Wauchope a memoir of twenty pages to fortify him against the writings in favour of *Unigenitus*.[100]

Thus the orthodoxy of the students of Scots College, Paris, was far less than perfect; no fewer than eleven students of the college (quite a high proportion, considering the very small number of students) are known to have opposed the Constitution at least for a time. This is perhaps the greatest indictment against the college. While the staff never refused outward obedience to Church authority, their inner convictions were not strong enough for them to restrain or sufficiently discipline the students. It is true that three were eventually expelled for holding Jansenist views, but even in that case, their dissent went unchecked for long enough, and Thomas Innes actually approved of their attitude. On their failure to properly direct the students, more than anything else, the college staff were remiss.

Part 3: Jansenist Problems after 1736

Jansenist problems had culminated in the unfavourable decision of Propaganda on 10 Sept 1736 when all missioners were enjoined to sign the Formulary for the second time, and to subscribe to the condemnation of both Carnegie's and Hacket's catechisms. One might have expected the difficulties to end there, but problems continued both in Paris and in Scotland.

Problems continue in Paris

From Paris, less than six months later, on 4 March 1737, Monsignor Lercari, acting-Nuncio at Paris, forwarded to Rome the report that had been demanded by Propaganda in the previous September.[101] The report was damnatory. It asserted that the three Inneses were all Appellants, that the college was a hotbed of the Jansenist heresy, and that through the college, the Scottish mission had become infected with Jansenism. The report, however, was not the fruit of a Visitation of the college; in fact, it admits that information had been hard to obtain. Many errors of facts in the report do not lead to confidence in its accuracy. Some of these are mentioned by McMillan.[102] The report said that George Innes and Thomas Innes were brothers, and that Louis is their uncle, whereas it was Louis and Thomas who were brothers, both uncles of George; Charles Whyteford was said to be Procurator instead of Principal; Robert Gordon was not, as stated, the co-author of Hacket's catechism, though he had helped Carnegie with the 1724 catechism. Hackett's name was given as Hasset. There are, however, many more errors than those listed by McMillan. It said that John Tyrie apostatised, whereas it was his brother James. The report stated that the three Inneses had always resided in the college, but for many years, Louis Innes had stayed at St Germain, and Thomas Innes had been out of the college since October 1733. The report wrongly averred that Bishop Gordon had approved Hackett's catechism after it had been condemned by Rome. It was falsely alleged that Bishop Gordon had 'opposed more than anyone else, the subscription to the formula sent from Rome', and that he employed missioners without demanding subscription, whereas the bishop had been punctilious in obeying the decree, and all the Scottish missioners had signed the formula. Lercari further stated that Alexander Smith had been consecrated without any of the Catholics in Scotland knowing anything about it, but Alexander Smith had written to all the missioners asking them if they thought that he should accept the post, and had received their support It is hard to believe that an acting Nuncio could have sent such an inaccurate report to Rome, and it is so full of errors as to be useless for evidence. Lercari gave no indication to the College that he was sending such a report, and outwardly appeared to be so much of the opposite opinion that George Innes later believed him to be the College's greatest friend.

The report of Lercari alleged that pure Jansenism was taught in the college, before the publication of *Unigenitus*. There is no evidence of this, and as we have already seen, accusations made before 1713 were trivial indeed. Lercari also wrongly alleged that all the Inneses were Appellants. To Lercari's allegations that Alexander Smith was a Jansenist, suffice it to say that Propaganda after investigation dismissed similar charges, and approved the appointment of Alexander Smith as Bishop. Despite the apparent weightiness of a condemnation by an acting Nuncio, Lercari's report can be discounted. After examination, it can be seen as the accusation of enemies, rather than the fruit of an independent inquiry.

The pilgrims, who had not been informed of Propaganda's decision of Sept 1736, continued their accusations in Rome. After the death of Louis Innes on 22 June 1738, they presented a memorial denouncing the deceased as a rank Jansenist. Whereupon Thomas and George Innes procured an attestation of his complete soundness in faith signed by the Curé of S. Étienne du Mont and by L. de Romigny, Vicar General of the Diocese of Paris. The church authorities in Rome became more and more nauseated with the doings of the pilgrims who were ordered to leave Rome. Before they left on 9 Oct 1738, however, they managed, through the intercession of Sir Thomas Durham, to obtain a benefice from the Pope. The Cardinal Protector of Scotland was furious, declaring that it never would have happened had he not been out of Rome at the time.

Meantime in Paris, the Sorbonne was making plans to revoke the Appeal against the Constitution that had been recorded in the University in 1718. Much to George Innes' annoyance, Cardinal Fencin had got the idea that the new Principal of the Scots College was against the revocation of the Appeal,[103] and on the day of the Revocation, 11 May 1739, a mishap occurred. John McKenzie, who had gone to Troyes for minor orders in 1733, had attended the Assembly of the University against his doctor's orders, but happened to be out of the room when his turn to vote came. This could easily have led his enemies to spread everywhere, not only in Paris, but in Rome and in Scotland, the strongest accusations that he was a Jansenist. John McKenzie went to the Rector of the University whom he satisfied as to his orthodoxy. He then declared his acceptance of *Unigenitus* and of the Revocation of the Appeal before the Procurator of the German Nation, and obtained from him a certificate to that effect, sealed with the seal of the Nation. Not content with that, at the next meeting of the Assembly of the Nation, he insisted on making a public declaration of his entire and full adhesion to all the heads of the conclusion made by the Nation in the General Meeting held on 11 May. Finally he sent his accounts of the affair to Rome and to the Scottish Bishops.[104] Orthodoxy was amply declared, but, in view of all the suspicion against the College, a very unfortunate mistake had been made.

When Colin Campbell had returned to Scotland, John Tyrie took up residence in Paris where he made trouble for the College.[105] He contacted two students, James Falconer and Charles Farquhar, and communicated with them by letter, but the letters were intercepted. This led to a formal Visitation of the College on 15 May 1740 by the Prior of the Carthusians, Pascale Le Tonnellier, who brought the Procurator of the Carthusian community, Hatenville, to act as secretary. The students were given no warning of this visit;[106] everybody in the community was interviewed individually with the sole exception of Thomas Innes who was considered to be neither staff nor student.[107]

At the scrutiny, two letters were produced, one from John Tyrie to Falconer and Farquhar, and the other from the students to John Tyrie. In the letter, the students had claimed that they did not get the same facilities as other students to visit friends in Paris, but under questioning they admitted that they had been granted the permissions they had asked for, and had not asked for others that were specified in the letter. They had also said in writing that their grievances if recorded would exceed the bounds of a letter. They were asked to give particular instances. Falconer's reply throws light on some domestic arrangements in the College. He said that he had been refused permission to have a fire in his room, although permission had been granted to another student. John McKenzie was claimed to have said that if Falconer lit another fire, he would block up his chimney, to which McKenzie replied that he did not remember this, but that he would have refused him permission, because Falconer had not bought his own wood, but had taken it from the studying room.[108] The result of the scrutiny was the expulsion of James Falconer and Charles Farquhar on 23 May 1740. The decree of expulsion was very formal, even bordering on the melodramatic, the operative phrase reading:

> We have expelled and do expel from the College of the Scots the said James Falconer and Charles Farquhar, prohibiting them from staying here any longer, or from coming here under any pretext whatsoever and we return them to Scotland, praying them besides, in the Bowels of Jesus Christ, to repent themselves of what has happened.[109]

A report of the scrutiny was to be sent to Rome which the Prior believed would end forever accusations against the College.

The College staff soon discovered that the two 'young pilgrims', as the expelled students were now called, intended to collect their viatic money for the journey to Scotland, but then stay in France. So the College decided not to hand over the viatic money until they were actually on their way. Accordingly Andrew Riddoch accompanied James Falconer to the Boulogne coach which was to leave in the morning after their arrival. After seeing Falconer place his baggage on board, Riddoch gave him his viatic money. Next day, however, Falconer had disappeared, and it was discovered that he had been back at the coach to retrieve his baggage. This episode further demeaned the young pilgrims in the eyes of the College, and convinced the staff that they were well rid of them.

The expulsion, however, which had been viewed as a grand gesture of vindication, was in several ways a blunder. For one thing, James Falconer had mentioned in his deposition that he had been given a theological work of Dupin as a text book, though he had admitted that the staff had warned him of errors in the book which they would rectify. As Dupin had been accused of Jansenism and Gallicanism, some of his works being condemned, and a full report of the College scrutiny was to be sent to Rome, George Innes grew fearful, and wrote to Peter Grant, the Scots agent in Rome, explaining his position, and asking the agent to treat with Hatenville before the report was sent to Rome. He also explained that he had in the past used the Montpellier catechism, but only in corrected editions, and he had now abandoned it altogether.[110]

Another unfortunate aspect of the expulsion was that, as Charles Farquhar had been personally recommended to the College by the Stuart King, there had been a breach of etiquette in not informing His Majesty of the expulsion.[111]

What caused most embarrassment, however, was that both the expelled students were received into other seminaries; James Falconer entered St Nicholas du Chardonet, his fees being paid by Abbé Hugh Sempil, a Scots priest in Paris who had left the Jesuit Order; Charles Farquhar joined the community of St. Barbara.[112] Now the Principal of St. Barbara was Mr Gailland, an agent of the Holy See with whom George Innes particularly wanted to be on good terms. This led to a reappraisal of the case against Farquhar who was now deemed to have been led astray by Falconer.[113] Farquhar was recommended for Scalan and received into the Scottish seminary,[114] while Falconer was described as 'an arrant knave.'[115] Even in the case of Falconer, however, there was for some time a softening of heart. Falconer petitioned Bishop Gordon for a title to ordination,[116] and George Innes did not know how he was going to tell him that the Bishop had refused.[117] Peter Grant, the agent in Rome, supported his case, but was unsuccessful. The student was now described as 'poor Falconer'.[118] Later, however, after trying his vocation with the Benedictines in Germany, Falconer returned to Scotland, apostatised from the Catholic faith, and assisted a Presbyterian minister.[119]

Meantime there were more accusations against the College. Abbé Melfort, William Drummond, son of the first Earl Melfort, who was Abbé of Liege, but appears to have been staying in Paris, accused the staff of reading Montgerous' book in the refectory, and of supplying Lord John Drummond with Jansenist books including that of Montgerous, to which George Innes replied that the students had never seen Montgerous' book. Thomas Innes, believing his presence in the college to be the cause of its troubles, wanted to leave, but George Innes persuaded him to stay.[120] Abbé Sempil was another who caused trouble for the college[121] by leading Cardinal Fencin to have doubts about its orthodoxy.[122] Little wonder that the Prior of the Carthusians was alarmed at all the ill opinion.[123]

In February 1742, three students left the College together. They were Clanranald, John Cairney and George Gordon of Beldornie. George Innes wrote to Bishop Gordon explaining their reasons for leaving, and hoping that they might still be educated for the priesthood.[124] Unfortunately this letter has not survived and so we cannot be certain what the reasons were, but it is likely that the students were nauseated by the Jansenist quarrels, as later in the year, George Innes wrote, 'Even our youngest students are upset by mischiefs intended against Grisy.'[125]

In this same year, Cardinal Rivera, the Cardinal Protector of Scotland, gave orders to Peter Grant that no students destined for the Scots College Rome should go there via Scots College Paris. When George Innes pressed for a reason for this, the Cardinal said that it was to stop him being harangued by complaints and calumnies against the College.[126] The answer suggests that he suspected the College of heresy, but had no concrete evidence against it. George Innes was quite content to respect the order, and advised Bishop Smith that Roman students might be directed to Aeneas or Angus Macdonald, a banker in Paris, and the bill for them be sent to Propaganda.[127] When the Principal heard that Bishop Smith intended to ignore the Cardinal's order, he declared that he would fight 'tooth and nail, for why should we exasperat Mr Rivers [Cardinal Rivera], and loose our money besides?'[128] Nevertheless Bishop Gordon and Bishop Smith decided to send two students via Paris 'whatever Mr Rivers may think.'[129] This put George Innes on the horns of a dilemma. He still hoped to direct them to Aeneas Macdonald, but the two students, Alexander Macdonald and John Macdonald arrived on his doorstep. George Innes asked Peter Grant to explain to Cardinal Rivera that he had had no choice but to take them in, as they had no other mortal to apply to, nor a farthing in their pockets'; if he had acted otherwise, he would have been accused of their death.[130] Even after this explanation, Cardinal Rivera expressed his great displeasure.[131]

No more students were sent to Rome until 1749 when William Guthrie and John Geddes, the future bishop, set out for the Eternal City. Cardinal Rivera still insisted that Roman students should not pass by Scots College Paris.[132] They were directed to avoid Paris, and were sent by boat round Spain and through the straits of Gibraltar, which led to great anxieties for their safety, and at one point, it was feared that they were lost.[133] This resolved Bishop Smith not to use the long way again. In 1750, he sent Roderick Macdonald and John Macdonell via Scots College, firmly declaring, 'Necessity has no law.'[134] The College looked after the youths whom they found to be two hopeful boys of sixteen years of age, and provided them with recommendations in French and Latin for their journey.[135] This time Rome did not complain.

In fact, after the 'forty-five' rebellion, there were not many accusations of Jansenism, other problems taking precedence. In 1748, however, the Nuncio sent for Innes to ask if there were any Jansenists in the Scottish mission, which Innes emphatically denied. The Principal thought that the Nuncio must have heard something from Scotland or from Rome, but when he asked the Nuncio of this, nothing particular was instanced.[136]

Problems continue in Scotland

In Scotland too, problems persisted. Accusations of Jansenism, that had reached such a climax in 1733, continued to be made, although there was less foundation than ever, since all had subscribed to *Unigenitus*. The quarrels greatly disturbed the peace of the mission in Scotland, just as they had sapped the life-blood of the College in Paris. In 1738, Bishop Gordon was embarrassed by Alexander Drummond, an *alumnus* of the Paris College 'making noise against Unigenitus and refusing to sign' the formulary of acceptance.[137] Thomas Innes was said to be in the greatest perplexity about a letter he got from Alexander Drummmond and Robert Gordon concerning Jansenism, and feared that if the pilgrims heard of it, all would be lost.[138] In the following year, Drummond was described as exclaiming against the Constitution as if he were mad. Colin Campbell, also an *alumnus* of the College although its chief accuser, returned to Scotland, but 'instead of owning his fault and asking pardon', 'strove all he could to justify his doings.'[139] He kept up his campaign, preaching a seditious sermon in Aberdeen which denied the Bishop's right to change missionaries from one station to another, and writing to Rome that the bishop's desire to move William Shand was motivated by his preference for his own party.

The 'Pick-pocketed' Letter

In 1739, a letter with the gravest accusations against the Inneses, the Paris College, and Bishop Gordon, was forwarded to Bishop Gordon by James Leslie, a Highland priest, stationed in Glengarry. The letter had been in the possession of a Jesuit priest called Patrick Gordon who said that Leslie had picked the letter from his pocket while he was speaking to Bishop Macdonald.[140] Leslie, however, said that he had found the letter in a garden. It was never established which version was true, nor who was the author, but it was the contents of the letter that gave most offence. The letter contained many accusations of Jansenism, those against the Paris College being so serious as to warrant quoting this section of the letter verbatim:

> Mr Ch: Whiteford, Mr Lewis & Mr T Innes did all three appeal agst the Constitution Unig: Mr Whiteford sign'd it aterwards. Mr Lewis dy'd being only absolved by his

Br Mr Th tho' suspended, & gave no other proof oh his Orthodoxy but by repeating the Athanasian Creed when the Parish Priest of S. Etienne a Genovevan Monk & Jansenist gave him the Viatick & extream Unction & Mr Tho. who was suspended by Arch-Bp glorys to this day in his open revolt.

In the Scots College at Paris they still continue to teach bad principles to their students. The book of Instructions made use of there is the Montpelier Catechism (judge by that of the other books) of wch practice Mr Gailland Principle of the College de Plessis & Ste Barbe private Agent of the H See gives proof.

The present ArchBp of Paris having in the year 1737 asked Mr Robinet one of his Grand Vicaires the character of the Scots College, Mr Robinet answer'd that it was the very worst in Paris, because they were as much poison'd as any Comunity in Paris & that they use greater care to conceal it.[141]

This is about one seventh of the letter, the rest being mainly accusations against the Scottish Bishops and missioners, though some members of the laity are accused as well. The revelation of the contents of the letter caused great animosity, and although the accusations against the Paris College were never substantiated, they show that the Scots College Paris was still a primary target for the malcontents. The contents of the letter infuriated Bishop Gordon who had himself been unjustly accused.

Suspension of Father Riddoch

Father John Riddoch, a Jesuit in Aberdeen was suspended by Bishop Gordon on 7 January 1741 for refusing to withdraw accusations of Jansenism against the secular clergy, and in particular against George James Gordon Scalanensis who had been sent to work in Aberdeen. His suspension brought lay people into the disputes as seventeen of them signed a protest to Bishop Gordon, declaring that the suspension was unjust save for one word uttered rashly 'against the author of impious, heretical and blasphemous verses'. They declared that George Gordon (Scalanensis) was more deserving of suspension, seven of the signatories adding after their names 'hearer of the Secular Clergy till Mr Gordon's arrival'.[142] Bishop Gordon lifted the suspension 2 Sept 1741 when he received John Riddoch's submission.

Heretical and Blasphemous Verses

The 'heretical and blasphemous verses', that the Aberdonians mention in their appeal, had become an object of concern in the troubles, although undoubtedly composed in a humorous vein. When read straight across each line, the verses mock the Catholic Church and praise Jansenism, but when read as parallel columns, the reverse is true. These were the verses in question:

Sir I believe Beelzebub preaches	The faith which Rome does now maintain
Each article Jansenius teaches	Is just what Christ did first ordain
Thus came from hell the cursed positions.	Such as in Roman Creeds are shown
The one & hundred propositions.	All saving faith to me make known
Cursed be the stinging race of vipers	The Pope & his believing band
Sprung from Jansenius of Ypres	Are those who to Christ's gospel stand[143]

These verses were composed by James Leslie who sent copies to Father Patrick Gordon and Fr Alexander Gordon, both Jesuits, while George Gordon, a secular priest, made and distributed further copies. Incredible as it seems, these verses were taken seriously and gave great offence to the extent of complaints sent to Rome. Abbé Sempil even translated the verses into Latin, in rhyming couplets, for the benefit of the Roman Cardinals.[144] Leslie was required to apologise to Bishop Gordon for the offence caused, although he declared that he had 'never believed them as read at lenght [sic]'.[145]

Several complaints and accusations of Jansenism were sent to Propaganda by secular priests, especially in the year 1740[146], which led to a third special congress of Propaganda on Scottish affairs on 10/24 April 1741. No wonder Bishop Gordon felt that there would be 'no end to the jars'.

The seriousness of the controversies in Scotland lay chiefly in the divisions amongst the clergy, and the high percentage of priests involved. In the numerically tiny mission, ten priests in Scotland, including the two lowland bishops, as well as all the staff in the Scots College, Paris, were accused of Jansenism, while about sixteen were involved, at least to some extent, in making the accusations. Only about five of the secular priests managed to keep their names out of the disputes. The divisions lasted from 1733 until the 'forty-five'; even after that, there were whimpers although they did not amount to very much.

The influence of the Scots College Paris in bringing these quarrels to Scotland can hardly be denied. Several ulterior motives for bringing accusations have been discerned, and have been stressed almost to the point of refusing to see any foundation for the accusations, and denying that any might have been sincere in their concern for orthodoxy. The foundation for complaints was provided by the Scots College Paris in so far as Thomas Innes did not accept *Unigenitus*, and other members of staff were most reluctant to accept it. Their failure to discipline students in this regard was even more serious, so that several were holding unorthodox views at least for a time. John Gordon had been allowed to receive the subdiaconate from Jacques Bénigne Bossuet, and later John McKenzie and William Duthie had been allowed to receive minor orders from the same prelate. A cult of the deacon Pâris had been brought into Scotland.

The Montpellier Catechism had been used as the foundation of the Scottish Catechisms of 1724 and 1725, and although neither of the authors were *alumni* of the Scots College Paris, the influence of the college in this choice is highly probable. Even the anti-Constitution stand of George James Gordon who had never been out of the country would never have germinated were it not for the books that Colin Campbell left at Scalan. Before examining the ulterior motives, it is therefore necessary to recognise the foundation, and to envisage the possibility that some complaints were made in all sincerity out of a regard for sound doctrine.

Nevertheless ulterior motives also played a part in the Jansenist quarrels. James McMillan has examined these under the aspect of divisions amongst the clergy, and in particular rivalries between Jesuits and Secular priests, Highland clergy and Lowland Clergy, Roman-trained and Paris-trained priests.[147] The old rivalry with the Jesuits had for a long time led to Jansenist accusations against the seculars. We have seen that the earliest accusations in Paris had been made by Jesuits, while in Scotland almost all the accusations prior to 1733 had been made by members of that order. As most of the Jesuits subscribed to Molinism which was not very palatable to most of the secular clergy, it is easy to see how such charges were made. What was radically new in 1733 was that secular priests complained about seculars. Although Jesuits and ex-Jesuits gladly joined in the fray,[148] their involvement cannot explain the deep division amongst seculars themselves.

The divide between priests educated at Rome and priests educated at Paris cannot fully explain the disputes, since one of the principal complainers, Colin Campbell, had been educated at Paris, and Aeneas MacLachlan, who also had pursued all his studies in Paris at first sided with 'the Pilgrims' though he later changed his mind. Not all attackers were Romans, and not all attacked were Parisians.

Highland versus Lowland tensions certainly existed, but complaints were not made against all the Lowland clergy, and at the Clashinore meeting of 8 June 1733, the Highlanders present were anxious to claim the support of six Lowlanders.

In seeking underlying motives, it is to the opening stages of the quarrels that we must turn, examining the persons making the attacks, the persons attacked, and the objectives in view. The first complaints made in 1732 were said to be made by Highlanders, and the instigator was said to be one of their number, Alexander Paterson. The key figures at the Scalan meeting of 6 June 1733 were the Highlanders, Bishop MacDonald, John McDonald, Colin Campbell and James Leslie, and John Tyrie who was transferred to the Highland district in August the following year. George

Gordon Scalanensis and George Duncan appear to have been present only because they were teachers at Scalan where the meeting was held; never afterwards did they join in the accusations. The only other Lowlander present was Thomas Brockie from the nearby Cabrach.[149]

At the Clashinore meeting two days later, the groups accused were first of all the staff of the Scots College Paris denounced in the letters to Rome, and then a group of six designated as the 'Paris Club'. 'Paris Club' could not have simply meant *alumni* of the Scots College Paris since two of the six, Andrew Hacket and George Gordon Scalanensis, had not studied there. Moreover the mere fact of having studied at Paris could never have been cited credibly as a reason for them being barred from holding ecclesiastical office. To belong to the Paris Club meant to be suspected of Jansenism, in much the same way as in the sixteenth century 'to have been drinking at St Leonard's Well' meant to be tinged with Reformed ideas whether or not one had been to St Andrews. The use of the expression 'Paris Club' does, however, show some bias against the Scots College that stood near the Seine. While there was perhaps some foundation in the accusation against Alexander Drummond, George Gordon Scalanensis, and Andrew Hacket, the only conceivable reason for including the other three, Alexander Smith, George Gordon Mortlach and Robert Gordon was their association with the Scots College Paris. The only Paris-ordained priests excepted from the indictment were the Highlanders Colin Campbell and Aeneas MacLachlan.

The concerns expressed, apart from that of heresy, were the Highland ambition that the whole body of Scottish clergy should be consulted before the appointment of a Vicar Apostolic or Coadjutor for either district, and secondly a change of Procurators at both Rome and Edinburgh which reflects the financial discontent mainly felt by the Highlanders.

What this suggests in terms of group divide is neither Roman versus Parisian, nor Highland versus Lowland, but rather Highland versus Parisian. The Highland clergy were aggrieved at the financial distribution, and believed that the Scots College Paris had too much influence on Bishop Gordon and too much say in the affairs of the mission. There was also suspicion of the college's handling of finance, at least partly caused by a failure to realise how John Law's bequest was almost all lost with the crash of his system.

Apart from the 'group divide' that existed, it is generally recognised that another ulterior motive was Colin Campbell's personal resentment at being passed over first of all for the Highland vicariate, and secondly as coadjutor in the Lowlands. Believing Bishop Gordon was guided from Paris, he blamed the Parisians, but in fact they were still promoting his case after Bishop Gordon had decided otherwise. His continued accusations had most pernicious results. The 'pilgrims' can indeed be blamed for fomenting and continuing the factions, but not for what is often considered an over-reaction on the part of the Roman authorities. This was not due to the 'pilgrims' whom Rome soon saw through, but it was due to the Clashinore letters signed by the bishops themselves. It was their precipitate act that led to the compulsory signings of the Constitution and the investigation of the Scots College Paris. They should have investigated before acting, and they should have given the staff of the College a chance to speak for themselves. Instead they gave the college a false account of the Glenlivet meetings, and never did tell the staff of the college what they had written about them.

The Jansenist controversy was a sad episode in the history of Scottish Catholicism, and sadly it was largely occasioned by the Scots College Paris, partly out of jealousy on account of its influence, which was not the fault of the college, but partly on account of the attitude of the staff towards *Unigenitus*, and their failure to instil sound doctrine into their students.

NOTES

1.   Denzinger, H., *Enchiridion Symbolorum* (Friburg1932), No 1379 p.393.

2.   Pius XII, *Mystici Corporis Christi*, Tr. Smith, G.D., (London 1951), para. 102, p.61.

3.   Abbot, W.M., *The Documents of Vatican II* (London, Dublin, Melbourne 1967), p.23

4.   McMillan, J.F., "Thmas Innes and the Bull 'Unigenitus'", *Innes Review* 32 (1982), p.23.

5.   Eggenberger, D.(Ed.), New Catholic Encyclopedia (New York, St. Louis, San Francisco, Toronto, London, Sydney 1967), Vol 7, pp.820–824.

6.   SCA/Bl Lett 2/274/4, 25 Feb 1725, Bishop Gordon to Thomas Innes

7.   SCA/Bl Lett 1/102/14, 5 July 1687, Louis Innes to Charles Whyteford.

8.   SCA/Bl Lett 2/44/3, 13 Sept 1699, George Adamson to Louis Innes

9.   SCA/Bl Lett 2/78/11, 12 Aug 1702, Robert Fr Mearnes [Strachan], Ja Augustinus Gibson [Carnegie], Alex Jo Bapt Frazer [Drummond].

10.   SCA/Bl Lett 2/192/8, 11 June 1714, Thomas Innes to William Stuart

11.   SCA/Bl Lett 2/192/13, 1 Oct 1714, Thomas Innes to William Stuart

12.   SCA/Bl Lett 2/224/7, 23 Feb 1719, Thomas Innes to William Stuart

13.   SCA/SM 3/13/3, 26 Sept 1719, sermon of Bishop Gordon

14.   SCA/Bl Lett 2/288/11, Thomas Innes to William Stuart

15.   Gordon, J.F.S., *The Catholic Church in Scotland,* (Glasgow 1869), p. 533

16.   SCA/Bl Lett 2/302/7, 27 Sept 1727, George Innes to Thomas Innes

17.   SCA/Bl Lett 2/335/11, 17 Oct 1732, Thomas Innes to Bishop Gordon

18.   SCA/BlLett 2/335/7, 19 Dec 1732, Thomas Innes to Bishop Gordon

19. SCA/Bl Lett 3/5/13, 27 July 1733, Thomas Innes to William Stuart

20. SCA/Bl Lett 3/4/15, 14 Aug 1733, Louis Innes to Bishop Gordon

21. Propaganda Archives, Rome, CP 86, f.270.

22. March 1736 Bp Gordon & BP Smith to Propaganda, quoted by Clapperton, 'Memoirs of Scotch Missionary Priests', SCA, Unpublished,pp. 1995–6.

23. SCA/Bl Lett 3/82/10, 24 July 1744, Bp Macdonald to Bp Smith

24. Clapperton, W., op. cit., Vol 2, pt 1, p.861

25. SCA/SM 4/1/4.

26. Propaganda Archives, Rome, CP 86, ff. 269 R et V & 274.

27. Ibid., f.270.

28. Ibid., f.270.

29. SCA/Bl Lett 3/4/2, 26 February 1733, Bishop Gordon to George Innes

30. SCA/Bl Lett 3/4/16, 16 Oct 1733, Louis Innes to Bishop Gordon

31. SCA/Bl Lett 3/4/15, 14 Aug 1733, Louis Innes to Bishop Gordon

32. Ibid.

33. Propaganda Archives, Rome, CP 86, ff. 271–272, R et V.

34. SCA/Bl Lett 3/4/15, 14 Aug 1733, Louis Innes to Bishop Gordon

35. SCA/Bl Lett 3/4/15, 14 Aug 1733, Louis Innes to Bishop Gordon

36. SCA/Bl Lett 3/2/5, 31 Aug 1733, James Carnegie to William Stuart

37. Ibid.

38. Ibid.

39. SCA/SM 4/1/4.

40. SCA/SM 4/1/2.

41. SCA/Bl Lett 3/6/5, 17 Nov 1733, Bp Macdonald to Bp Gordon

42. Bl Lett 2/332/8, 23 Nov 1731, Thhomas Innes to Bp Gordon

43. SCA/SM 4/1/4.

44. Clark, R., *Strangers & Sojourners at Port Royal* (Cambridge1932), pp. 230f.

45. SCA/Bl Lett 2/192/12, 19 Sept 1714, Thomas Innes to Bishop Gordon

46. SCA/Bl Lett 2/238/15, 29 Oct 1721, Thomas Innes to Bishop Wallace

47. SCA/BlLett 3/5/7, 27 May 1733, Thomas Innes to Bishop Wallace?

48. SCA/Bl Lett 3/302/11, 8 July 1727, Louis Innes to Thomas Innes

49. Clark, R., op. cit., p.231.

50. SCA/Bl Lett 3/5/16, 31 Aug 1733, Thomas Innes to William Stuart

51. Denzinger, H., op. cit., No 1441, p. 397

52. SCA/Bl Lett 2/335/6, 9 Dec 1732, Thomas Innes to Bishop Wallace

53. SCA/Bl Lett 2/238/18, 11 Nov 1721, Thomas Innes to William Stuart

54. SCA/Bl Lett 3/12/4, 6 Sept 1734, Thomas Innes to Bishop Gordon

55. SCA/Bl Lett 2/265/4, 28 July 1724, Thomas Innes to James Carnegie

56. SCA/Bl Lett 2/335/10, 1 Sept 1732, Thomas Innes to William Stuart

57. Denzinger, H., op. cit., 'Errores Paschasii Quesnel n.29', p. 393.

58. SCA/Bl Lett 3/31/7, 3 June 1737, George Innes to William Stuart

59. SCA/Bl Lett 3/23/11, 15 Dec 1736, Thomas Innes to Robert Gordon
60. SCA/Bl Lett 3/5/16, 31 Aug 1733, Thomas Innes to William Stuart
61. SCA/Bl Lett 3/5/17, 21 Sept 1733, Thomas Innes to William Stuart
62. SCA/Bl Lett 3/12/4, 6 Sept 1734, Thomas Innes to Bishop Gordon
63. SCA/Bl Lett 3/17/9, 9 Nov 1735, Thomas Innes to George Gordon
64. Gordon, J. *Memoirs of the Life of John Gordon of Glencat* (London 1733), p. 26
65. SCA/BlLett 3/717, 4 Jan 1733, Gilbert Wauchope to Thomas Innes
    SCA/BlLett 3/13/15 6 June 1734, Gilbert Wauchope to Thomas Innes
66. Dictionnaire de Biographie Francaise (Paris 1954), Tome VI, pp.1156f.
67. Clark, R., op. cit., p.234.
68. SCA/Bl Lett 2/192/12, 19 Sept 1714, Thomas Innes to Bishop Gordon
69. SCA/BlLett 3/717, 4 Jan 1733, Gilbert Wauchope to Thomas Innes
70. SCA/Bl Lett 2/207/17, 9 Apr 1716, Louis Innes to Thomas Innes
71. SCA/Bl Lett 2/312/11, 21 Sept 1728, Louis Innes to Thomas Innes
72. SCA/Bl Lett 2/312/13, 20 Oct 1728, Louis Innes to Thomas Innes
73. SCA/Bl Lett 2/332/7, 21 Sept 1731, Louis Innes to Bishop Gordon
74. SCA/Bl Lett 3/4/15, 14 Aug 1733, Louis Innes to Bishop Gordon
75. Ibid.
76. SCA/Bl Lett 2/321/6, 22 Feb 1729, Louis Innes to Thomas Innes
77. SCA/Bl Lett 2/215/5, 9 Mar 1717, Robert Gordon to William Stuart
78. Bellesheim, A., *History of the Catholic Church of Scotland* (Edinburgh & London 1887–1890), Vol IV, p. 413
79. SCA/Bl Lett 2/78/11, 12 Aug 1702, Robert Fr Mearnes [Strachan], Ja Augustinus Gibson [Carnegie], Alex Jo Bapt Frazer [Drummond].
80. not on 30 October as stated in J.F.S. Gordon, op. cit. p.552 who is relying on Bishop Geddes' MS,
81. SCA/Bl Lett 2/265/14, 4 Dec 1724, Thomas Innes to William Stuart
82. Clark, R., op. cit. p.236, n.4.
83. Bellesheim, op. cit., Vol IV, p. 413
84. SCA/SM 4/2/13, John Tyrie to Monsignore, draft, n.d., Italian.
85. SCA/Bl Lett, 1750, Peter Grant
86. SCA/Bl Lett 2/312/13, 20 Oct 1728, Louis Innes to Thomas Innes
87. SCA/Bl Lett 2/312/14, 30 Oct 1728, Louis Innes to Thomas Innes
88. SCA/Bl Lett 2/321/3 25 Jan 1729, Louis Innes to Thomas Innes
89. J.Gordon, (Glencat), op. cit., p.9. (This penance was given as a disciplinary measure, and not in the Sacrament).
90. Ibid. p.12.
91. Ibid. p.17.
92. Archives Historiques du Department de l'Aube, TROYES, Registre G. 53, ff.26v &27
93. SCA/Bl Lett 3/10/8, 24 July 1734, Bishop Gordon to Louis Innes.
94. SCA/Bl Lett 2/48/11(2), Undated, Letter 'found' by James Leslie

95. SCA/Bl Lett 3/7/17, 4 Jan 1733, Gilbert Wauchope to Thomas Innes
96. SCA/Bl Lett 3/13/15, 6 June 1734, Gilbert Wauchope to Thomas Innes.
97. Clark, R., op. cit., p. 180.
98. SCA/Bl Lett 3/7/17, 25 July 1733, Gilbert Wauchope to Louis Innes
99. SCA/Bl Lett 3/13/15, 6 June 1734, Gilbert Wauchope to Thomas Innes
100. Clark, R., op. cit. p.180.
101. Bellesheim, A., op. cit., Vol IV, pp.408–13.
102. McMillan, J., 'Jansenists & Anti-Jansenists in Eighteenth Century Scotland: The Unigenitus Quarrels on the Scottish Catholic Mission 1732–1746', *Innes Review*, Vol 39, (1988), pp.12–45
103. SCA/Bl Lett 3/53/12, 4 May 1739, George Innes to Peter Grant
104. SCA/Bl Lett 3/56/12, 23 March 1739, John Mackenzie to Bishop Gordon
105. SCA/Bl Lett 3/53/4, 26 Jan 1739, George Innes to Peter Grant
106. SCA/Bl Lett 3/62/7, 27 Mar 1740, George Innes to Peter Grant
107. SCA/Bl Lett 3/65/1, 1740, Thomas Innes to Peter Grant
108. SCA/Bl Lett 3/62/10, April 1740, George Innes to Bishop Gordon.
109. SCA/CA 1/16/3, 23 Mar 1740, Copy of Sentence of Expulsion.
110. SCA/Bl Lett 3/62/7, 27 Mar 1740, George Innes to Peter Grant
111. SCA/Bl Lett 3/65/4, 23 May 1740, Thomas Innes to Peter Grant
112. SCA/Bl Lett 3/62/10, April 1740, George Innes to Bishop Gordon
113. SCA/Bl Lett 3/62/11, 13 May 1740, George Innes to Bishop Gordon
114. SCA/Bl Lett 3/62/13, 30 May 1740, George Innes to Bishop Gordon
115. SCA/Bl Lett 3/62/11, 13 May 1740, George Innes to Bishop Gordon
116. SCA/Bl Lett 3/69/3, 17 Mar 1741, George Innes to Bishop Smith.
117. SCA/Bl Lett 3/69/44, 3 Apr 1741, George Innes to Peter Grant
118. SCA/Bl Lett 3/74/8, 3 Jun 1741, George Innes to Peter Grant
119. SCA/Bl Lett 3/79/4, 2 Sept 1743, George Innes to Peter Grant
120. SCA/Bl Lett 3/62/7, 27 Mar 1740, George Innes to Peter Grant
121. SCA/Bl Lett 3/63/16, May 1740, George Innes to Peter Grant
122. SCA/Bl Lett 3/69/10, 14 Aug 1741, George Innes to Peter Grant
123. SCA/Bl Lett 3/69/8, 24 July 1741, George Innes to Peter Grant
124. SCA/Bl Lett 3/75/4, 23 Feb 1742, Thomas Innes to Bishop Gordon
125. SCA/Bl Lett 3/74/9, 2 July 1742, George Innes to Peter Grant
126. SCA/Bl Lett 3/75/1, 12 May 1742, George Innes to Bp Gordon & Bp Smith
127. SCA/Bl Lett 3/75/2, 26 Nov 1742, George Innes to Peter Grant
128. SCA/Bl Lett 3/74/13, 8 Oct 1742, George Innes to Peter Grant
129. SCA/Bl Lett 3/74/16, 19 Nov 1742, George Innes to Peter Grant
130. SCA/Bl Lett 3/74/17, 24 Dec 1742, George Innes to Peter Grant
131. SCA/Bl Lett 3/78/3, 11 Feb 1743, George Innes to Peter Grant
132. SCA/Bl Lett 3/94/3, 24 May 1749, George Innes to Peter Grant
133. SCA/Bl Lett 3/100/2, 26 Jan 1750, George Innes to Peter Grant

134. SCA/Bl Lett 3/100/19, 7 Dec 1750, George Innes to Peter Grant
135. SCA/Bl Lett 3/100/20, 13 Dec 1750, George Innes to Peter Grant
136. SCA/Bl Lett 3/41/10, 27 Sept 1748, George Innes to Peter Grant
137. SCA/Bl Lett 3/37/4, 16 Nov 1738, Bishop Gordon To George Innes
138. SCA/Bl Lett 3/44/6, Aug 1738, George Innes to Bishop Smith
139. SCA/Bl Lett 3/48/5, 10 April 1739, George Innes to Bishop Gordon
140. SCA/Bl Lett 3/48/11, 26 Nov 1739, Patrick Gordon to Bishop Gordon
141. SCA/Bl Lett 3/48/1(2), Pickpocketed letter, no signature or date.
142. Jesuit Arcives, Rome, ANGLIA 5, Missio Scotica: Epistolae 1740–1749, f.262
143. Ibid. f.243.
144. Propaganda Archives, Rome, SC Scozia 2 (1701–1760), f.311v.
145. SCA/SM 4/1/17, James Leslie to Bishop Gordon
146. Propaganda Archives, Rome, CP 86, f.260 R et V, George James Gordon to James Campbell, Glengarry, 24 May 1732.
Propaganda Archives, Rome, CP 87, f.529.
Propaganda Archives, Rome, CP 87, ff.511–513.
Gordon, J.F.S., op. cit., pp.554f.
Propaganda Archives, Rome, Letter of William Reid, 18 Sept 1740.
Ibid. Letter of Charles Crickshanks, 17 July 1740.
147. McMillan, op. cit., pp.12–45
148. Propaganda Archives, Rome, CP 86 f. 299, Fr Hudson to Mr Wolf, 16 Sept 1735. Mr Wolf was not Fr de Lupis in Rome as presumed by Clapperton and McMillan, but an ex-Jesuit in Paris. Therefore either Hugh Sempill or William Drummond, Abbé Melfort.
Propaganda Archives, Rome, CP 86, ff.295f, 12 Jan 1736 Fr John Maxwell to Colin Campbell.
SCA/Bl. Lett. 3/21/8, 16 Nov 1735, William Stuart to George Innes.
149. Propaganda Archives, Rome, CP 86, f.272 V.

CHAPTER 8

The Principalships of
Charles Whyteford and George Innes

Part 1: The College under Charles Whyteford (1713–1738)

When Louis Innes resigned the principalship at the beginning of 1713, his place was taken by Charles Whyteford who until that time had been Procurator, while Robert Gordon was chosen to succeed Whyteford.[1] The new Principal and new Procurator were installed by the Carthusian Prior on 27 Feb 1713.[2] The choice of Whyteford was indeed strange after his past record, but the authority to appoint lay solely with the Carthusian Prior, and Whyteford had won his confidence. Whyteford seems never to have been more than a figurehead, and the real power lay with Thomas Innes who was addressed in letters as Vice-Principal. Louis Innes himself retained a room in the college, was often consulted, and still exercised considerable control. This was unfair to Whyteford, unhealthy for the college, and enabled his brother Thomas to exercise control of the seminary. Louis Innes still wrote to Bishop Gordon in Scotland about the suitability or non-suitability of prospective students. In 1728, when it had already been decided that Alexander Smith who was Procurator was to be replaced by James Carnegie, Louis Innes had to remind Bishop Gordon that he must write to Whyteford who had not yet been told of it, to give him the reasons for the change.[3] In the following year, James Carnegie appealed to Louis Innes against a decision of Whyteford who wanted to employ an expensive master-builder to rebuild the garden wall, on the grounds that although more expensive than others, the master-builder would not immediately submit his bill.[4] To many, Louis Innes still appeared to be head of the college, and John Gordon of Glencat, a student who came in 1722 and of whom we shall say more later, wrote that Louis Innes was First Principal and Charles Whyteford Second Principal.[5]

Thomas Innes, in addition to acting as Vice-Principal, was also Prefect of Studies from 1718 until 1727 when he went back to Britain to publish his book. He was succeeded in this post by his nephew, George Innes, who had started the small seminary at Morar, and had been the first rector of Scalan from 1717 to 1721. Both Louis Innes and Thomas Innes were very pleased with their nephew's discharge of his duties.

Robert Gordon, who had become Prefect of Studies in 1712, was both Procurator and Prefect from 1713 until 1718. He was not comfortable in the college, and as early as 1715, expressed his desire to leave, but he stayed on out of respect for Louis Innes. His successor as Procurator was Alexander Smith, the future bishop. Both Louis and Thomas Innes regarded Smith as an excellent character, but they were not happy with his book-keeping methods, and considered him to be in the wrong job; thus they recommended him as a future principal when it was feared that Whyteford was dying.[6] Smith was succeeded by James Carnegie, but this was not a good choice. It was true that Carnegie had been very successful on several diplomatic missions, and that he had, at his own expense, published a new edition of the Catechism that he and Andrew Hacket had prepared; the college could not have had an abler priest, but he was now advanced in years, and his health was not good. He returned to Edinburgh in 1734 where he died at the beginning of 1735. His place was taken by George Innes who was already Prefect of Studies.

The efficiency of the college was handicapped during this period by tensions amongst the members of staff. Periodically Charles Whyteford complained that he was being ignored or bypassed, and there is little doubt that this was the case. Thomas Innes often complained about Alexander Smith's book-keeping, and he found James Carnegie's little better. Matters came to a head in 1732, when, in the words of Louis Innes:

> M. Blacks [Whyteford's] judgement (wch was never very great) is extreamly failld of late. And as to M. Gibson [James Carnegie], the affairs of Grisy [Scots College] have been so managed since he medled with them that nothing has thriven in his hands.[7]

It was resolved to have a Visitation of the college, conducted by the Carthusian Prior. This took place in December 1732, and every member of the college was interviewed. The result was that all members of staff were confirmed in their offices (and it is significant that the first resolution was to confirm Louis Innes in his place; the place is undefined, but, being mentioned first, he is clearly regarded as the overlord of the college). It was decided to appoint George Innes as coadjutor to Whyteford, and John McKenzie, though still a student, as assistant to Carnegie, the procurator. Neither Whyteford nor Carnegie were pleased with the new appointments, but at least there was a practical solution for the management of the college.[8]

It is clear that Bishop Gordon was dissatisfied with the staff, and in particular Thomas Innes. His letters of rebuke have already been mentioned in the chapter on Jansenism, although Jansenism was not an accusation. A letter of 1722, which from its contents was not the first, can now be quoted:

> But to tell you freely, as I have done once all ready, & 'tis necessary to speak freely in a matter of such importance; my opinion is, that the defect lyes not in the choice made of such as are sent to you, (for a great many that have miscarried have been the

very hopefullest that ever I knew sent,) but in the manner they are cared for there, for of those who are best disposed most ruine their health by excessive studys, & for want of corporal exercise, (& both these defects are essential in point of health, & yet little look'd after wt you) & another the most considerable of all defects is that a proper Director does not take sufficient care of them, leaves 'em allmost entirely to 'emselves, or if good advices once or twice given be not followed, they are allmost utterly abandon'd, wch can't be but of most pernicious consequence, and above all things I have ever been astonished that M. Fleming [Thomas Innes] who has a call to that to direct by his post, & has much genius and capacity for it, has little applyed to it, (while most of the time they had none other tolerable) & yet as I have heard, he applyes a great deal to that kind of business elsewhere: and unless his advices be followed readily by the young ones, he gives 'em quite over; & yet that seems also most unaccountable, & it can't be expected while better measures are not followed that things are as we would wish, I beg you'l consider the things maturely, & apply the necessary remedys for no difficultys will excuse those who are oblig'd to look after these things, if possibly they can be remov'd: other mens humors must be born patiently; but we must not for them neglect any essential point of our own duty.'[9]

The number of students can be better determined in this period than hitherto; compared to other periods, the numbers were good in the first half of this principalship, with ten when Whyteford took over in 1713,[10] rising to twelve (and possible thirteen) in 1724.[11] The student roll fell to six in 1729,[12] and to as low as two in 1732,[13] but by the end of this principalship in 1738, in which year five new students arrived, the college had fourteen students.[14]

A feature of the college at this time, which reflected the success of earlier days, was that several students came whose fathers, uncles or grandfathers had been in the college. Amongst those whose fathers had been students were Patrick and Alexander Gordon, Letterfourie's sons, and John Gordon, the son of Dorlaithers. There were two Gordons of Beldorney whose grandfather had been a student. Those whose uncles had been students included James Innes, the nephew of Louis and Thomas, and James Gordon, nephew of Bishop Gordon. Members of the nobility still came to the college as students. These included Charles Stewart who was Lord Linton, later fifth Earl of Traquair, and John Stuart, the Earl of Bute's brother. Also students were James Drummond, third Duke of Perth, and his brother John, later fourth Duke, whose father had not only been a student, but was buried in the college chapel. The young Drummonds were the occasion of political machination. In 1721, attempts were made to take the Duchess of Perth's sons from her to have them educated as Protestants. Seeing the great danger, she took her sons, James and John, to Paris to ensure their Catholic education, and they were later received into the Scots College. They are frequently mentioned in letters, but never with their proper names, but under the *alias* of Gray.

Another political catalyst was James Gordon of Glastirim. The whole story is best told in a letter of Thomas Innes of January 1734, in which he explained to William Stuart in Rome the reason for James Carnegie's voyage to London:

The occasion of this new unfeavorable voiage was to convey to Lond. M. Ja Gordon of Gl[a]stirim nevew to our anent Bp M. Fife [James Gordon] and Heir of his family. The Bp had sent that young Gentleman about 6 months ago to this college to be bred up in piety & thoroughly instructed in Cath. Religion in order to preserve it (as it hath full continued hitherto since the Reformatn) in his family. the end of the institution of this College (as no doubt you know) being no less the education of the children of Caths, especially the Heirs of familys, in piety & Cath. Religion, than that of Churchmen and this College is particularly oblidgd to render service to that family. Meantime the Kings advocate in Scotld gives out an order to bring back before the end of Decr this youth with certification, that if he come not back by that time, he'l pursue & take up all the Church men & particularly the Bp & raise a violent persecution agt all Caths. upon which the Bp hath written letter upon letter to send the youth home in all hast, and M. Smith, who brought him, not being able to travel in winter, M. Gibson [James Carnegie] hath been so good as to undertake the commision. We made application to the Nuncio here and he was so good as to write to the Ambassadors of the Emperor & other Princes at London in our favors, but by new and more pressing letters from the Bp we see a necessity of sending back the youth, there being little or no doubt but the Dhsse of Gordon (tho shee wd be angry if it were publishd and do more mischief) is at the botom of all this. You'll easily gues the reason viz for fear of a precedent to her own Sone.[15]

The health record of the students during this principalship was deplorable; no fewer than three students died in the college: George Gordon, a subdeacon, who returned to Paris after illness against Bishop Gordon's wishes died on 27 Nov 1721, John Dixon died on 29 Aug 1728,[16] and John Augustine Arthur died on 9 Jan 1729.[17] In addition to these, John Joseph Veillan, who had to leave for health reasons in July 1716, died on 18 Oct 1719,[18] and Andrew Parkins, who left the college in 1723, and was professed in Ratisbon in 1726, died in 1728.[19] Over and above these five deaths, at least five others had to be sent home for health reasons: Archibald Anderson who left as a deacon in 1718, immediately took ill of a brain fever, and was detained for a year at Rouen, and on account of this, he was never promoted to the priesthood; Aeneas MacDonald was sent home with bad health in September 1722,[20] George Duncan had to leave for health reasons in September 1726, but was ordained at Scalan in 1732, and William Lindsay and John Farquharson were both sent home for health reasons in 1727. John Gordon of Birkenbush often had to be sent to the country on account of his health. From the small number of students, a big proportion had serious health problems.

Discipline in the college was not what it should have been, reaching its nadir in the case of John Gordon of Glencat who had been advanced as far as the diaconate. In 1733, three years after he had left the college, he published a diatribe against the Catholic Church[21] in which he maintained that he had been taken to the college against his will, had been held prisoner there for thirteen years, and that after being refused ordination to the priesthood because he would not subscribe to *Unigenitus*, saw and took his chance to escape from the college. In an Aberdeen journal, he published the further detail that his escape had been from a window of the college onto a waiting cart. Apart from the unlikelihood of his being kept prisoner in the college, there are discrepancies in his story. Since he left the college in 1730, thirteen years stay would place his entry in 1717, but he states that before he went to France, he stayed with Mr Shaw, a secular priest. Shaw is an *alias* for William Shand who did not come back to Scotland until August 1719. Also Glencat failed to tell us that he had subscribed to *Unigenitus* before his diaconate, although some of his student contemporaries refused to do so. A letter of his own to Thomas Innes admits with regret that he had been expelled from the college.[22] The reason for this was his embroilment with an adventuress who called herself the Countess of Gordon,[23] a notorious swindler. In writing about this to Bishop Gordon in 1731, Thomas Innes said 'I need not refresh his [Glencat's] past unaccountable vagaries after that pretended Lady Gordon which for several months was here the town talk of all our three nations.'[24] How it could have reached such a pitch without the college taking action is beyond comprehension, but Glencat was finally expelled on 11 August 1730.

After his expulsion, he repented for a time, went to confession above six times in ten days (signs of Jansenist piety?), and was going to join the Lazarites, but changing his mind again, he came to Scotland with his 'countess'. Racy details of the pair's wild doings were published in London in 1734 by Elizabeth Harding under the title, *The Masterpiece of Imposture, or the Adventures of John Gordon of Glencat and the Countess of Gordon, alias Countess Dalco, alias Madam Dallas, alias Madam Kempster etc.*[25] By her own account, Elizabeth Harding was a widow who had become friendly with John Gordon who had promised to keep up a correspondence with her. It seems that she was a woman scorned, and so might be inclined to exaggerate the adventures.

John Gordon's subsequent career illustrates a facet of the Jansenist piety that was nurtured in the college, namely its power to lead to repentance. Despite all the wide publicity of his apostasy (his book had a second edition published in 1734) Glencat repented, published a recantation of his book, was reconciled with the Catholic Church, and was made an agent in London for the Scottish bishops. When a third edition of his book was published against his will, he bought up the whole edition and burned it in his house. Ever the extremist, he set fire to his house in the process.[26] The pseudo-Countess stayed with him till her death on 26 Dec 1765; the Scottish bishops tried to get a dispensation from Rome so that John Gordon might marry her, but they were unsuccessful. Glencat did much good for the mission in London until his death on 26 December 1770; as will be recorded later, he helped to rehabilitate a defected priest of the college, and he was also the one who introduced George Hay, the future famous bishop, to Bishop Challoner.

If the college superiors were dilatory in discovering the misdemeanour of Glencat, they even more tardy in the case of Neil MacEachan. George Innes wrote to Bishop Smith:

> I knew not till long after he was gone, that by his false treacherous ways, whilst here, he persuaded by hook or by crook the 3 Westerns sent last to Hamburg [Rome] to give him under culor of pretended scants and wants to the matter of 15 livres of their viatik money, for he was insatiably greedy for money whatever way it should come.[27]

Finance

Lack of finance, a perennial problem, was blamed for restricting student numbers. In 1727, when Alan Macdonald, who had previously been a student at Scots College, Rome, wished to resume his studies for the priesthood, the Paris college could not receive him for lack of funds. This seems to have been a ruling of the Carthusian Prior, but the college got round it by feeding him during the day while at night he slept near the college,[28] an arrangement that was probably more expensive than keeping him as a student. In July that same year, Louis Innes wrote to William Stuart in Rome, 'And actually now we are obliged to lessen our number, not being able to maintain all those we have.'[29]

It was in this period that the college lost nearly all the bequest of John Law after the fall of his system, and a further loss was sustained by the withdrawal of the pension of 1600 livres from the French clergy.[30] The financial position was not improved by the chaotic book-keeping of Alexander Smith. Seldom did he mark down transactions as they took place. Being of a generous disposition, he would be asked for charity, and would grant it without recording the matter. It was not unknown for him to ask people whether or not he had paid them, because he simply could not remember.

Poor results and the causes

This period was not very successful in producing priests. In the twenty-five years of Whyteford's principalship, there were only four ordinations in Paris, and three other *alumni* were ordained at Scalan, Alexander Gordon (Coffurich) and John Gordon (Birkenbush) who had pursued almost all their studies at Paris, and George Duncan who had studied there for two years. One other, William Farquharson, having been dismissed from the Scots College on account of his Jansenist views, was ordained for the Diocese of Troyes in 1735.[31]

There were several reasons for this poor harvest. One reason, in no way discrediting to the college, was the establishment of seminaries in Scotland; the first began at Loch Morar in 1714, and, on account of its destruction after the Fifteen, recommenced at Scalan in Glenlivet in 1717. After a separate Highland Vicariate was created, Bishop Hugh MacDonald, in 1732, founded a Highland seminary which was first situated on the old Loch Morar site, but was moved to Guidal in 1738. The college felt no rancour at these developments, and without the financial backing of Louis Innes, neither would have been possible. Four of the first six rectors of Scalan were Paris trained, George Innes (1717–1721), Alexander Gordon (Coffurich) (1738–1741), William Duthie (1741–1758) and George Duncan (1758–1761). This was a most important contribution of the Scots College, Paris to the Scottish mission.

Other reasons were not so praiseworthy. Absorption with Jacobite affairs was one of them. The sojourn in the college in 1716 of Lord Nithsdale, recently escaped from the Tower of London, must have been a distraction to the students. It was in the same year that the Jacobite King desired Innes to write a complete history of Scotland. One would expect the staff to write, but not to exclusion of care for the students, which seems to have happened in the case of Thomas Innes. It is extraordinary that such a religious person should have considered his King's command more binding than that of the Pope. Shortly after the birth of Prince Charles Edward, there was a magnificent day of thanksgiving in the college, with two dukes and over a hundred gentlemen present, although the college had to borrow money to make this possible.[32] It was not surprising that so many *alumni* from this period were involved in the Forty-five; they outnumbered those who became priests.

The Jansenist difficulties were an even more disturbing factor. *Unigenitus* was promulgated in the same year as Whyteford became Principal, 1713. Although the staff endeavoured to hide their doubts from the students, there were factors that must have made this well-nigh impossible. The fact that an annual subsidy of 1600 livres from the French clergy was discontinued on account of refusal to subscribe to *Unigenitus* could hardly have remained secret, and the students could not have been unaware that the staff were secretly distributing copies of the Jansenist newspaper

Nouvelles Ecclésiastiques. Thomas Innes favoured those who rejected the Constitution, especially the three who were eventually dismissed, John Gordon of Birkenbush, John Farquharson and William Farquharson. Their expulsion was probably ordered by the Carthusian Prior who made more rulings than has generally been realised, although the staff were masters in circumventing what he decreed. When Thomas Innes opened his heart and discussed his misgivings with James Campbell, could this have remained secret from all the other students? Thomas Innes approved of John Gordon's going to Troyes for the subdiaconate ordination,[33] and he must also have approved of John McKenzie and William Duthie going there for the tonsure and minor orders.[34] Thomas Innes believed that the 'miracles' at St Médard endorsed his view, and his correspondence with Gilbert Wauchop reveals that by 1733, he was becoming more outspoken as an opponent of *Unigenitus*. All of this must have been confusing to the students who were constantly receiving different signals. Not surprisingly quite a number (at least nine in this period) took an anti-Constitution stand at one time or another. Others must have been nauseated, if not confused, by all the debates. One can see why numbers slumped in the late twenties and early thirties.

Part 2: The College under George Innes (1738–1752)

Charles Whyteford died on Christmas Day 1738.[35] Since the adversaries of the college wanted to influence the choice of staff (the pilgrims Campbell and Tyrie had arrived in Paris that month[36]), no time was lost, and the new office-bearers were installed by the Carthusian Prior on 30 December 1738.[37] The new Principal was George Innes who had been appointed coadjutor in December 1732. He was now fifty-five years of age, had pursued all his theological studies at Paris, and had been ordained there in 1712. He had been Rector of the first seminary in Scotland at Loch Morar, and first Rector of Scalan. In Paris, he had been Prefect of Studies from 1727 until 1738. The new Prefect of Studies was John McKenzie. He was a convert to Catholicism, had come to the college in 1729, and was ordained in Paris in 1737. Since 1732, although still a student, he had been assistant bursar. The new Procurator was Andrew Riddoch. After leaving the College, he had been received back in 1734, and was now a subdeacon. He was not ordained priest until June 1740. All three had given proofs of submission to *Unigenitus* both to Rome and to the Archbishop of Paris, and as Thomas Innes wrote to Mr Edgar in Rome, were faithful servants of His Majesty, James VIII.[38]

Thomas Innes considered that an excellent choice of staff had been made, but that is very doubtful. John McKenzie was no doubt academically clever (George Innes informed Bishop Gordon in 1739 that he and John

Gordon Dorlaithers were with himself members of the nation of the Sorbonne University[39]), but as he was one of the two who had received minor orders from the Bishop of Troyes in 1733, his appointment was a tactical error, and he was soon to be the target of attack. Later, in September 1743, he had to go back to Scotland on account of bad health, and was one of those present at a clergy meeting in Edinburgh in 1745, but then he disappeared. Great enquiries were made, but all to no purpose. He was not heard of until November 1750 when he sent a letter to John Gordon of Glencat in London asking him to meet after dark. Then he told his story. He had gone to London with Peter Leith, and then had fallen into bad company. He had married a woman of bad character who had died in Newgate prison for stealing. Being so disgraced by this, he had been dismissed from his post as tutor to a family, and had been left with no option but to enlist as a common soldier in a marine regiment in Portsmouth. The regiment was now broken, and he had tried to live by teaching in Portsmouth, but without success. He was then destitute and in rags.[40] John Gordon did what he could for him, and obtained financial help from Bishop Smith. They got John McKenzie into the monastery at La Trappe,[41] Glencat suggesting that henceforth in letters McKenzie might be known by the *alias* of Dumoulin which is clearly derived from his mother's name which was Helen Milne. After being received into La Trappe in the second week of Lent 1751, John McKenzie was clothed with the novice habit on the Vigil of the Feast of the Annunciation.[42] In November 1753, he was visited by John Gordon Dorlaithers, by then Principal of the Scots College, Paris, and he was still in La Trappe in March 1772.

Andrew Riddoch was still Procurator of the College in 1776, but does not seem to have been as satisfactory as the long tenure of office suggests. He had experienced great doubts and hesitations about becoming a priest, and even after his ordination Thomas Innes wrote, 'M. Riddoch besides his puny health boggles still at being made Laborer'[43] Although he was ordained priest on Saturday 7 June 1740,[44] he did not say his first Mass until 19 June.[45] This in itself, however, although quite different from practice today, need not indicate any diffidence, as a similar interval between ordination and first Mass is found in the case of John Gordon Dorlaithers who was raised to the priesthood in 1743. John Gordon of Glencat, with information received from a relative who was a student, told Bishop Gordon that Andrew Riddoch could not get out of his bed in the morning, dined very well in the afternoon, insisted on mocha coffee after his meal, and only said Mass on Sundays. After visiting the college in 1761, Glencat realised that all of these problems were occasioned by Riddoch's very poor health. Dozens of letters from the college refer to this, and Andrew Riddoch was often unable to do any work at all. He was far from being the ideal person to have on the staff.

George Innes, the Principal, was given a fine character by Abbé MacPherson:

> A better clergyman, a man of greater activity, learning and piety, or of greater zeal for the good of his country can seldom be found. His letters to Agent in Rome are a monument of his superior talents and virtue. They supplied what his uncles gave, and now when they are gone, the materials for mission history are scarce.[46]

Yet at the beginning of his seminary career at Scalan in 1718, Bishop Gordon considered him not entirely suitable for the post of rector, but the best he could find:

> for nev. [nephew] Geo…he has so little health, & is so timorous & helpless in these hard times, is not of that genius entirely that were necessary for that post, not having much discretio spiritus, & he understands so little economy, that another must be with him to help him, & yet with all his infirmity we have not another labourer so fitt[47]

No doubt he grew with the job, and he appears to have been very conscientious, and punctilious in correspondence. Yet his fellow priests in Scotland were dissatisfied with him in 1750, and he believed that Bishop Smith and Bishop Macdonald were trying to get him dismissed, although this does not seem to have been the case. His principalship was not a prosperous time for the college, and during it only two students reached the priesthood, these being Andrew Riddoch (1740) and John Gordon of Dorlaithers (1743). Times were hard, and there were set-backs after the Forty-five, but one may opine that he lacked the extra spark to rise above his difficulties.

The only change of staff that occurred during this time was that John Gordon Dorlaithers replaced John McKenzie as Prefect of Studies in 1743, at first temporarily, but as his predecessor never returned, the post became permanent. Dorlaithers, as he is nearly always called because there were so many 'John Gordons', came to the College in 1727 at the age of fourteen. Like Andrew Riddoch, he had great doubts about his vocation to the priesthood, and had obtained a temporary leave of absence to visit Scotland and there consider his future. He was not ordained priest until 1743, which was sixteen years after his first entry into the College. Before his ordination, he made great efforts to obtain a benefice, but without success. He was to succeed George Innes as Principal, a post he held until his death twenty-five years later, but his relationship with the Scottish Bishops was strained. Academically brilliant, perhaps his best work was improving the College library.

Thomas Innes still resided in the College until his death on 8 February 1744, but held no office. In the controversies of the time, his presence in the College was sometimes felt to be an embarrassment.

Students

There were fourteen students in the college when George Innes took command in 1738, but when three left, probably on account of the Jansenist quarrels, in 1742, the number dropped to six. Poor discipline was exemplified in the case of Alastair Ruadh Macdonnell, young Glengarry, of whom George Innes wrote:

> As G/y [Glengarry] has no governor tho his exercises takes him out frequently and by the by may fall into bad compy for aught we can hinder especially he having no p[rinci]ples of religion to be a bar upon him: therfor if any accident should befall him abroad, we can't answer for it tho I'm sure we have our own fears constantly about him. His having no genious for letters, but only for fencing, dancing, rideing etc, nothing can be harder than to apply him to reading and studying the Scots law[48]

He was not the only culprit as his lack of discipline was attributed to the bad example of Clanranald and John Gordon Dorlaithers. George Innes found the conduct of Glengarry and John Gordon Dorlaithers so bad that he placed them in a house by themselves, as their frequent absences from the College, and not wearing the College garb, were having a bad effect on the discipline of the house. This was a terrible admission of failure and a very bad solution to a discipline problem. Innes himself lived to regret it:

> I have been so oft reflected upon for Jn Dorl and his [Glengarry's] being excused from the common rule that no one henceforth shall be received on the like terms. All the reasons one can give for their dispensation are of little avail and I have promised faithfully the like shall never happen for the future[49]

Considering Glengarry's future activity as Pickle the spy, it can only be concluded that this expedient was very bad for his character formation.

By contrast, another student deserves mention. This was Seignelay Colbert of Castlehill, near Inverness, who came to the college in 1747.[50] Though Bishop Geddes believed that he had been in the college for only three years, there was mention of a Colbert leaving in September 1761.[51] He was ordained priest in 1762, and became Bishop of Rodez in 1781.[52] As often is the case with very well behaved students, no details of his student career in the college have been recorded.

The future principal, Alexander Gordon, also came in this period, and was in the college by at least 1749.

The Forty-five and aftermath

Two issues dominate this period, Jacobitism and Jansenism, of which the details, having been recorded in the respective chapters, will only be summarised here to show their effect on the college.

George Innes, who was Principal of the college during the Forty-five in which so many *alumni* were fighting for Prince Charles, took an avid interest in the campaign, after which the college became a haven for priest refugees, including Bishop MacDonald. It seems highly likely that the college was also hiding Bonnie Prince Charlie.[53] Thus the college continued to serve the Jacobite cause in Paris.

The college also became involved in a celebrated case in Scotland, where, after the Forty-five, laws, which had lain dormant for years, were reinforced, often at the instigation of private persons. A student of the college called Alexander Bowers, heir of Methy and Kincaldrum in Angus, whose father had wanted him to go to the Paris College where he himself had been a student, was brought to the college after his father's death by an aunt. Her brother, however, wanted to have curators named for him by the Court of Session. Learning where the boy was, the Court first of all suspended Mr Hay of Monquhitter, the uncle's agent, from parliament house for six months, and then had Robert Innes, a Jesuit priest, arrested and tried. Being found not guilty in this affair, the Jesuit was nevertheless imprisoned for being a priest, and banished the following year. Then warrants were issued for the arrest of Bishop Smith who had been delated by the uncle of the boy. To avoid capture, the Bishop had to flee across the border into England. In this affliction, George Innes wrote to the Lord Advocate in Edinburgh on 13 January 1751, promising to send the boy home, and explaining that Bishop Smith could have had nothing to do with the student's departure from Scotland, being a hundred miles away at the time, and beseeching them to stop proceedings against him.[54] Innes wrote again on 10 February, complaining that the College staff had been represented as persons who had slighted the Court's authority, and stating that Bishop Smith had several times urged them to comply with the Court order, and hoping that the Bishop would not 'be brought to trouble on that score'. He also hoped that Mr Hay would be restored to favour.[55] Alexander Bowers was on his way home in March,[56] and proceedings against Bishop Smith appear to have been dropped as the Bishop was back in Edinburgh by June.

This case indirectly led to a mitigation of persecution in Scotland. Since it had occasioned the imprisonment and banishment of Robert Innes, and had forced Bishop Smith to flee the country, Peter Grant, the Scots priest-agent in Rome, urgently represented the case of the Scottish Catholics to the Cardinals of Propaganda who got the Pope to solicit the Catholic Powers to make their ambassadors at the British Court intercede for the Catholics of Scotland. The Ministers of the Imperial, Sardinian and Bavarian Embassies spoke to the British Government, while Dr Challoner got the

Duke and Duchess of Norfolk to plead with the Duke of Argyll.[57] These moves led somewhat to easing the situation for Catholics in Scotland.

Jansenist Problems

In the first six years of this principalship, the staff of the college were continually harassed by accusations of Jansenism. Some of the problems were of their own making, as were the use of the Montpellier Catechism and the work of Dupin, the absence of John McKenzie from the Revocation of the Appeal on 11 May 1739, and the melodramatic expulsion of Falconer and Farquhar. Others, like the complaints of Abbé Melfort and Abbé Sempil came from without, and there was little they could do about them. Abbé Hugh Sempil actually sent no fewer that twenty-nine letters to Rome between 15 December 1738 and 21 July 1744, complaining about the Scots College Paris and about the missioners in Scotland. Of these, however, the college need not have had any fear. Propaganda, who normally made translations and transcriptions of letters, had got tired of doing this with Sempil's letters and merely recorded that letters had been received. Perhaps the most hurtful thing for the college was the Roman ruling that students travelling to Rome were not to stop at the college on their way. That the Jansenist problems had a bad effect on the college is evident from the words of George Innes, 'Even our young students are upset by mischiefs intended against Grisy [Scots College Paris]'[58]

Jansenist problems eased as the Forty-five concerns overshadowed them. A further easing of tension came in 1752 with the death of Cardinal Rivera, The Cardinal Protector of Scotland, who had always strongly suspected the Scots College Paris of Jansenism, and the appointment of Cardinal Spinelli who was most favourable to the Scots. George Innes, however, was not to enjoy his benevolence. The Principal who appeared to have a strong constitution took ill suddenly and died a few days afterwards on 29 April 1752. He was 68.

The Principalship of George Innes had been very difficult, as he had been suspected of heresy by Cardinal Rivera, Cardinal Fencin, Abbé Sempil, Abbé Melfort and by the Nuncio from Rome. He appears to have been conscientious and hard working. Yet he did make mistakes. One of these was the choice of John McKenzie as Prefect of Studies; he was appointed by the Carthusian Prior, but this could scarcely have been done without the Principal's approval. Then there was the use of Dupin's book and the Montpellier Catechism, which was a dangerous error of judgement. The dramatised expulsion of Falconer and Farquhar was his greatest mistake, as the sympathies of Paris lay with the students. Instead of calling in the Prior for a Grand Inquisition (at which the students were given no time to prepare their defence), George Innes should have dealt with them privately on a much lower key. Lastly, there was the mistake that he recognised himself, of giving a separate house to Glengarry and Dorlaithers. This was bad for the discipline of the house, and detrimental to the students themselves. These were far too many mistakes for a man who was suspected of heresy.

George Innes can nevertheless be said to have weathered the storms and kept the College going (it was to survive for another forty years), and he had provided a haven for priests who were not safe in their own country after the Forty-five, but as with the Jacobite cause which the College had espoused, the day of glory was gone, and the College was no longer to be a vital influence on the Scottish Catholic Mission. Now that there were two seminaries in Scotland, Paris was not needed as much as before. With Colleges at Madrid and Rome as well, it was difficult for the tiny Scottish Mission to keep all her Colleges filled with students. One disadvantage for Paris was that the Scottish Bishops were reluctant to give it their patronage because they had no say in the appointment of staff. What really crippled the College, however, was the accusation of Jansenism. The unorthodoxy of the college had been overestimated at Rome on account of the two letters sent to the Pope and the Cardinal Protector by Bishop Gordon and Bishop Macdonald in 1733. This regime of the Ineses has been sharply contrasted to that of the next two Principals, John Gordon and Alexander Gordon, with the claim that there was harmonious co-operation between Bishops and staff while the Ineses were in charge. One can see, however, that the seeds of dissension had been planted by the Clashinore Letters, and George Innes thought that the Bishops were opposed to him. It is to the credit of George Innes, however, that he persevered amidst many difficulties. As the founder of Morar and Scalan, and as a Principal of the Scots College Paris, he has a place in Scottish Catholic history.

NOTES

1.   SCA/Bl Lett 2/184/1, 13 Feb 1713, Thomas Innes to William Stuart
2.   SCA/Bl Lett 2/184/2, 27 Feb 1713, Thomas Innes to William Stuart
3.   SCA/Bl Lett 2/312/6, 10 Feb 1728, Louis Innes to Bishop Gordon
4.   SCA/Bl Lett, 1729, James Carnegie
5.   Gordon, J., *Memoirs of the life of John Gordon of Glencat* (London 1733).
6.   SCA/Bl Lett 2/321/4, 28 Jan, Louis Innes to Thomas Innes
7.   SCA/Bl Lett 2/335/4, 1 Nov 1732, Louis Innes to Bishop Wallace
8.   SCA/Bl Lett, 2/335/7, 19 Dec 1732 Louis Innes to Bishop Gordon

9. SCA/Bl Lett 2/242/9, 15 Sept 1722, Bishop Gordon to Thomas Innes

10. SCA/BL Lett 2/184/4, 24 Apr 1713, Thomas Innes to William Stuart

11. SCA/Bl Lett 2/274/1, 30 Oct 1724, Alex Smith to William Stuart

12. SCA/Bl Lett 2/321/9, 10 Mar 1729 Louis Innes to Bishop Gordon

13. SCA/Bl Lett 2/335/11, 17 Oct 1732, Thomas Innes to Bishop Gordon

14. SCA/Bl Lett 3/44/7, 17 Sept 1738, George Innes to Bishop Gordon

15. SCA/Bl Lett 3/12/1, 4 Jan 1734, Thomas Innes to William Stuart

16. SCA/CA 1/7, Necrology of Scots College, Paris,
    SCA/Bl Lett 3/312/10, 1Sept 1728, Louis Innes to Bishop Gordon.

17. SCA/CA 1/7, Necrology of Scots College, Paris, where 1728 is in Old Style. cf.
    SCA/Bl Lett 2/231/2, 18 Jan 1729, Louis Innes to Thomas Innes.

18. SCA/CA 1/7, Necroloogy of Scots College, Paris.

19. *Records of the Scots Colleges*, p.268 & p.284.

20. SCA/Bl Lett 2/246/17, 22 Sept 1722, Alex Smith to William Stuart

21. Gordon, J., *Memoirs of the life of John Gordon of Glencat* (London 1733).

22. SCA/Bl Lett 2/328/4, undated, John Gordon to [Scots College Paris]

23. Her real name was Joaney More, and she was born in Edinburgh.

24. SCA/Bl Lett 2/332/9, 10 March 1731, Thomas Innes to Bishop Gordon

25. Harding, E., *The masterpiece of imposture* (London 1734).

26. SCA/Bl Lett 3/109/4, 26 Dec 1752, John Gordon to Bishop Smith

27. SCA/Bl Lett, 3/45/4, 11 Nov 1738, George Innes to Bishop Smith

28. SCA/Bl Lett 2/304/3, 16 Apr 1727, Thomas Innes to Bishop Wallace

29. SCA/Bl Lett 2/302/12, 14 July 1727, Louis Innes to William Stuart

30. Clark, R., *Strangers & Sojourners at Port Royal* (Cambridge 1932), p.234).

31. Archives Historiques du Department de l'Aube, Troyes, Registre G.53.

32. SCA/Bl Lett 2/238/1, 27 Jan 1721, Thomas Innes to William Stuart

33. SCA/Bl Lett 2/332/6, 26 July 1731, Thomas Innes to Bishop Gordon

34. Archives Historiques du Department de l'Aube, Troyes, Registre G.53.

35. SCA/Bl. Lett. 3/44/11, 29 Dec 1738, George Innes to Bishop Gordon

36. SCA/Bl. Lett. 3/44/10, 14 Dec 1738, George Innes to Peter Grant

37. SCA/Bl Lett 3/53/1, Jan 1739, George Innes to George Gordon

38. SCA/Bl. Lett. 3/45/5, 29 Dec 1738, Thomas Innes to Peter Grant

39. SCA/Bl. Lett. 3/53/9, 6 Apr 1739, George Innes to ?

40. SCA/BlLett 3/99/4, 24 Nov 1750, John Gordon Glencat to Bishop Gordon

41. Claperton thought that this McKenzie was not a priest, but hs letter to Glencat is
    still extant, and thehandwriting is conclusive proof that this is the same John
    McKenzie who was on the staff in Paris.
    SCA/Bl Lett 3/101/5, Nov 1750, John McKenzie to John Gordon Glencat.

42. SCA/Bl. Lett. 3/105/10, 27 Apr 1751, George Innes to John Gordon Glencat

43. SCA/Bl. Lett. 3/65/1, 1740, Thomas Innes to Bishop Gordon

44. SCA/Bl. Lett. 3/62/15, 12 Jun 1740, George Innes to Peter Grant

45. SCA/Bl. Lett. 3/62/17, 20 Jun 1740, George Innes to Peter Grant

46. SCA Clapperton, W., 'Memoirs of Scotch Missionary Priests', Unpublished, Vol 3, p.1773.

47. SCA/Bl. Lett. 2/221/1, 25 Mar 1718, Bishop Gordon to Thomas Innes

48. SCA/Bl. Lett. 3/79/6, 7 Sep 1743, George Innes to ?

49. SCA/Bl. Lett. 3/78/6, 5 Apr 1743, George Innes to Bishop Smith

50. SCA/CA 1/23/4, Bishop Geddes, 'Mémoire of Journey to Paris in 1791', p.65.

51. SCA/Bl. Lett. 3/155/8, 8 February 1762, George Innes to Bishop Smith

52. Ritzler, R. & Sefrin, P., *Hierarchia Catholica Medii et Recentioris Aevi* (Padua1958), Vol VI, p.361, n. Ruthenen, 5.

53. Lang, A., *Pickle the Spy* (London, New York & Bombay 1897) p.109.

54. SCA/Bl. Lett.3/105/4, 13 Jun 1751, George Innes to Lord Advocate (copy)

55. SCA/Bl. Lett.3/305/4, 10 Feb 1751, George Innes to Lord Advocate (copy)

56. SCA/Bl. Lett.3/105/5, 1 Mar 1751, George Innes to Peter Grant

57. SCA/Bl. Lett.3/105/8, 19 Apr 1751, George Innes to Peter Grant

58. SCA/Bl Lett 3/74/9, 2 July 1742, George Innes to Peter Grant.

CHAPTER 9

The Principalships of John Gordon and Alexander Gordon

In the last forty years of the College's existence, under Principals John Gordon and Alexander Gordon, there was a marked decline in its influence on the Scottish Catholic Mission. There were several reasons for this. On the political front, the Jacobite cause was finished. Although hopes and aspirations remained, it would be generally recognised that there was no real hope of a Jacobite restoration after the failure of the Forty-five. Marginal Jacobite activity continued. Befriending Jacobite exiles was a task that fell to John Gordon who was Principal of the College from 1752 until his death in 1777. Many of the exiles dined at the College, which occasioned some criticism,[1] but as John Gordon explained to his namesake Glencat 'since the year 1746 he laid under a necessity of being civil to many'.[2] The family history of *The Jacobite Lairds of Gask* bears witness to the college hospitality, 'the most hospitable fireside of all was that of the Scots College at Paris; thither every Scottish exile whatever might be his creed, turned as to an assured haven of rest'.[3] The most frequent of these visitors was the *alumnus*, Aeneas Macdonald, the banker in Paris who had been one of the seven men of Moidart.

In all probability Principal John Gordon was called upon to plead the case of impecunious Jacobites who had lost all in the Stuart cause. At least one such case is recorded when the Principal acted as intermediary for the Duchess of Perth in forwarding her letter to the Jacobite King in Rome who likewise used Gordon as intermediary when forwarding his reply. Many other services were requested by Jacobite friends. In 1759, Laurence Oliphant, the Laird of Gask, requested Principal Gordon to procure for him a lawyer so that he could write his will.[4] In the same year, the Principal was one of those who wrote many letters to extricate Charles Nairne, son of Lord Nairne, from a rash promise of marriage to the daughter of a Dutch tradesman.[5] When the sum of his redemption from the entanglement was fixed at 3000 livres, young Oliphant advised his uncle, Lord Nairne, to send the money through Principal Gordon.[6] In 1768, the Principal helped Mrs Oliphant and her son to buy an Italian post chaise, and gave the laird a furred gown to keep him warm.[7] These services to Jacobites, however, little affected Scotland where they would scarcely be known. In reality, they were a burden on the college rather than an asset.

By the time of the next Principal, Alexander Gordon (1777–1792), the historical scene had so changed that shortly after his appointment as Principal but before he came to Paris, Alexander Gordon undertook a strenuous tour of the Highlands of Scotland to find out how many Catholics would be prepared to serve in the British army, as it was hoped that this information would lead to a Catholic Relief Act. After Gordon reported that two or three thousand might be expected to enlist if the restrictions against Catholics could be lifted,[8] he maintained, in a letter to Bishop Hay, that allowing Catholics to serve in the British army was no more disloyal to the Stuart cause than the paying of taxes.[9] It was, however, a far cry from the old Jacobite spirit of the college. The college had been a nest of intrigue for Jacobite schemes, had provided military leadership from its lay students, and kept the Stuart hopes high. Inevitably this powerful influence died at Culloden.

Theologically, Jansenist quarrels were dying out. It had been through the Scots College, Paris that Scotland had been dragged into these disputes. This had been a baneful influence, now fortunately over and done with. There were some little echoes, but they were faint indeed. In a quarrel with Alexander Gordon, about which more will be said presently, Bishop Hay, with what Abbé MacPherson described as the bishop's 'scarcely excusable ignorance of history', quoted the accusations of Colin Campbell and his cabal as evidence against the college.[10] Principal Alexander Gordon replied by exposing the moral faults of Colin Campbell. This, however, was not a Jansenist quarrel, and was merely incidental in the argument. Later in the debate, when the Abbé de Rigaud asked Bishop Geddes if the Principal might be a Jansenist, Geddes replied that he most certainly was not.[11] Only one Scottish priest of this time showed reluctance to sign *Unigenitus*, and that was Alexander Geddes, ordained in Paris c.1764.[12] This eccentric was anything but typical of the clergy of the time. He expounded novel ideas on biblical criticism, but Scottish Catholic clergy and laity were far from ready to be influenced by these. Moreover Alexander Geddes offended by his breaches of Church discipline, and retired to London where he published a Hebrew Bible,[13] but was quite isolated from the main body of Scottish Catholic missioners. There was now no notable theological influence in Scotland on the part of the Paris educated priests.

A third reason why the Scots College Paris declined and lost it influence was the appalling health of both staff and students during the principalship of John Gordon (1752–1777). It would appear that tuberculosis had got into the college and spread from one to another in the small community. Robert Gray, a subdeacon from the Diocese of Moray, died of consumption on 21 April 1758.[14] Harry Innes had to go to Douai for his health in 1770, 'threatened with consumption.'[15] Alexander Gordon, later Principal, had all the symptoms of the same illness, spitting blood, pains in the chest and breathlessness. John Gordon, the Principal, was often so ill that he could not write. His illness was sometimes described as 'asthma', but it could easily have been tuberculosis. Andrew Riddoch, the Procurator, was chronically ill, usually described as 'very ill' at least from 1758 until his death on 11 July 1772.[16] A student called James Gordon of Auchleuchries died on 5 September, 1762 of a malignant putrid fever which had occasioned an imposthume on his breast.[17] Alexander Geddes was in bad health in 1762,[18] and later, one of the reasons for sending him to serve on the staff of Douai college was that he did not have the health for the rigours of the mission.[19] A student called Duff and Henry Innes both had malignant fevers in 1762.[20] Robert Gordon, a member of staff, was ill in December 1761 and for most of 1762. Bad health undoubtedly hampered the achievement of the college.

The main reason, however, for decline and loss of influence, was contention between the Scottish Bishops and the Principals of the College. Difficulties started in 1761 with the bishops' dissatisfaction with college accounts.[21] The argument went on for years.[22] In 1770, the college withdrew some of the money that it had been accustomed to send to the mission, namely revenue from Hackett's contract which the college pointed out was 'entirely at the disposal of Grisy [Scots College Paris]' according to a declaration before a public notary on 15 October, 1750, and the Scalan Rector's rent which had only been given as a favour and not as an obligation.[23] Naturally this withholding of funds did little to alleviate the tension, but the Principal stood his ground, telling the bishops that the college had lost a third of its revenue while the mission had doubled its income. The college was in debt in 1761, but only apparently to the extent of £500. Further losses came with the crash of the East India Company, which John Gordon described as 'gone to pot'.[24] Then, after some people had been killed by the fall of an old building in Paris, the college was forced by law to knock down one of its houses and to rebuild it at a cost of 40,000 livres.[25]

A more serious accusation was made against the college in 1762 when the bishops blamed the staff for the apostasies of *alumni*. John Gordon replied that since 1730, none had apostatised on leaving, and that if any had left after five, six, ten or twelve years, the blame should be placed against those whom they were under at the time.[26] It was a good rejoinder but hardly answered the case; there may have been something defective in the training or discipline of the college.

Serious and debilitating as these disputes were, they were as nothing compared to the feud between Bishop Hay and the next Principal, Alexander

Gordon. At the beginning of Alexander Gordon's principalship all seemed to augur well. Gordon was well qualified for the job; an *alumnus* of the college and an M.A. of Paris University, he had been Prefect of Studies in the college from 1764 until 1772 and Procurator of the college from 1772 until 1774, and at the time of his appointment, he was Procurator for the Scottish mission. He seemed to get on well with Bishop Hay who was still coadjutor, but assuming most of the responsibility for the Lowland District in the old age and infirmity of Bishop James Grant whom he succeeded on 3 December 1778. Hay was grateful to Alexander Gordon for defending him at a meeting of the clergy when all others seemed against the Bishop. Alexander Gordon was greatly encouraging Bishop Hay in his striving for a Catholic Relief Bill, and he wrote well of the bishop to John Reid, the missionary priest stationed at Preshome.[27] Although Gordon in his first letter to Bishop Hay from Paris, spoke truculently about getting no news from Scotland,[28] there was as yet no real hostility. On the contrary, after hearing that Bishop Hay had lost all his books in the burning of the Catholic chapel in Edinburgh in 1779, Alexander Gordon generously offered all his own books to the bishop.[29]

Disputes with Bishop Hay started very soon afterwards. Nearly all account of the squabbles put the blame almost entirely on Alexander Gordon, the exception being Fr William Anderson who believed that Bishop Hay was more to blame than the Principal.[30] Without attempting to excuse Alexander Gordon, we would incline to Anderson's opinion.[31] It must be admitted, however, that Bishop Hay had the kinder style in writing, whereas Alexander Gordon was abrasive and truculent, believing that he must bring every difference out into the open, and never turning the blind eye to an unfortunate remark. This might have been advantageous in conversation, but this lack of tact in letters caused great offence. There are certainly two sides to the story. In one of the early quarrels which was about the Principal's brother, there is little that can be said in defence of Bishop Hay's position. John Gordon, the Principal's brother who had served on the staff of the Scots College in Valladolid until 1775, had lost his reason. Bishop Hay at first wanted Principal Gordon to find a house of refuge for his brother in France, but the Principal replied that he could not do this. Bishop Hay then communicated John Gordon's desire to go to Scots College Paris, to which the Principal replied that the college could not take his brother as a sinecure, nor could he dismiss a member of staff to replace him with his own brother.[32] Then began the great debate as to where the obligation of maintenance lay. Whereas Alexander Gordon maintained that the obligation lay with the Scottish mission.[33] Bishop Hay first said that the onus of maintenance for John Gordon lay chiefly with the Principal as his next of kin, and later denied any responsibility on the part of the mission for Paris-ordained priests because they did not take the mission oath. Bishop Hay may have threatened to take the matter to a Roman ecclesiastical court, as Alexander Gordon wrote in September 1780, 'You may think that the interference of Rome will be of service to you on this occasion, but…Rome can be of no service either to you or me in this case.' He told the Bishop that if he did not accept the principal's proposal of shared costs, the only remedy was to try the justice of the case in a civil court, where he would lose and be forced to pay costs.[34] Hay then threatened to send no more students to the college, should Gordon take him to court. This was on 31 January 1781.[35] Eventually the matter was resolved with the decision that the Scottish Mission, Bishop Hay, Bishop Geddes and Alexander Gordon should each pay a share of John Gordon's keep.

For another dispute with Bishop Hay which began about the same time as the above, Alexander Gordon had only himself to blame. Bishop Hay wanted Henry Innes, the College Procurator, to return to the Scottish mission, but the Principal said that he could not spare him, but that he would gladly return to Scotland himself as he had never had any desire to go back to Paris.[36] When Bishop Hay tried to take him up on this offer, Alexander Gordon regretted what he had said, and stoutly maintained his right to stay in the college.[37] As with the other dispute, Alexander Gordon won his point,[38] which was unfortunate for him when his adversary had the temperament of Bishop Hay.

In 1783, Bishop Hay refused to send any more students to Scots College, Paris. This was said to be on account of complaints against the Principal and the College. Often after this, Bishop Geddes referred to damaging letters in the hands of Bishop Hay, although he never disclosed whom they came from. One complainant was Peter Hay, who had been Prefect of Studies in Paris from 1777 until 1781. In December 1782, he had written to Bishop Hay, complaining about French students that the Principal had boarded in the college, 'and the first he made choice of was of a notoriously bad character'.[39] At least two more letters were later sent, complaining not only about the boarders, but also about the Principal's violent temper, and 'the flagrant abuses which were daily introducing'.[40] It seems strange that these letters had so much influence, because Peter Hay had left the college when they were sent, and Bishop Hay had often complained about the melancholy character of his namesake. We do not know if other complaints were received, but Alexander Gordon was not asked to answer the charges, was not even told them in detail, and never knew who had complained. This he felt most deeply and declared, 'It is but common justice to hear before passing sentence what can be said by the person accused.'[41] The Principal maintained, although Bishop Hay later denied this, that Bishop Hay 'gave the first notice to Miss Drummond of our misunderstanding', you see he has likewise told her his reason for not sending her nephew [to the college].'[42] It would appear that Alexander Gordon believed that the lady had knowledge of the Bishop's decision before it was communicated to the Principal himself, which Hay did not do in person but through Bishop Geddes. Bishop Hay maintained that he could not in conscience send students to Paris. 'Better not to send them', he said, 'than have them be ruined'.[43] Who can judge motives? The fact that the bishop had made the threat not to send students in January 1781 during a personal dispute with the Principal and before he had heard the complaints from Paris must make one wonder.

The Principal replied by immediately withholding money left in trust to Scalan by Louis Innes, maintaining that this had been bequeathed to Scalan for students who would be sent to Paris.[44] Although the Principal has been severely criticised for doing this, he was legally in the right on this point. Louis Innes, the benefactor had pointed this out to Bishop Gordon. What really made this a bitter blow to the mission was that the Principal maintained that the college was not due to send any money to Scalan after 1778 when the last students had been sent to the college from Scotland. He therefore deducted three years rents, already paid (in total 822 livres) from money he was due to the mission. Whatever the legal and moral rights of this action, it must only have served to put all the missioners onto the Bishop's side. Alexander Gordon withheld other moneys too, namely what were known as the Glastirum moneys, the Hacket rents and the Deeside rents. In these cases, he was also legally in the right though vindictive and selfish. In 1780 he had been able to quote Louis Innes and George Innes to show that the distribution of the Glastirum and Hacket moneys was the prerogative of the Paris College,[45] and in 1789, the missioners in Scotland accepted the fact that they had no right to the Scalan and Deeside rents.

The quarrel dragged on and on, ever becoming more acrimonious. In a letter to the Carthusian Prior in 1784, Hay said that he was stopping students because of miscarriages of students and the bad conduct of the French boarders in the house, but went on to blame Alexander Gordon for things that he could not have been responsible for, including the scrupulosity of Alexander Geddes who had been ordained at the same time as the Principal, the melancholy temper of Peter Hay, and the madness of his brother John Gordon. Even Bishop Geddes, Hay's coadjutor, had to admit that his superior had gone too far.[46]

Right or wrong, for the good of the college, Alexander Gordon would have done better to resign office, or at least to have held his peace. This was a quarrel that he could not win. Instead he published a memorial[47] to defend himself which he circulated not only to the priests in Scotland, but to a few of the Catholic gentry as well. To this, Bishop Hay circulated a reply among the clergy, but neither sent the Principal a copy nor intimated to him its contents! Such was the prejudice against Alexander Gordon that when Henry Innes, the Procurator of the College, left the college in 1789 to become a chaplain to a Mr and Mrs Chichester in Devonshire, Bishop Geddes blamed the Principal. When the Principal replied that he personally disapproved of Innes' leaving, while Bishop Hay had given his consent, Bishop Geddes replied by saying that even although Bishop Hay had given his consent,[48] the Principal could still have prevented his going!

It was most tragic that the Scottish Bishops and the Principal of the Scots College, Paris were at such loggerheads at the time of the French Revolution. Co-operation was desperately needed, and had there been any, the outcome may have been different. At the outbreak of the Revolution, the future of the college seemed precarious indeed. It was expected that the religious orders would be suppressed, and if this happened, the Scots College Paris would lose its ecclesiastical superior, the Prior of the Carthusians. In these difficult times, Principal Gordon made some moves to sell the college and its property with a view to establishing the college elsewhere. This was a most wise thing to do, but he did not tell the bishops. He contacted the Papal Nuncio, and got the British Ambassador to present a motion to the French Parliament. When the Prior of the Carthusians discovered this from Alexander Innes, Prefect of Studies, he sent for Principal Gordon, but was satisfied when Gordon informed him that he had consulted the Papal Nuncio and the British Ambassador, and that he had authority from the bishops and clergy of Scotland to dispose of the college's property. The authority from the bishops, however, which had been granted in 1788, concerned only moveable goods, not the immovable property.[49] Bishops and clergy in Scotland were alarmed at the prospect of Principal Gordon acting on his own. Bishop Hay, therefore, drew up a letter which his coadjutor sent abroad, giving joint power to Principal Gordon, Principal Farquharson at Douai, and Alexander Innes, or to any two of them, to act for the Mission with regard to the College. Legally this would have been of no avail, because legally the Scots College Paris was a purely French establishment incorporated by Royal Charter of France, and it was not under the jurisdiction of the vicars-apostolic in Scotland. Principal Gordon was infuriated, and little wonder, since the clause 'or any two of them' was assigning authority (albeit illegally and ineffectually) to the Principal of Douai and the Prefect of Studies to dispose of the college without consulting him.

John Farquharson, the Principal of Douai who had invited Bishop Geddes to come to his college, had intimated that it might be necessary for the bishop also to visit Paris. Alexander Innes had written to Scotland in the same vein. Hence at a clergy meeting at Gibston near Huntly, Bishop Geddes was given a commission by the bishops and clergy of Scotland, and signed by twenty-four of the Catholic gentry as representing the 'Catholics of Scotland', giving him full power to deal with the situation, and if necessary to sell all the assets of the Scots College, Paris. This move displayed crass ignorance of the French law. As stated already, the bishops of Scotland, although they had an interest, had no jurisdiction over the college, and had no legal standing in France. 'The Catholics of Scotland' were not a corporate body and could not become so. They had no 'locus standi' in French law, though they did have an interest in the matter. It is even rather amusing to conceive of the mind of the Catholics of Scotland being ascertained by the signatures of twenty-four gentry. Principal Gordon, on the other hand, in virtue of his office, had all the rights and privileges of a French citizen, and as Principal of the college, had a legal position in the matter. The college, however, could not have been sold without the permission of the French Parliament. This would have necessitated a hearing, in which the Scottish bishops would have been heard, but only as a party with an interest. Even if sold, the money realised could not have been transferred out of the country in order to establish a college elsewhere. This would have required a change in French law by enactment of the French Parliament. Bishop Hay had no inkling at all about the legal position. Characteristically, the bishops decided that Principal Gordon was not to be appraised of their decisions until Geddes arrived in France lest he should make any counter preparations.

Bishop Geddes arrived in Paris on 23 December, 1791.[50] Being a mild mannered man, he has deservedly won a reputation as a good mediator, but in this affair, he was far from being at his best. From the outset he was disadvantaged on account of his concurrence with the previous actions of Bishop Hay which did not make him very acceptable to Principal Gordon. For example, he utterly failed to see the insult in the 'joint-power' document that he had forwarded to Paris. During the negotiations with the Principal, on his own admission, he had daily talks on the subject under discussion with Alexander Innes. How he could have failed to see that this was bound to be most irritating to the Principal, who was Innes' superior in the college, is almost incomprehensible. There were lengthy negotiations with the Prior of the Carthusians, Principal Gordon, and others who were called in to help including Floirac, vicar-general of Paris, the Abbé de Rigaud and Bishop Colbert of Rodez who had once been a student in the college.[51] No agreement could be reached. It was the turn of Principal Gordon to be unreasonable in his demands. He tried to maintain that if the office of Prior of the Carthusians ceased, then the superiority of the college devolved upon himself. One can to some extent understand why he did not want the college to be subject to the Scottish bishops; it never had been since Beaton's foundation in 1603, even although there had been a bishop in Scotland since 1694; after his previous dealings with Bishop Hay, that Bishop's jurisdiction would be most unwelcome, and it was most likely that Gordon would be dismissed. Nevertheless it was unreasonable to deny the bishops' interest in the college, especially if the office of Prior were to disappear, and even more unreasonable to claim the superiority for himself. When Gordon realised that he could not fall heir to the superiority of the college, he claimed that the Archbishop of Paris became superior if the office of Prior of the Carthusians disappeared. In this he was probably right, not because the Archbishop was the successor of either the Bishop of Moray or the Bishop of Glasgow (which Geddes thought that the Principal was claiming), but because he was the local Ordinary. (It is significant that the amalgamation of the Moray and Beaton foundations in 1639 had been made by the first Archbishop of Paris).

The situation was exacerbated by Alexander Gordon being at this time both Principal and Procurator of the College. Bishop Geddes made too much of the fact that this was forbidden by the statutes of the college. The statutes did not have legal force in the same way as the foundation of the college or the amalgamation of the Moray and Beaton benefactions in 1639. The statutes, drawn up by Louis Innes in 1707 expressed the ideals of the college, but over the years, it had been found necessary to make exceptions to almost every regulation. It was therefore rather pedantic to insist on the statutes in this instance. Nevertheless, given the Principal's aspirations, a separate Procurator was desirable. The Prior wanted to appoint Alexander Innes who was now Prefect of Studies, but Alexander Gordon quite naturally objected since Alexander Innes had taken the bishops' side against him in the dispute. The Principal declared that he would accept Henry Innes, but the latter refused, claiming that he could not desert Mr. Chichester. In fact, he did not want to come. The end result was that the Prior did appoint Alexander Innes, and Alexander Gordon was reluctantly forced to accept the fact.

Bishop Geddes left Paris in May 1792. Despite all the pretence, at the time and in subsequent writings, that it had been a most useful visit,[52] really, nothing had been achieved. In fact, external forces were quickly leading events to a conclusion quite different from that desired by Scottish ecclesiastics. In August 1792, the college was twice invaded by armed *banditti,* and on the first occasion Principal Gordon was taken to the Section by four national guards to be presented with the new oath. He refused to take the oath, but agreed to take an oath to do nothing against their *liberté, egalité et proprietés.*[53] Alexander Gordon decided to leave Paris. Having obtained a passport for Alexander Innes, he tried to force the Procurator to leave too, but the latter refused. Although Gordon is usually blamed for running away, and Alexander Innes praised for his bravery in staying,[54] the Procurator was very rash to remain and was lucky to survive. After an edict of 9 October 1793, Alexander Innes was made prisoner under his own roof. He was condemned to death and his grave was dug in the college garden, but he was unexpectedly reprieved on the downfall of Robespierre on 27 July 1794.[55] Alexander Gordon left Paris at the end of September 1792, taking with him the 'Book of Grisy' and the 'Statutes of the College', regarding these as title-deeds to his office as Principal. It was the end of the Scots College Paris as an educational institute.

The last forty years were an unhappy time for the Scots College Paris, but there were during this time seven ordinations to the priesthood in Paris, and another two who had studied at the college were ordained at Valladolid, John Baptist Gordon who had done nearly all his studies in Paris, and Alexander MacDonald who had been there for three years. There was also the ordination in 1762 of Seignelay Colbert who had started his studies in the college, and later became Bishop of Rodez. These ordinations, however, cannot disguise the decline. Although objections to *Unigenitus* were at an end, the spectre of Jansenism still haunted the college, as Roman trained Bishops suspected its orthodoxy, and were further frustrated by their inability to appoint the staff. When the Delilahs of Jacobitism and Jansenism had ceased their temptations, it was the adversary of internal dissension that struck the fatal blow.

NOTES

1. SCA/Bl Lett 3/119/18, 3 Apr 1755, John Gordon Glencat to Bishop Smith.
2. SCA/Bl Lett 3/150/12, 1761, John Gordon Glencat to Bishop Smith.
3. Oliphant, T.L.K., *The Jacobite Lairds of Gask* (London: 1870), p.230.
4. Ibid. p.298.
5. Ibid. p.307
6. Ibid. p.309.
7. Ibid. pp.356f.
8. Gordon, J.F.S., *The Catholic Church in Scotland* (Glasgow 1869), p.250

9. SCA/Bl Lett 3/301/2, 1 April 1778, Alexander Gordon (Drummond) to Bishop Hay (Edinburgh)
10. Gordon, J.F.S., op. cit., p.250.
11. SCA/CA 1/23/2, Account of Bishop Geddes' Journey to Paris, p.43.
12. Anderson, W., 'Notes on Illustrations', *Innes Review* Vol XIV (1963), p.207.
13. Anderson, W., 'The Book of Zaknim', *Innes Review* Vol XIV (1963), p.139.
14. SCA/CA 1/7, Necrology. of the Scots College, Paris, 1694
15. SCA/Bl Lett 3/213/9. 9 July 1770, John Gordon to Bishop Grant,
16. SCA/Bl Lett 3/134/2, 3/181/4, 3/181/6, 3/193/8, 3/193/11, 3/213/9, 3/238/14.
17. SCA/Bl Lett 3/155/13, 5 Sept 1762, John Gordon to Bishop Smith
18. SCA/Bl Lett 3/155/12, 25 July 1762, John Gordon to Bishop Smith
19. SCA/Bl Lett 3/174/10, 10 Oct 1765, Bishop Grant (Edinburgh) to John Geddes (Scalan)
20. SCA/Bl Lett 3/155/13, 5 Sept 1762, John Gordon to Bishop Smith
21. SCA/Bl Lett 3/150/16, 6 Sept 1761, John Gordon to Bishop Smith
22. SCA/Bl Lett 3/165/14, 27 July 1764, John Gordon to the Missioners
23. SCA/Bl Lett 3/213/8, 30 Apr 1770, John Gordon, Andrew Riddoch & Alex Gordon to Bishop Grant,.
24. SCA/Bl Lett 3/213/7, 15 Apr 1770, John Gordon to Bishop Grant,
25. SCA/Bl Lett 3/251/18, 11 July 1773, John Gordon to Bishop Grant
    SCA/Bl Lett 3/251/19, 21 Nov 1773, John Gordon to Bishop Grant.
26. SCA/Bl Lett 3/155/8, 8 Feb 1762, John Gordon to Bishop Smith
27. SCA/Bl Lett 3/301/4, 26 Sept 1778, Alex Gordon (Edinburgh) to John Reid (Preshome)
28. SCA/Bl Lett 3/301/5, 4 Dec 1778, Alex Gordon (Paris) to Bishop Hay (Edinburgh)
29. SCA/Bl Lett 3/313/3, 28 Feb 1779, Alex Grodon (Paris) to Bishop Hay
30. SCA/CA 1/23/2 p.1., Anderson, W., unpublished remarks.
31. SCA/CA 1/23/2 p.1., Anderson calls both Hay & Gordon 'silly old men'.
32. SCA/Bl Lett 3/329/6, 12 Apr 1780, Alex Gordon (Paris) to Bishop Hay
33. SCA/Bl Lett 3/329/8, 8 May 1780, Alex Gordon (Paris) to Bishop Hay
34. SCA/Bl Lett 3/330/11, 11 Sept 1780, Alex Gordon (Paris) to Bishop Hay
35. SCA/Bl Lett, 31 Jan 1781 (copy), Bishop Hay to Alexander Gordon
36. SCA/Bl Lett 3/329/1, 1 Jan 1780, Alex Gordon (Paris) to Bishop Hay
37. SCA/Bl Lett 3/329/6, 12 Apr 1780, Alex Gordon (Paris) to Bishop Hay
38. 'I have had already two paper wars with him [Bishop Hay] al tho' in both I obtained my ends, yet I am no ways inclined to have a third.' (SCA/Bl Lett 3/379/5, 3 Nov 1783, Alex Gordon to John Geddes)
39. SCA/Bl Lett 3/362/2, 10 Dec 1782, Peter Hay (Kininvie) to Bishop Hay
40. SCA/Bl Lett 3/386/2, 16 Oct 1783, Peter Hay (Fochabers) to Bishop Hay
    SCA/Bl Lett 3/386/2, 20 Oct 1783, Peter Hay to Bishop Hay
41. SCA/Bl Lett 3/379/5, 3 Nov 1783, Alex Gordon (Paris) to Bishop Hay

This was a common theme of the Principal, used on behalf of others as well as himself. It is very interesting to see this in The Book of Zaknim, a burlesque written by Alexander Geddes referring to the mission administators of 1778 (i.e. shortly before Gordon went back to Paris as Principal. Chapter IV.

10. And they all cried out with one voice: Let him [Alexander Geddes] be tarred and feathered.

11. And there was in the council chamber a young man of the tribe of Gordon, and his name was Alexander

12. And the thing displeased him, and he stood up and said: You wot [know?] not what you do.

13. It is against all Law, to condemn a man till he has spoken in his own defence. [Italics mine.]

42. SCA/Bl Lett 3/379/5, 3 Nov 1783, Alex Gordon (Paris) to Bishop Hay

43. SCA/Bl Lett, 26 June 1784, Bishop Hay to Mr Thomson

44. SCA/Bl Lett 3/378/12, 12 Dec 1783, Bishop Geddes to Bishop Hay

45. SCA/Bl Lett 3/329/3, 26 Jan 1780, Alex Gordon (Paris) to Bishop Hay

46. SCA/Bl Lett 3/409/5, 4 Dec 1784, Alex Gordon to Bishop Geddes

47. SCA/CA 1/21/4, *Memoire de M. Gordon, Pricipal du College de Ecossois a Paris,* (1785).

48. SCA/Bl Lett 4/6/10, 14 March 1789, Alex Gordon to Bishop Geddes

49. SCA/CA 1/23/4, p.8, Account of Bishop Geddes' Journey to Paris.

50. SCA/CA 1/22/1 p.13, Account of Bishop Geddes' Journey to Paris.

51. SCA/CA 1/23/3 p.55, Account of Bishop Geddes' Journey to Paris.

52. Gordon, J.F.S.,op. cit., Vol IV, p.333.

53. Alex Gordon to Andrew Lumisden, 2 Sept 1792, Glasgow Registrum i, viii, quoted in McRoberts, D., 'The Scottish Catholic Archives 1560–1978', *Innes Review*, Vol. XXVIII (1971) p.88.

54. McRoberts, D., 'The Scottish Catholic Archives 1560–1978', *Innes Review*, Vol. XXVIII (1971), p.88

55. MS of James Dennistoun of Dennistoun in National Library, Edinburgh, quoted in Hay, M.V.,*Blairs Papers* (1603–1660) (London & Edinburgh.1929), pp.11–12.

CHAPTER 10

The College Library and Archives and the Historical Work of Thomas Innes

1. The Beaton Bequest and Early Accessions

No account of the achievement of the Scots College Paris would be complete without some account of the College Library and archives and the archival work of their most illustrious keeper, Thomas Innes. Acknowledgement must be made to Monsignor David McRoberts for his excellent article, 'The Scottish Catholic Archives, 1560–1978', in the *Innes Review*,[1] and to subsequent articles by Alistair Cherry.[2] This chapter builds on these foundations.

It is appropriate to begin with the bequests of Archbishop Beaton which are simultaneous with the second foundation of the College. Archbishop James Beaton of Glasgow, taking advantage of the terms of the Treaty of Edinburgh of 6 July 1560, whereby those who wished could leave the country with the French troops, sailed from Leith on 18 July 1560 and arrived in Paris on 3 August 1560. He managed to take with him silver art treasures from Glasgow Cathedral along with original charters and records of the Archdiocese from the Cathedral Muniment Room. In Paris, the Archbishop tried to sustain a kind of 'government in exile' for Scottish Catholics, and before he died, achieved the second foundation of the Scots College, Paris by leaving the poor Scottish students a house in the *Rue des Amandiers*, now *Rue La Place*.[3] In his will, he bequeathed the art treasures of Glasgow Cathedral and the original charters and the records of the Archdiocese of Glasgow to the Carthusian Priory, while to the Scots College he left his own personal and diplomatic papers, and his library of six hundred books which Thomas Dempster described as *'Bibliotheca Sua Selectissima'*. This legacy was the foundation stock of the Scots College Library.

David McRoberts made mention of a document of 1660 in the Archives Nationales which lists thirty printed volumes and 225 manuscripts, including the Cartulary of Glasgow Church, the Hours of Anne of Brittany, and the Beaton Psalter. In the Étude Muret Collection of the same archives, the present writer has seen an earlier list, dated 5 July 1655,[4] which appears to be a inventory at the transmission of authority from Principal George Leith to Principal Robert Barclay, in which the publication dates of some of the volumes (1608, 1614, 1616, 1623, 1641, 1644) prove, as one would have expected to find, that the College had added to the original collection.

Some of the books added to the Beaton Collection are worthy of special mention. The 'Book of Grisy', now preserved in Columba House, Edinburgh is a cartulary relating to the College between 1564 and 1580 with masterful illustrations assembled by Thomas Wynterhop, the priest scholar who, with the help of Mary Queen of Scots, saved the first college foundation from ruin; additional charters of 1640 and 1692 have been added. The Album Amicorum of George Strachan, the oriental scholar, has epitaphs in various hands collected by Thomas Chambers who gifted the book to the College before 1651. There are two manuscript copies of Gilbert Blakhal's *Breiffe Narration*, the original written by the author c.1666–7 and a transcript by 'APL' dated 9 May 1671. The present writer has identified the handwriting of the transcriber as that of Alexander Leslie, the famous Visitator of Scotland mentioned in Chapter 4.[5] There was, before it was lost at the time of the French Revolution, a History from James I's death to James VI's death by William Sinclair, who was the Edinburgh advocate with whom St John Ogilvie lodged in the Canongate, Edinburgh. This was bought for the College Library by John Paul Jamieson, a Scottish priest sometime after 1685. It attracted the attention of scholars, until it was last seen by Andrew Stewart in 1789. Also in the College was a manuscript entitled 'Portrait of True Loyalty Exposed in the Family of Gordon without interruption to the present year 1691' which was written by David Burnet who had been Prefect of Studies in the College from 1676 until 1680. The present writer has also seen in the College des Irlandais Paris, a manuscript copy of a work of Abbot Gilbert Brown,[6] which is one of the books which have come to that College from the Scots College. The manuscript consisting of 252 folios is entitled 'Answere to Welches forged lyes'. It is written in two different hands, and judging by the handwriting style, the writer believes that it is a copy made much later than the original. Much of the narrative suffers from the defect of the times in accusing opponents of heinous crimes. It refers to a previous work of Gilbert Brown now lost that we knew existed from lengthy quotations in the work of Welches. What is of interest is that it gives the title of that lost work, hitherto unknown, as 'The Hunting of the Foxe'. Another curiosity is that it gives a translation of *hyperdulia*, a technical word for devotion to Mary, as 'superdouly'.

One fairly early visitor to the Scots College Library was Sir Robert Sibbald (1641–1722), President of Edinburgh Royal College of Physicians, first Professor of Medicine at Edinburgh University, and co-founder of the Edinburgh Botanical Gardens, who visited the College in 1661–2 where he noted the 'Book of Grisy' and the huge collection of letters from Queen Mary to Archbishop Beaton. It may be of some interest that Sir Robert

Sibbald embraced Catholicism for a short time due to the influence of the Earl of Perth, but later, seeing the intrigues of the Jesuits and their bad influence on King James VII, returned to the religion of his birth.[7]

2. Memoirs of King James VII and Other Jacobite Papers

A most important addition to the Scots College Library came on 24 March 1701 when King James VII deposited in the College a collection of his memoirs and papers. The extent of this collection can be seen from a list which was prepared by Alexander Innes for Charles James Fox in 1802. The list read:

> Four volumes folio [and] six volumes quarto: [containing] Memoirs in James the Second's own handwriting, beginning from the time that he was sixteen years of age. Two thin quarto volumes: containing letters from Charles the Second's ministers to James the Second (the Duke of York), when he was at Brussels and in Scotland, MS. Two thin quarto volumes: containing letters from Charles the Second to his brother, James Duke of York, MS.

Thomas Innes wrote in 1740 that the Memoirs which had been written on papers of different sizes were arranged by Louis Innes under the King's directions, and bound into three volumes. The discrepancy between the fourteen volumes listed by Alexander Innes and the three volumes mentioned by Thomas Innes, can be explained by the further information provided by the latter that the Memoirs he was referring to stopped at the Restoration in 1660. A transcript of this smaller collection was made in 1686 by Charles Dryden, son of the famous poet, and was also bound into three volumes. This fair copy was also deposited in the Scots College archives.

In 1707, memoirs of James VII 'as relate to the year 1678 and downwards' were taken from the College to St Germain by order of King James VIII so that a biography of James VII could be compiled. Although a late tradition of the College attributed this biography to three authors (Sir David Nairne, Lord Caryll and William Dicconson), James Edgar and Thomas Innes both referred to it simply as the work of William Dicconson, and we may refer to it as 'Dicconson's Life'. The Scots College manuscript, which still exists, was bound in five folio volumes, marked on the spine as 'Memoirs, Tom I', Memoirs Tom II' etc. When researchers at the College Archives referred to 'Memoirs of James VII', they were referring to 'Dicconson's Life.' Thomas Carte in 1740 was the only person given the King's permission to see the Original Memoirs.

Following the King's placing of his Memoirs and papers in the College, other Jacobite collections also came to its archives. These included papers of Queen Mary of Modena, papers of the Erskines of Mar, papers of Francis Atterbury, Bishop of Rochester which came in 1732, letters of

Lord Rochester, and about twelve volumes of Nairne Papers which came after the death of David Nairne in 1741.

By entrusting his papers to the College, the King had made the College the home of the official royal archives, and these papers along with other Jacobite collections now attracted historians of state affairs as well as ecclesiastical researchers.

3. Thomas Innes

The great archivist of the College was Thomas Innes, the third son of James Innes wadsetter of Drumgask, and Jane Robertson. He was born at Drumgask in the parish of Aboyne, Aberdeenshire, in 1662, the year of his birth being inscribed on the fly leaf of a missal belonging to the late family of Ballogie. The editor's preface to the Spalding Club edition of the *Civil and Ecclesiastical History* states that Thomas Innes went to Paris in 1677 at the age of fifteen,[8] but the date seems unlikely, as Thomas Innes has left 'A memoriall of my travels in England'[9] which gives an account of his journey from his departure from Edinburgh on 27 June 1679 until setting sail from Harwich on 15 August 1679. In itself, it is an interesting journey; the first stage to London is direct and ordinary enough, going through Berwick, Newcastle, Durham, York, Nottingham, Huntingdon and Cambridge, but then he travelled west visiting Windsor, Oxford, Bath, Bristol, Plymouth, Exeter, Salisbury and Portsmouth, and then to the east of London, visiting Maidstone, Sittingburn, Canterbury, Dover and Rochester. Thus Innes saw several of the old Cathedrals of England, and even at that early stage of his career revealed his interest in history. Apart from cases of illness, it was very rare for Scots students of those times to go back to Britain after only two years abroad, and Innes wrote as if seeing places for the first time. So, failing other documentary evidence, Thomas Innes' first coming to Paris can be dated in 1679, when he was seventeen years old. Several printed accounts state that he did not enter the Scots College Paris until 12 January 1681 as he pursued his studies at the College of Navarre. It was, however, the common custom of the Scots College to send students out to the College of Navarre for lectures and tuition, and it seems unlikely that Thomas Innes was not enrolled in the Scots College when he first went to Paris, especially as his brother Louis was already there. This tends to be confirmed by the fact that Thomas Innes is not listed as a resident student of the College of Navarre in lists that exist for that time.[10] From the outset, he appears to have been a brilliant pupil, and there is in the Blairs Collection, a copy of Dion Cassius, awarded to him by the College of Navarre on 19 August 1681 for a Greek oration. He was ordained to the priesthood on 10 March 1691, then went for some months pastoral training with the Oratorians at Notre Dame des Vertus. Having returned to the College in 1692, he took his M.A. at the Sorbonne in 1694, and in the following year matriculated into the German nation of the University.

Thomas Innes is, like most other Catholic priests of the period, commonly designated by *aliases*, the two most common being Fleming and Melville. Of these, we know the origin of the former as Skene records that Malcolm IV 'did grant the lands of Innes, extending from the Spey to the Lossie, to Berowald, the Fleming by a charter granted at Perth', while Duncan Forbes of Culloden qualifies this by saying that 'Berowald was a native Scotsman of the province of Murray, and had the name Fleming added as a 'to name' because he had travelled in that country'.[11]

Thomas Innes recorded that he first saw the archival documents of the College in 1686 or 1687 when they were in a considerable state of disorder, and that he managed at that time to recover some important papers from a Scots gentleman's house in the country. In 1692 and 1693, he was able to begin his work of arranging the archival documents, and he made copies of Bulls and Charters in the Carthusian Priory, which were bound into volumes, consisting of 1238 pages.

In 1694 he made the great discovery of a charter of Robert II whereby the King founded a chaplaincy in Glasgow Cathedral to fulfil the conditions of the Pope in granting the King a dispensation from consanguinity and affinity so that he could marry Elizabeth More. This proved the legitimacy of the Stewart dynasty which had been called in question on account of the matrimonial impediment. Louis Innes showed the document to King James, and on 26 May 1694 at St Germain, he submitted the charter to an examination by the most famous antiquaries of France, including Camille le Tellier de Louvois, the King's Librarian; Eusèbe Renandot, the Historiographer Royal; Étienne Baluze, the Colbertine Librarian; Honoré Caille, a lawyer and counsellor to King Louis XIV; and the leading Maurist Scholars Jean Mabillon and Thierry Ruinart, who declared the charter authentic. Louis Innes then published the proceedings in *Charta Authentica Roberti Seneschalli Scotiae ex Archivo Collegii Scotorum Parisiensis Edita* (Paris 1695). From the phrase in the title *'ex Archivo Collegii Scotorum'*, it would appear that the charters had then been transferred from the Charterhouse to the College, possibly by command of the Jacobite King.

It was in the same year as the discovery of the charter, 1694, that James, Earl of Drummond presented the College with one of its most treasured possessions, a 15th century manuscript of the Scotichronicon.

From 1695–1697, Thomas Innes worked as a curate in the parish of Magnay in the diocese of Paris. After a further brief stay in the College, he was back in Scotland from June 1698 until October 1701, labouring mostly in the mission of Strathavon. It must have been in this period that the incident occurred which is mentioned in the diary of Thomas Hearne, the English Antiquary, under the date 26 February 1721:

> some years agoe being in England and Scotland, he [Thomas Innes] lost his papers in Scotland (being an excellent collection made and written by himself, a work of 10 years,) where the house was beset upon account of his being a priest, whereupon he leapt out of a window, and his papers were seized and brunt, they being left behind. He bore this loss with great patience, being a man of excellent temper.[12]

1701 was a time of persecution when Walter Innes, a brother of Thomas was arrested and imprisoned, and this year would fit well with 'a work of 10 years' since Thomas Innes was ordained in 1691, and we know that he began work on the Glasgow Charters in 1692. A later date is ruled out, as Thomas Innes was not back in Scotland until 1727. In the year 1700, Thomas Innes accompanied Bishop Nicolson on a visitation of the Highlands that lasted six months; he later spoke of the Island of Barra with great nostalgia, and declared that it was his earnest wish to spend all his days working for Catholics in the Islands of Scotland. In the autumn of 1701, he returned to Paris where he was made Prefect of Studies in the Scots College.

Thomas Innes has left two major works, only one of them being published in his lifetime. His *Critical Essay on the Ancient Inhabitants of the Northern Parts of Britain or Scotland* was published in two volumes by William Innes in London in 1729 at the expense of Louis Innes.[13] The work was not without its critics; neither *Waddel's Remarks on Innes' Critical Essay on the Ancient Inhabitants of Scotland, Edinburgh 1733*,[14] nor *Tait's Roman Account of Britain and Ireland in Answer to Father Innes & c, Edinburgh 1741*,[15] accepted the author's conclusions, but the consensus of historians is that the *Critical Essay* very successfully used good historical methods, which Innes had learned from Mabillon, to refute the mythic history of the Scottish kings. Yet Innes had his own agenda, and his substitution of the Pictish line of kings is certainly not without its problems.[16] The second work, which may be considered a continuation of the first, existed only in manuscript form until published by the Spalding Club in 1853 under the title, *The Civil and Ecclesiastical History of Scotland*.[17] The Spalding Club was criticised for publishing this work as it was clearly Innes' intention to defend aspects of Catholicism. Yet, as was the case with the first work, historians have recognised its merit.

Other items by Thomas Innes that have been published include his 'Letter on the Ancient Manner of holding Synods in Scotland', printed in Vol I of Wilkins' *Concilia, a short narrative of the Scottish Reformation,* published by William Anderson in the *Innes Review* (1956),[18] and some papers in the Miscellany of the Spalding Club, Vol II, pp. 353–380.

Many eminent scholars visited the archives of the Scots College Paris or wrote for information. Most of the scholars dealt with Thomas Innes. Some instances have been recorded. In May 1697, Étienne Baluze, Librarian of the Colbertine Library made a transcript of the 'Registrum Vetus' of Glasgow which is now MS Latin 5540 in the Bibliothèque Nationale; he also transcribed some Scots Synodal Decrees. Peter Fea, an Edinburgh Law student, spent four or five hours with Thomas Innes on 22September 1716, and saw the Charter of King Robert II, 13 or 14 Charters of Scots Kings, letters of Queen Mary, holograph papers of James VII and the manuscript of Fordun's 'Scotichronicon'. In 1719, Thomas Innes 'sent 60 sheets of the most valuable Scotch matters to Mr William Hamilton of Wischaw', an antiquary who wrote *Descriptions of the Sheriffdoms of Lanark and Renfrew*, published posthumously by the Maitland Club in 1831.[19] These sixty sheets were in turn borrowed by James Oliphant. In 1727, Thomas Innes supervised a transcript of the 'Registrum Vetus' for Harry Maule, the titular Earl of Panmure who had fought at Sheriffmuir, and was collecting at Kellie Castle chronicles, chartularies and historical documents of Scotland.[20] In 1734 Thomas Innes supplied Bishop Robert Keith with material for his History. In this work the Bishop in acknowledging his obligations to Thomas Innes, takes the opportunity of mentioning the good service that he and his brother Louis had done in arranging the papers of the Scots College. Dr. Wilkins' first volume of *Concilia Magnae Britanniae et Hiberniae*, published at Paris in 1735 contains Thomas Innes' 'Letter on the Ancient Manner of Holding Synods' in Scotland, already mentioned; the letter is addressed to Dr. Wilkins, and it is known that Innes also supplied Dr. Wilkins with canons of the later Scottish Councils.

Thomas Innes corresponded with the Maurist scholar, Thierry Ruinart, and there are in the manuscript section of the Bibliothèque Nationale in Paris five letters from Thomas Innes and one from his brother Louis to Thierry Ruinart.[21] Mostly they are in praise of his fellow Maurist Jean Mabillon. The letter from Louis Innes is dated 5 August 1708; unfortunately, Thomas Innes did not state the year of writing. Professor John Ker of Kings College Aberdeen was another of Thomas Innes' correspondents. Both Atterbury and Ruddiman admired his work. Robert Wodrow who observed Innes in the Advocates' Library and described him as 'a monkish, bookish, person' seems to have liked him, though there is no evidence that they ever conversed. Thomas Innes was on terms of intimacy with Bishop Archibald Campbell, and Bishop Keith spoke of him as 'his worthy and learned friend'.

It was an occasion of the greatest joy to Thomas Innes when Robert and Andrew Foulis visited the College as emissaries from Glasgow. The brothers, later so famed for publishing, dined at the College at least once a week and sometimes oftener, while Innes sometimes had tea at their lodgings in Paris. The brothers were presented with a copy of the Charter of Robert II that had been prepared for the University of Glasgow in 1694, but had never been delivered on account of the religious troubles in Scotland. In the following year, the brothers returned to the College to present Thomas Innes with a silver case, engraved with the arms of the city of Glasgow, containing a Certificate from the Provost and Magistrates to attest that Thomas Innes had been made a Burgess of the City of Glasgow. Thomas Innes in return made a transcript of some of the ancient charters relating to Glasgow and this was duly presented to the city.

In 1740, Thomas Carte, a non-juring cleric of the Church of England who had been secretary to Bishop Atterbury, visited the College to consult Jacobite papers. His case was unique as he is the only one known to have received the King's permission to read his Original Memoirs, and because the Memoirs were in some places difficult to read on account of age and poor quality ink, Thomas Innes also allowed Carte the use of Dryden's 'fair copy', made in 1686. It would appear that Carte abused the privilege of using the College Archives by stealing about a dozen volumes of royal correspondence deposited in the Scots College Archives after the death of David Nairne, royal secretary. These Nairne papers were sold with the rest of the Carte papers, and are now in the Bodleian Library at Oxford.

Thomas Innes' interest in archives and historical publications never diminished even in old age and failing health. On 5 April 1742, he devoted the best part of a letter to Bishop Smith in defence of the reputation of King Malcolm IV, as he had been saddened by the poor treatment of the subject in Duncan Stuart's elaborate Collection of the Royal Family. Innes explained to the Bishop how a grave historical error had been generated:

> A monk of Kelso copeing the Chartulary intending (as it was often used) to write the Kings names in the beginning of each charter in capital or greater letters, left a blanc for them to be filled up afterwards with a greater pen. Among others, a Charter of K. David I where he gives Innerleithen to the Abbay of Kelso for the soul of his beloved son Prince Henry who was buried there at Kelso…the stupid monk in filling up the King's name of this Charter putts by mistake the name of K. Malcolm instead of K. David at the head of it and as it happens in course that K. David mentions in it corpus filii mei meaning that of his Son Prince Henry th's Chartulary falling into a certain great lawier's hand he concluds that Malcolm had a Son, and as he was certainly never married I leave you to judge of the consequences.[22]

A fortnight later, Innes wrote his Bishop again, praising Ruddiman's *Introduction to Diplomatik*, but making an observation of disagreement on one point, which he asked the Bishop to communicate only to Ruddiman. It was about:

' K. Kenneth MacAlpin's death which I am still persuaded happened AD 859–860 and not 854 as Fordun reckons in which he is contradicted by our most ancient witness as well by the Extract of our old Chronicle of the 12 first Kings of all Albany.[23]

Innes followed this up by sending on 15 August 1743 what he described as a 'piece' relating to the date of Kenneth MacAlpine's death in answer to Ruddiman, along with two 'pieces' relating to Queen Mary.[24]

Thomas Innes died in the College on 8 February 1744. His nephew George related with sadness that scarcity of money had obliged him to sell part of his uncles' collection of books and papers. Principal George Innes blamed the accusations of Jansenism by the 'pilgrims', Campbell and Tyrie, for hastening his uncle's end (he was 81!), and severely damaging his historical works which he deemed so imperfect that little use could ever be made of them. In the latter we know that he was mistaken, as the Spalding Club published Thomas Innes' *Civil and Ecclesiastical History* in 1853.

4. The Archives after the time of Thomas Innes

After the death of Thomas Innes, the principal of the college acted as keeper of the archives. Researchers were still welcomed. Thus Laurence Oliphant of Gask, a forfeited Jacobite laird, spent part of his exile after Culloden transcribing forty-two charters from the Glasgow cartulary, and had them authenticated by Principal John Gordon on 24 May 1753. A more distinguished visitor was David Hume who was making revisions for the 1770 edition of his History of Great Britain. Of his visit to the College, he wrote:

From the humanity and candour of the principal of the Scotch College at Paris, he was permitted to peruse James the Second's Memoirs kept there. The amount of several volumes of small folio, all writ with that Prince's own hand and comprehending the remarkable incidents of his life from his early youth till near the time of his death.

Lord Shelburne visited the College on 23 November 1771 when he was shown Dicconson's Life which he describes as 'five very thick folio volumes which appear to be a history of James's Life, compiled about sixty years ago from his journal'. Sir John Dalrymple, defending his writings against the Earl of Dartmouth claimed to have seen the same work (although he thought that it was written by Mr Caryll).

In 1768 Mr Erskine of Alva applied to the College for family papers. A search revealed a sealed box and a sealed bundle of papers, both of which required royal permission to open. Prince Charles Edward gave the permission, but when the packet of Mar correspondence was found to be individually sealed, Principal Gordon thought that it should only be opened in the presence of Mr Erskine, and the matter was referred to the royal court in Rome for a decision.

James Macpherson, of Ossianic fame, who in 1775 published *Original Papers Containing the Secret History of Great Britain from the Restoration to the Accession of the House of Hanover. To which are prefixed Extracts from the Life of James II as written by Himself*, visited the College to get information from Dicconson's Life which he augmented with material from the Nairne Papers and the Carte Papers.

At the very time of the capture of the Bastille in July 1789, Andrew Stewart was working in the College archives searching for material on Stewart genealogy.

One of the last visitors was M. Mercier de Saint-Léger who was there on 29 April, 1790 when Principal Alexander Gordon showed him the 'Heures d'Anne de Bretagne, reine de France'.

There is every reason to believe that Principals John Gordon and Alexander Gordon were deeply interested in the archives. The confusion of papers mentioned by David McRoberts referred only to the papers that had been taken from the Carthusian Charterhouse in 1764. Although by 1789 there had been plenty of time to arrange these and make an inventory, the fact that it had not been done seems insufficient ground for an accusation of general neglect. The impression one gets is that in the last two principalships, the Scots College Archives were well known, and fairly well consulted.

5. The French Revolution

Historians can only regret the great damage inflicted on the College collections at the time of the French Revolution. At least some of the losses might have been prevented had the principal, Alexander Gordon acted more prudently. The Scottish Bishops were not unaware of the danger, but the poor relationship between Bishop Hay and Principal Gordon was not conducive to a satisfactory solution. One very constructive suggestion was that the Cardinal Duke of York who was now the owner of the Stuart Papers might be persuaded to sell them to the British Museum. The Cardinal seemed to be willing, but the sale never took place.

Another opportunity of rescue arose when the British Ambassador, Lord Gower, offered to take the Stuart Papers to Britain when he left France in August 1792, but it seems that Principal Gordon would only accept the offer if the Ambassador took the silver plate of the College as well, although the Principal himself denied that he had made this condition. In any case, this last chance was lost. On the 2 September 1792 the Principal wrote that the College had been invaded twice by armed *banditti*.[25] He decided to flee, taking only the Statutes of the College and the Book of Grisy, which contained the College charters. Alexander Innes, the procurator, and the great-grand-nephew of Louis and Thomas Innes, was left to face the hostile forces.

Alexander Innes made a serious effort to get the Stuart papers to safety, and it was most unfortunate that the plan failed. Gregory Stapleton, president of the English College at Saint Omer, thought that he could take the manuscripts to England. They were accordingly sent by mail coach to M. Dourlens, Stapleton's lawyer. When Stapleton was arrested, they were transferred to the house of Mr Charles Mostyn. When Mostyn came under threat of arrest, a M. Carpentier was made the custodian of the collection, though Mostyn retained two books, a prayer book and a missal which had both been presents from the Pope to Mary Queen of Scots. Carpentier felt it was necessary to take the bindings from the books as they bore the royal coat of arms. His wife, fearing for her husband's safety, burnt the books and manuscripts.

At the college, the library was ravaged. In September 1793, it was decreed that all British subjects were to be arrested, and their goods confiscated. Alexander Innes became a prisoner in the College from 9 October 1793. On 4 January 1794, it was decreed that the college library and archives were to be removed to the civic depot. After various sortings of the material in January and June, a certain number of books and manuscripts were removed to the national depot in the *Rue de Beaune*. A small inventory of fifty items, twenty-three printed books, twenty-five manuscripts and two other items was prepared by an ex-Benedictine, Germain Poirier. The list included Dicconson's 'Life of James II', the two Glasgow cartularies, the 'Registrum Vetus' and the 'Liber Ruber'. Alexander Innes was able to recover the items on the list from the civic depot three years later.

The second removal from the College was less discriminate, and Alexander Innes described how a large collection was taken away in several carriages and in twenty-four boxes or small coffers, the despoilers refusing to number or label what was taken. Another English speaking prisoner in the College, whose identity is unknown but who signed himself C.F.S.M. described in a letter how the vandals (he called them Goths) sold precious books and manuscripts by the quintal, and burnt others, while prisoners pilfered. He himself had found Jacobite correspondence, but as he tried to sort it, the gaoler came and carried it off.

A little over two years later, laws against British subjects were abrogated, but all that Innes could recover from the French authorities were the fifty items that had been listed by Germain Poirier.

In May 1798 Abbé Paul MacPherson, rector of Scots College Rome, passed through Paris while taking home British students from Rome. Alexander Innes asked him to take home a quantity of manuscripts which filled a box measuring about two feet by three feet. The box included the *Protocol Book of Cuthbert Simon* and the *Rental Book* of Glasgow and the two cartularies of Gleasgow, which MacPherson lent to George Chalmers in London, and five manuscript volumes of historical collections, compiled by Thomas Innes, which, for some unknown reason, MacPherson regarded as his personal property. The rest of the collection was claimed by Principal Alexander Gordon who was then staying at Traquair, but Bishop Cameron refused to surrender the documents, and before his death transferred them to the custody of Bishop Kyle at Preshome.

The Scots and Irish Colleges in Paris were merged for a time, though the Scottish Bishops were never happy with the arrangement, and this led to the remainder of the Scots College Library being transferred to the Irish College. Bishop Paterson's appeal to the French government in 1830 led to the recovery of some historical portraits, and the negotiations of Bishop Gillis in 1839 led to the surviving remnant of the Scots College Paris Library being transferred to Blairs College, Aberdeen. Not surprisingly, a few volumes were overlooked, and are still to be seen in the College des Irlandais, 5 Rue des Irlandais, Paris.

6. The Remnant

After all the havoc wrought by the French Revolution and its aftermath, it is astonishing that anything of the college library and archive collection survived, yet even the remnant is quite considerable. About seven hundred and sixty of the works in the Blairs Collection, now lodged in the National Library in Edinburgh, bear the bookplate of the Scots College, Paris, and it is quite probable that many others among the twenty-seven thousand volumes were once on the library shelves of the Scots College Paris.

Included in the Blairs Collection are the Album Amicorum of George Strachan which was carried to Scotland by John Farquharson, and the Book of Hours that was once thought to have belonged to Anne of Brittany, but we now know to have been owned by Marie de Rieux. Also in the National Library, though not in the Blairs Collection but by a separate deposit from Columba House on 11 April 1991, are six very special items. The first is the fifteenth century manuscript of the 'Scotichronicon' which had been presented to the Scots College, Paris by James Earl of Drummond in 1694. This had been rescued from Paris and was kept in the Archbishop's Library, Edinburgh, until placed in Columba House by Cardinal Gray. The second item is the Beaton Psalter. With these were deposited the four Glasgow cartularies, the sixteenth century *Rentale* or rental book of Glasgow; the *Protocol Book of Cuthbert Simon*; the *Registrum Vetus* which was the ancient Register of the See of Glasgow; and the *Liber Ruber*. These four Glasgow registers had been entrusted to Abbé MacPherson by Alexander Innes so that he could take them to the Scottish bishops, but the Abbé lent them to George Chalmers in London, with the result that the Catholic bishops had great difficulty in getting them back. One indeed, the *Liber Ruber*, had been lent by Chalmers to Thomas Thomson and found its way into the Scottish Record Office, and it was only in 1991 that Mark Dilworth, then keeper of the archives in Columba House, on production of receipts succeeded in getting it returned to the Scottish Catholic Archives. Now after two centuries, the four cartularies are together again, and lodged for safety in the National Library. The contents of the *Registrum Vetus* and of the *Liber Ruber* were published by the Bannatyne and Maitland Clubs among the muniments of the Church of Glasgow in 1843,[26] and the *Protocl Book of Cuthbert Simon* and the *Rental Book* of the Diocese of Glasgow were published by the Grampian Club in 1875.[27]

A few bound volumes, mostly manuscript rather than printed, from Paris are still lodged in Columba House, Edinburgh. They are as follows: the 'Book of Grisy', already described; the 'Necrology' of the Scots College, Paris, which had been lost, but was unexpectedly found in a grocer's shop in Paris; the manuscript of Gilbert Blakhal's *Breiffe Narration* brought from Paris by John Farquharson and the transcript by 'A.P.L.' (Alexander Leslie); a manuscript of Thomas Innes' *Civil and Ecclesiastical History* transcribed by Andrew Carruthers in 1794 from which the Spalding Club Edition of 1853 was largely taken; the manuscript of David Burnet's 'The Portrait of true Loyalty Exposed In the Family of Gordon, without interruption to this present year 1691' with 'A Relation of the Siege of the Castle of Edenbrughe in the year 1689'; the five volume 'Life of James II' by Dicconson; memoirs of Cardinal de Retz, entitled 'Suite Des memoires De Mr Le Cardinal de Retz'; a collection, mostly of printed items but including two in manuscript, concerning the Life and Death of King James VII and II, which has inscribed on the spine 'Recueil D'éloges Funèbres Jacques II Marie Therese Dsse D'Aiguillon &.&.'; two volumes of 'The Psalms of David, Translated from the Vulgate' in manuscript, beautifully bound in red leather with gold tooling and gold edges; a volume entitled 'Loci Communes'; another entitled, 'Méthode en abrégé pour bien faire le Catechisme'; and finally 'A Catalogue of the several Treatises written by JS for Catholic Faith'.

Three volumes from the library of the Mission of Chapeltown can be seen by their inscriptions to have come from the Scots College, Paris; they are catalogued as follows:

> Cicero, M.T. [Selecta opera. Parisiis, 1725]
> Ex lib. Coll. Scot. Parisiis; Joseph Henry, Chapeltown.
> Cartius Rufus, Qu. Historiarum libri. Amstelodami, 1644.
> Ex lib. Collegij Scotor Parisys; other names Scalan, Chapeltown.
> Le manu[el] de Grammarie[ns] Nouv. ed. Paris, 1712. Ex libris
> Collegii Scotorum; John Gordon. Chapeltown.[28]

These three works are now in the library of the Catholic Bishop of Aberdeen.

Maurice Caillet has published in the *Innes Review*[29] a list of books in the College des Irlandais which have a Scottish connection. 262 printed items and ten manuscripts are listed, but of these, only the works of the second section, listed under the heading 'owners' (Nos 49 to 100) can be said with certainty or probability to have belonged to the Scots College Paris. Twenty three works (Nos 49–71) have either the engraved or manuscript *ex libris* of the Scots College Paris. The library contains one other, a work by Denis Granville, not mentioned by Caillet, presumably omitted or overlooked because there is a second *ex libris* of the English College. The full entry in the card index catalogue reads

> B616 GRANVILLE (Denis) doyen de Durham, The Resigned and resolved christian and faithful and undaunted royalist... — Printed at Rouen, 1689, 4 part. en I vol, in–4. Ex libris ms. Ex biblioth, Colleg. Scot. Paris. ex dono illmi D.D. Edi Drumond de Perth — Ex libris gr. s. c. Ex bibliotheca Seminarii Anglorum Parisiis.[30]

These *ex libris* works are followed by four others (Nos 72–75) which probably came from the Scots College Paris. No.76 is inscribed 'ms. ex-libris: Miss. Scot. Soc. Jes.', and is the only work listed in the second section which cannot be said with probability to have belonged to the Scots College Paris. The individual owners of Nos 77–100 all had intimate connection with the Scots College Paris either as staff, students or benefactors, and there is thus a strong likelihood that these came from the Scots College. In total, fifty-two works now in the Irish College (certainly in some cases, probably in others) were once in the Scots College library.

The list, though small has much of interest. It includes a 'Cartularium Ecclesiae Glasguensis, T.2.', which is a manuscript collection of records concerning the Church in Glasgow and the University of Glasgow (probably the work of Thomas Innes). It is the second of two volumes, the first of which had found its way to St Andrew's College, Drygrange, but is now deposited in the Scottish Catholic Archives in Edinburgh. Three of the books were donated by Edward, Duke of Perth, and two by Gilbert Wauchope, both donors being highly regarded *alumni*, although both were Jansenists. It is not surprising to find one book in the collection, *Causa Quesneliana*, dealing with the Jansenist controversy, but we would not subscribe to the view of Professor McMillan that the presence of pro-Jansenist books in the College would reveal the views of the staff;[31] one would expect a College library to possess works of both sides in a controversy. The College possessed many works that defended Protestantism, but no one would make the deduction that the staff therefore adhered to the views of the authors. One book was won as a prize from the College of Navarre by Robert Grant in 1739. One work had been in the collection of David Chambers who had been Principal from 1637 until 1641. Another was from the books of Patrick Leith who had spent some time in the college in 1751, while on the way back to Britain from Rome. The manuscript books are of special interest. Some details of the work of Gilbert Brown have already been given. Three other manuscript volumes contain doctrinal tracts transcribed in his student days by Alexander Gordon, showing early propensity for theological studies. He became a Doctor of the Sorbonne, and died in the Scots College in 1724.

Maurice Caillet also lists two works in the Bibliotheque Sainte-Genevieve which bear the *ex libris* of the Scots College Paris, and a further two works in the Bibliothèque Nationale which bear the arms of Archbishop James Beaton who bequeathed his library to the Scots College Paris.

One volume, originally in the Scots College collection, is now in the Huntingdon Library, San Marino, California; it is the Book of Hours believed to have belonged to Mary Queen of Scots, purloined by Charles Mostyn at Saint Omer.

Thus over eight hundred works from the library of the Scots College Paris are still extant, and are now housed in the seven locations outlined above viz. The National Library, Edinburgh; Columba House, Edinburgh; Bishop's House, Aberdeen; Collège des Irlandais, Paris; Bibliothèque Sainte-Geneviève, Paris; Bibliothèque Nationale, Paris; and Huntingdon Library, San Marino, California.

The collection of documents rescued from Paris is no less impressive, and of more importance to historians. Most of the manuscript collection is now in the Scottish Catholic Archives in Columba House, Edinburgh,[32] having previously been kept partly at Preshome and partly at Blairs College, Aberdeen. Bishop James Kyle, Vicar Apostolic of the Northern District of Scotland from 1828 until 1869, began the sorting of the letters that came from Paris at his home in Preshome. He identified 'a considerable number' as older than the others and evidently part of Beaton's papers which included holograph letters of Mary Queen of Scotland.[33] He deciphered the secret letter code used in the diplomatic correspondence of Mary Stuart, thus rendering invaluable service to historians of her period. A large part of Archbishop Beaton's papers are now available in print.[34]

There are also in the Scottish Catholic Archives thousands of letters pertaining to the Scottish Mission and Colleges abroad. It would be extremely difficult now to ascertain the exact number of letters that came from the Paris College, as these were amalgamated into a general collection in which the letters are arranged chronologically in alphabetical order (of authors) for each year. Certainly from Paris are Historical Papers of Thomas Innes, now kept in two cardboard boxes and arranged under twelve headings. Perhaps the most impressive of these are twelve sewn sections of papers entitled 'Annales Scotiae ab AD 43 ad 1120'.

The five manuscript volumes of historical collections compiled by Thomas Innes, which were brought to Scotland by Abbé MacPherson, were given by him to George Chalmers in London, where they were bought by David Laing in 1842, and they are now in Edinburgh University Library.

The Nairne Papers being a dozen volumes of copies of royal correspondence, already referred to, which were purloined from the College by Thomas Carte, are now in the Bodleian Library at Oxford.

Two letters of Mary Queen of Scots which were once in the Scots College are now in the Pierpont Morgan Library, New York.

One of these letters, dated 12 February 1576, was purchased by Mr Morgan, about the year 1900, from a London dealer named J. Pearson. The other letter, dated 10 September 1571, was presented to the Pierpoint Morgan Library in 1974 by John P Fleming, a New York dealer, who had purchased it at Sotheby's in 1959, where it was described as having come from the collection of George Moffat (1806–1878) of Goodrich Court, Ross.[35]

Some letters from the Paris college were published in the *Miscellany of the Spalding Club*, Vol II pp.353–380. These papers had been brought to Ballogie by Henry Innes, a former Prefect of Studies at the College.

Other manuscript material from the college was used by Robert Watson who in 1820 anonymously published *Memoirs of the Rebellion in 1745 and 1746 by the Chevalier de Johnstone Translated from a French MS Originally deposited in the Scots College at Paris and now in the hands of the Publishers* (London: 1820). Robert Watson, having been employed by Napoleon to teach him English, had got himself appointed 'President of the Scotch College' in Paris, a nominal appointment which would nevertheless have given him access to any documents remaining in the College. Some other of the papers he obtained were later purchased and published in *Stuart Papers, Pictures, Relics, Medals and Books in the Collection of Miss Marion Widdrington.*

The manuscripts and letters from Paris are of extreme importance for the study of Catholicism in Scotland, are very valuable to Jacobite scholars, and have even been found a most useful source of information for aspects of Jansenism. The library and archival collection of the Scots College, Paris, was a magnificent achievement, and despite all the ravages of the French Revolution, the remnant is a most useful asset for the historian.

NOTES

1. McRoberts, D., 'The Scottish Catholic Archives, 1560–1978', *Innes Review* 28 (1977), pp.59–128.

2. Cherry,A., 'The Library and Archives of the Scots College, Paris.', *Bulletin de Bibliophile*, 1984, pp.327–364.
    Cherry, A., 'The Library of St Mary's College, Blairs, Aberdeen', *The Bibliotheck* 12, No. 3, (1984), pp.61–69.

3. Hochereau, *Nomenclature des Voies Publiques et Privées* (Paris 1885), p.309.

4. Archives Nationales, Paris, Etude Muret No. 91 liasse 306, 5.7.1655.

5. Chapter 5 of this thesis, p.101. p.109.

6. College des Irlandais, Paris, MS 63.

7. *Dictionary of National Biography* (London 1885–1900) (Henceforward referred to as D.N.B.), 'Sir Robert Sibbald' Vol 52, pp.179–181.

8. Innes, T., *The Civil and Ecclesiastical History of Scotland; A.D. LXXX–DCCCXVIII*, (Aberdeen 1853), p.IX and p.X.

9. SCA/P–TI 4/1.

10. Archives Nationales, Paris, H 3, 2552, Register of College de Navarre

11. Brand, J., *A short Account of the Life and Writings of the Rev. Thomas Innes,* (Glasgow 1905).

12. McLaren, R., 'Father Thomas Innes: Lost Papers', *Innes Review* 5, (1954), p.78.

13. Innes, T., *A Critical Essay on the Ancient Inhabitants of the Northern Parts of Britain or Scotland* (London 1729).

14. Waddel, A., 'Waddell's Remarks on Innes Critical Essay' (Edinburgh: 1733), *Tracts Illustrative of Traditionary & Historical Antiquities of Scotland* (Edinburgh) pp. 225–256.

15. Tait, A., *'Taits Roman Account of Britain and Ireland Answer to Father Innes & c,* (Edinburgh: 1741)',
    Tracts Illustrative of the Traditionary & Historical Antiquities of Scotland, (Edinburgh), pp. 305–326.

16. Mason, R.A., 'Scotching the Brut: Politics, History and National Myth in Sixteenth-Century Britain', Scotland and England 1286–1815, Edinburgh: John Donald, 1987, p.77.
    Kidd, C., 'Antiquarianism, religion and the Scottish Enlightenment', *Innes Review* 46 (1995), p.147.

17. Innes, T., *The Civil and Ecclesiastical History of Scotland; A.D. LXXX–DCCCXVIII* (Aberdeen 1853).

18. Anderson, W.J., 'Narratives of the Scottish Reformation, II. Thomas Innes on Catholicism in Scotland 1560–1653', *Innes Review* 7 (1956), pp.112–121.

19. *D.N.B.*, 'William Hamilton of Wishaw', Vol. 24, p.220.

20. *D.N.B.*, 'Harry Maule', Vol. 37, pp.85f.

21. Bibliotheque Nationale, Paris, 19639 'Letters & Memoirs on the Life of Mabillon'
    f.156 Louis Innes to Thierry Ruinart, 5 Aug 1718
    f.158f Thomas Innes to Thierry Ruinart
    f.160 Thomas Innes to Thierry Ruinart
    f.162 Thomas Innes to Thierry Ruinart
    19666 'Thierry Ruinart Correspondence'
    f.46 Thomas Innes to Thierry Ruinart
    f.48 Thomas Innes to Thierry Ruinart

22. SCA/Bl Lett 3/75/5, 5 April 1742, Thomas Innes to Bishop Smith.

23. SCA/Bl Lett 3/75/8, 18 Apr 1742, Thomas Innes to Bishop Gordon.

24. SCA/Bl Lett 3/79/16, 15 August 1743, Thomas Innes to Bishop Smith.

25. Alexander Gordon to Andrew Lumsden, 2 Sept 1792, Glasgow Registrum i, viii, quoted in McRoberts, D., 'The Scottish Catholic Archives 1560–1978', *Innes Review*, Vol. 28 (1971), p.88.

26. Registrum Episcopatus Glasguensis: Munimenta Ecclesie Metropolitane Glasguensis, Vols 1 & 2, Edinburgh: Bannatyne & Maitland Clubs, 1843.

27. Bain, J. & Rogers, C., Liber Protocollorum M. Cuthberti Simonis...also Rental Book of Diocese of Glasgow, Vols 1 & 2, London: Grampian Club, 1875.

28. SCA/GD 50, Copy of Chapeltown collection catalogue.

29. Caillet, M., 'Scotland in the Antiquarian Collection of the Library of the Scots College in Paris', *Innes Review* Vol. 43 (1992), pp.18–52.

30. College des Irlandais, Paris, Card Index (Provenances).

31. McMillan, J., 'Scottish Catholics and the Jansenist Controversy: The Case Reopened', *Innes Review*, Vol. 32 (1981), p.31.

32. Dilworth, M., 'The Scottish Catholic Archives', *Catholic Archives* 1 (1981), pp.1019.

33. Dilworth, M., 'Archbishop Beaton's Papers in the Scottish Catholic Archives', *Innes Review* 34 (1983), p.3.

34. Beaton Papers have been published in:
    Miscellaneous Papers principally illustrative of events in the reigns of Queen Mary and King James VI, Glasgow: Maitland Club, 1834.
    Labanoff, A., *Lettres, instructions et mémoires de Marie Stuart, Reine d'Ecosse*, 7 Vols, (London 1844).
    Hosack, J., *Mary, Queen of Scots and her Accusers*, Vol 2, (Edinburgh & London 1874), pp.502–565.
    Some of the Labanoff documents were published in English in:
    Turnbull, W., *Letters of Mary Stuart, Queen of Scotland* (London 1845).

35. McRoberts, D., op. cit., p.112.

Epilogue

In Retrospect

At the beginning of the seventeenth century, the Scots College Paris appeared to be in a most advantageous position to further the success of the mission. Situated in the University of Paris, the college could enable the students to receive a high standard of education and a broadness of mind. It could have been confidently expected that its graduates would be able to remedy the great dearth of Catholic literature. With the College of Douai in the hands of the Jesuits, and, after 1615, Jesuit Rectors in charge of the Scots College in Rome, the Scots College Paris was the one college that the secular clergy could claim as their own. It was the one best placed to provide secular priests for the Scottish mission.

Although very few priests came to Scotland from Paris in the first half of the seventeenth century, most of the small group of secular priests who were successful in obtaining a permanent subsidy from Rome, and in gaining the establishment of a Prefecture with a secular priest in charge, had pursued at least some of their studies in the Paris College, where they had come under the influence of David Chambers who was Principal from 1637 to 1641.

In the principalship of Robert Barclay (1655–1682), the college began to realise more of its potential. Although the college still did not produce very many priests, numbers were quite favourable when compared with those from Rome, and two religious works were produced by the staff of the college, the apologetic work of John Walker entitled *The Presbytery's Triall* and the devotional work of William Ballantine entitled *Preparation for Death*. The new building commissioned by Robert Barclay gave the college such prestige that more of the gentry and nobility began to send their sons.

With Louis Innes at the helm, numbers of ordinations could again be favourably compared with those from Rome, though partly because neither college was doing exceptionally well. What gave the Paris College more influence was that three of the priests who were trained there became bishops. After 1713, however, there was a decided decline.

The most common assessment of the Scots College Paris is that it had what might be called 'a golden age' in the time of the Inneses, but later fell into decline through the truculent and stubborn behaviour of the two Gordon principals who selfishly refused to co-operate with the Scottish

195

Bishops. The Inneses are indeed renowned, but not on account of their good government of the college. Louis Innes is famous as a Jacobite politician and royal almoner, and also for his personal generosity to the Scottish Mission which enabled the establishment of seminaries on Scottish soil. As Principal of the college, he was seldom there; even before the Revolution of 1688, he was more away than present, and after the Revolution he stayed mostly at St Germain. Thomas Innes is famous as an archivist and an historian. Bishop Gordon found him very remiss in the exercise of his duties, and it would appear that his antiquarian interests led him to neglect the care of the students. George Innes deserves credit for starting the seminary at Morar, and restarting the seminary at Scalan in most difficult times. This achievement outweighs that of his principal-ship (1738–1752) during which only two students reached the priesthood. It could even be argued that the Scots College Paris would have flourished better without the Inneses, and that there was a certain nepotism in their continued control over such a long period (1682–1752). It would be hard to defend the way in which Louis Innes continued to influence the college after his resignation of office in 1713.

The decline of the Scots College Paris can be attributed chiefly to the excessive pre-occupation with the political cause of Jacobitism, and the reactionary stance on Jansenism. Louis Innes and Thomas Innes were the men best able to lead the college, but they both made the Jacobite King's interests their priority, the first by sacrificing his college life for his political endeavours, and the second by devoting most of his energies to writing his history 'at the King's command'. The Jacobite outlook of the whole college was best seen by the percentage of *alumni* involved in the Forty-five, which it could be argued, could never have taken place were it not for the early initiatives of Aeneas Macdonald, young Clanranald and the Duke of Perth.

The reluctance of the staff, especially Thomas Innes, to accept *Unigenitus* led to bitter and damaging quarrels on the Scottish Mission, but was even more damaging to the college itself. As the priests of the college had honourably refrained from any open dissent, they were most unfortunate to get involved in public disputes. There is little doubt about the presence of ulterior motives, particularly the episcopal ambition of Colin Campbell, and the erroneous belief of some of the Highland clergy that the college had misappropriated part of the Law bequest that was due to them, but the accusations and quarrels might have had far less impact had not Bishop Gordon and Bishop Macdonald denounced the college to Rome in the so-called Clashinore letters. What they said was not untrue, but the method of denunciation to Rome and asking for the removal of staff before the college itself was contacted was both unnecessary and underhand. The cover-up afterwards was worse. In every other respect, Bishop Gordon was a wonderful bishop and a great credit to the Scots College Paris which trained him. He was accustomed to acting with impartiality, and listened with sympathy, but as this incident showed, too ready to accept the viewpoint of those who were present with him, and it was tragic that an *alumnus* dealt such a blow.

Although Jacobitism and Jansenism were very different in essence, they interacted. Both were to some extent anachronistic, looking back to the glories of the past. Wedded together they produced a kind of royal Gallicanism in which the crown was seen as a necessary safeguard against ecclesiastical encroachments. Thus Louis Innes had maintained that subscription to *Unigenitus* should not have been enforced without the royal consent. Both movements had the effect of making the college secretive, and of fostering a kind of persecution complex, neither of which contributed to the good image of the college.

To a lesser extent, quarrels with the Jesuits had also been detrimental. In the first fifty years and in Robert Barclay's time, there were several attempts by the Jesuits to gain control of the college, and a tussle for students between Jesuits and seculars. Charles Whyteford as Principal indulged in criticising the Jesuits to his students which had the opposite effect to what he intended as it turned the students against himself. In the Jansenist debates, Jesuits and ex-Jesuits joined forces with the accusers of the college, and sent many letters of complaint to Rome.

Along with secular-Jesuit frictions, there were tensions amongst the secular clergy themselves, and the Scots College Paris experienced the antipathy of several priests trained in Rome. In the seventeenth century, there were criticisms from William Leslie, the Scots agent in Rome, and from Alexander Dunbar, Prefect of the Mission, and in the latter days of the college, bishops who were educated in Rome had little time for a college over which they had no control. Although most Catholic historians blame the principals, especially Principal Alexander Gordon, it is hard to exonerate Bishop Hay who went as far as to say that the Scottish Mission had no responsibility to meet the needs of Paris-educated priests in sickness or old age. The internal squabbles were unnecessary and very damaging, and it was in fact these divisions that led to the ineffectiveness of the college in its last years.

Taking an over-all look at the achievement of the college, it is hard to deny a sense of disappointment that the college did not realise its full potential. As the Stuart cause finally failed, the Jacobite activities of the college did not prove beneficial to the Scottish Catholic Mission, but left

Catholics very much disadvantaged. The Jansenist quarrels were damaging to the mission. Yet the college did contribute to the education of about seventy priests, most of whom gave useful service to the Church, and the Scots College Paris did produce three of the first five bishops in Scotland. It gave both the finance and the personnel to get the native Scottish seminaries started, with four of the first six rectors of Scalan being *alumni* of the college. The development of the library and archives was a magnificent achievement, and although the collection was severely ravaged at the French Revolution, the remnant remaining is a very valuable resource for historians. The college also left the heritage of a robust spirit of independence whereby priests were unafraid to voice their disagreements with bishops. There has been no attempt to disguise the weaknesses and very human difficulties of the members of the college, but even in these, to all who are struggling against the odds, the Scots College Paris may serve as an inspiration.

Bibliography

Primary Sources Unpublished

Archives Historiques du Depnt de l'Aube, Troyes
    Registre G. 53.

Archives Nationales, Paris
    Étude Muret XCI
    Register of College of Navarre, H 3, 2552.
    L 502, cote 31–33.

Bibliothèque Nationale, Paris
    19639 Letters & Memoirs on the Life of Mabillon
    19666 Thierry Ruinart Correspondence

Collège des Irlandais, Paris
    MS 63.
    Card Index (Provenances)

Scottish Catholic Archives, Columba House, Edinburgh
    Avery, A collection of documentary information about the Scots College, collected in Paris by Fr Avery, SCA./GC 13/1
    Blairs Letters
    Book of Grisy CA 1/1
    Clapperton, William, 'Memoirs of Scotch Missionary Priests, Compiled from original letters', Revised and Transcribed by Very Revd George Canon Wilson, Four Volumes, Elgin: 1901.
    Colleges Abroad Letters
    College Oath, CA 1/11
    Copy of Chapeltown collection catalogue, GD 50/1 &2.
    Farquharson, J. 'History of Scots College, Paris' MS CA I/29.
    Guides, Cipher Aliases, D 3.
    Hamilton, E.J., Letter to W.J. Anderson 16 January 1960, W.J. Anderson correspondence (in process of cataloguing)
    Leslie, Alexander, 'Itinerary of Alexander Leslie, Visitor of the Scots Mission', SM 2/9/1, copy from Aberdeen University, Kings College, 2260 Box R., transcript, original presumably in Rome, Archives Propaganda Fide.
    Necrology of the Scots College, Paris. CA 1/7
    Scottish Mission Letters
    Statutes of the Scots College, Paris, CA 1/10/2.

Jesuit Archives, Rome
    ANGLIA 5, Miss. Scotica Epistolae 1740–1749.
    NEAP. CAT. TRIEN 85, 1665–1669.

Mairie, Bourguinons
    Registre des marriages et des sépultures 1773–1686

Propaganda Archives, Rome
    ACTA

CP 86 CP 87.
SC (Scozia Vols 1 & 2

Scottish Record Office, Edinburgh
GD 18/2364/6

Vatican Library, Rome.
Barberini Latini 8614.
Barberini Latini 8628

Primary Sources Published

Abbott, W.M.(Ed.), *The Documents of Vatican II* (London, Dublin, Melbourne, 1967)

Anderson, P.J. (Ed.), *Records of the Scots Colleges at Douai, Rome, Madrid, Valladolid and Ratisbon,* Vol I (Aberdeen 1906)

Anderson, P.J. (Ed.), *Roll of Alumni in Arts of the University and King's College of Aberdeen 1596–1860* (Aberdeen 1900)

Bain, J. & Rogers, C., *Liber Protocollorum M. Cuthberti Simonis...also Rental Book of Diocese of Glasgow*, 2 Vols (London 1875)

Birch, T. (Ed.), *A Collection of the State Papers of John Thurloe, Esq.; secretary, first to the Council of State, and afterwards to the Two Protectors, Oliver and Richard Cromwell in Seven Volumes, etc.* (London 1742)

Blakhal, G., *A Breiffe Narration of the Services done to Three Noble Ladyes, 1631–1649* (Aberdeen 1844)

Botfield, B. (Ed.), *Original Letters relating to the Ecclesiastical Affairs of Scotland chiefly written by, or addressed to His Majesty King James the Sixth after his accession to the English Throne*, 2 Vols (Edinburgh 1851)

Daniell, F.H.(Ed.), *Calendar of the Stuart Papers belonging to His Majesty the King preserved at Windsor Castle*, 5 Vols (London 1902–1912)

Dickson, W.K., *The Jacobite Attempt of 1719, Letters of James Butler, second Duke of Ormonde, relating to Caerdinal Alberoni's project for the invasion of Great Britain on behalf of the Stuarts, and to the landing of a Spanish expedition in Scotland* (Edinburgh 1895)

Gordon, A., *Mémoire de M. Gordon, Principal du Collège de Écossois à Paris, pour servir de réponse a l'invective de M. l'Évêque Hay, contre les supérieurs et élèves du dit Collège* (1785)

Hamilton, W., *Descriptions of the Sheriffdoms of Lanark and Renfrew compiled about MDCCX* (Glasgow 1831)

Hosack, J., *Mary Queen of Scots and her Accusers*, Vol 2 (Edinburgh & London 1874), pp. 502–565.

Johnstone, J.F.K., *The Alba Amicorum of George Strachan, George Craig, Thomas Cumming* (Aberdeen University Studies: No. 95) (Aberdeen 1924)

Labanoff, A., *Lettres, instructions et mémoires de Marie Stuart, Reine d'Écosse*, 7Vols (London 1844)

Leslie, W. A., *Laurus Leslaeana explicata sive clarior enumeratio personarum utriusque sexus cognominis Leslie etc.* (Graz 1692).

Miscellaneous Papers principally illustrative of events in the reigns of Queen Mary and King James VI (Glasgow 1834)

Panzani, G., *The Memoirs of Gregorio Panzani; giving an account of his agency in England in the Years 1634, 1635, 1636* (Birmingham 1793)

Pius XII, *Mystici Corporis Christi*, Tr Smith, G.D. (London 1951)

Registrum Episcopatus Glasguensis: Munimenta Ecclesie Metropolitane Glasguensis, 2 Vols (Edinburgh 1843)

Registrum Episcopatus Moraviensis (Edinburgh 1837)

Turnbull, W., *Letters of Mary Stuart, Queen of Scotland* (London 1845)

Secondary Sources

Anderson, W.J., 'The Scots College, Paris: Seal and Book-Plates', *Innes Review* 18 (1967), pp. 64–66.

Anderson, W.J., 'Presbyteries Triall', *Innes Review* 8 (1957), pp. 86–90.

Anderson, W.J., 'Abbé Paul Macpherson's History of the Scots College, Rome', *Innes Review*, Vol 12 (1961), pp. 3–172.

Anderson, W.J., 'The Book of Zaknim', *Innes Review*, Vol 14 (1963), pp. 134–164.

Anderson, W.J., 'Notes on Illustrations', *Innes Review*, Vol 14 (1963), pp. 205–212.

Anson, P.F., *Underground Catholicism in Scotland 1622–1878* (Montrose 1970)

Ararat, R., *The Jacobite Peerage, Baronetage, Knightage, & Grants of Honour* (London & Edinburgh 1974)

Barclay, H.F. & Wilson-Fox, A.(Eds), *A History of the Barclay Family with Pedigrees from 1067 to 1933*, 3 Volumes (London 1934)

Barclay, R., (Mill, H. ed.), *A Genealogical Account of the Barclays of Urie for upwards of seven hundred years etc.* (London 1812)

Bellesheim, A., tr. Blair, O. H., *History of the Catholic Church of Scotland from the introduction of Christianity to the present day*, 4 Vols (Edinburgh & London 1887–1890)

Blaikie, W.B., *Itinerary of Prince Charles Edward Stuart from his landing in Scotland July 1745 to his departure in September 1746. Compiled from The Lyon in Mourning supplemented and corrected from other contemporary sources* (Edinburgh 1975)

Brand, J., *A Short Account of the Life and Writings of the Rev Thomas Innes, Sometime Rector of the Scots College of Paris, with copy af A Correspondence with the University of Glasgow, dated 1738* (Glasgow 1905)

Bulloch, J.M., *The House of Gordon*, 3 Vols (Aberdeen 1903–1912)

Caillet, M., 'Scotland in the Antiquarian Collection of the Library of the Scots College in Paris', *Innes Review*, Vol 43 (1992), pp. 18–52.

Carr, J.L., *Le Collège des Écossais à Paris (1662–1962)* (Paris 1963)

Chambers, D. *De Fortitudine Scotorum* (Paris 1631)

Cherry, A., 'The Library and Archives of the Scots College, Paris', *Bulletin de Bibliophilie*, 1984, pp. 327–364.

Cherry, A., 'The Library of St. Mary's College, Blairs, Aberdeen', *The Bibliotheck*, 12, No. 3,(1984), pp. 61–69.

Clark, R., *Strangers & Sojourners at Port Royal; Being an account of the connections between the British Isles and the Jansenists of France and Holland* (Cambridge 1932)

Complete Baronetage Vol II (1625–1649), ed. G.E.C. (Exeter 1902)

Dellavida, G.L., *George Strachan, memorials of a wandering Scottish scholar of the seventeenth century* (Aberdeen 1956)

Dempster, T., *Historia Ecclesiastica Gentis Scotorum: sive, de Scriptoribus Scotis*, 2 Vols (Edinburgh 1829)

Denzinger, H., *Enchiridion Symbolorum definitionum et declarationum de rebus fidei et morum*, Editio 18–20 (Friburg 1932)

Dictionary of National Biography, 63 Vols, Ed. Lee, S. (London 1885–1900)

Dictionary of Scottish Church History and Theology, ed. Cameron, N.M. de S. (Edinburgh 1993)

Dilworth, M., *The Scots in Franconia* (Edinburgh & London 1974)

Dilworth, M., 'The Scottish Mission in 1688–1689', *Innes Review* Vol 20 (1969), pp. 68–79.

Dilworth, M., 'The Scottish Catholic Archives', *Catholic Archives*, Vol 1 (1981), pp. 10–19.

Dilworth, M., 'A Jesuit that calls himself Ogilvy', *Innes Review* Vol 34 (1983), pp. 5165.

Dilworth, M., 'Archbishop James Beaton's Papers in the Scottish Catholic Archives', *Innes Review* Vol 34 (1983), pp. 3–8.

Dilworth, M., 'The Counter-Reformation in Scotland: A Select Critical Bibliography', *Scottish Church History Society Records*, Vol 22 (1986), pp. 85–100.

Dilworth, M., 'Archbishop James Beaton II: A Career in Scotland and France', *Scottish Church History Society Records*, Vol 23 (1989), pp. 301–316.

Durkan, J., 'Rev. Alexander Gordon', *Innes Review* 1 (1950), pp. 68–70.

Durkan, J., 'Scots College, Paris', *Innes Review* 2 (1951), pp. 112–113.

Durkan, J., 'Grisy Burses at Scots College, Paris', *Innes Review*, 22 (1971), pp. 50–52.

Durkan, J. (as McLaren, R.), 'Father Thomas Innes: Lost Papers', *Innes Review* 5 (1954), p. 78.

Eggenberger, D.(executive editor), *New Catholic Encyclopedia*, 17 Volumes (New York, St Louis, San Francisco, Toronto, London 1967)

Felibien, M., *Histoire de la ville de Paris* (Paris 1725).

Forbes-Leith, W., *Narratives of Scottish Catholics under Mary Stuart and James VI* (Edinburgh 1885)

Forbes-Leith, W., *Memoirs of Scottish Catholics during the XVIIth and XVIIIth centuries*, Vols I & II (London, New York, Bombay & Calcutta.1909)

Fraser, Alexander, *The Frasers of Philorth*, 3 Vols (Edinburgh 1879)

Giblin, C., 'The "Acta" of Propaganda Archives and the Scottish Mission, 1623–1670', *Innes Review*, Vol 5 (1954) pp. 39–76.

Gibson, J.S., *Playing the Scottish Card; The Franco-Jacobite Invasion of 1708* (Edinburgh 1988)

Gordon, A., *History of Peter the Great, Emperor of Russia*, 2 Vols (Aberdeen 1755)

Gordon, J.F.S. (Ed.), *The Catholic Church in Scotland, from the suppression of the hierarchy till the present time, being memorabilia of the Bishops, Missioners and Scotch Jesuits* (Glasgow 1869)

Gordon, J. of Glencat, *Memoirs of the life of John Gordon of Glencat, in the county of Aberdeen in Scotland: who was thirteen years in the Scotch College at Paris, among the secular clergy* (London 1733)

Groome, F.H., *Ordnance Gazeteer of Scotland, a survey of Scottish topography, statistical, biographical and historical* (London, Edinburgh, Glasgow 1882–1885)

Halloran, B. M., 'Neil MacEachan at Scots College Paris', *Innes Review*, Vol 43 (1992), pp. 176–181.

Halloran, B. M., 'Spirited Scottish Students: the Scots College Paris in 1639', *Innes Review* Vol 45 (1994), pp. 171–177.

Harding, E., *The masterpiece of imposture, or the adventures of Gordon and the Countess of Gordon, alias Countess Dalco, containing...an answer to the late memoirs of...J. Gordon of Glencat, etc* (London 1734)

Hay, M.V., *The Blairs Papers (1603–1660)* (London and Edinburgh 1929)

Hay, R. A., *Genealogie of the Hayes of Tweeddale* (Edinburgh 1835)

Helyot, *Histoire des Ordres Monastiques, Religieux et Militaires et des Congregations seculiers de L'un & de l'autre sexe, qui ont été établies jusqu'à present*, 8 Vols, (Paris 1718)

Hemphill, B., *The Early Vicars Apostolic of England 1685–1750* (London 1954)

Hochereau, M., *Nomenclature des Voies Publiques et Privées*, 3rd Edition (Paris 1885)

Innes, T., *A Critical Essay on the Ancient Inhabitants of the Northern Parts of Britain or Scotland containing An Account of the Romans, of the Britains betwixt the Walls, of the Caledonians or Picts, and particularly of the Scots. With an Appendix of ancient MS Pieces*, Vols I & II (London 1729)

Innes, T., *The Civil and Ecclesiastical History of Scotland; A.D. LXXX–DCCCXVIII*, (Aberdeen 1853)

Innes, T., 'The Inneses of Balnacraig. A Family of Deeside Jacobites', *The Deeside Field*, fifth number (1931), pp. 76–83.

Johnson, C., *Developments in the Roman Catholic Church in Scotland 1789–1829* (Edinburgh 1983)

Johnson, C., 'Secular Clergy of the Lowland District 1732–1829', *Innes Review* 34 (1983), pp. 66–87.

Lang, A., *Pickle the Spy or The Incognito of Prince Charles* (London. New York and Bombay 1897)

Lees, J.C., *The Abbey of Paisley, from its foundation till its dissolution* (Paisley 1878)

Lenman, B., 'The Scottish Episcopal Clergy and Ideology of Jacobitism', Cruickshanks, E., *Ideology and Conspiracy: Aspects of Jacobitism, 1689–1759*, pp. 36–48.

Leslie, K.H., *Historical Records of the Family of Leslie from 1067 to 1868–9 etc.* (Edinburgh 1869)

MacEachain, N., 'The Young Pretender', *The New Monthly Magazine and Humorist* 60 (1840), pp. 323–343.

MacKenzie, A.M., *Robert Bruce King of Scots* (London 1935).

Maclean,A., *A Macdonald for the Prince; the Story of Neil MacEachen* (Stornoway 1982)

McMillan, J.F., 'Scottish Catholics and the Jansenist Controversy: the Case Reopened', *Innes Review* 32 (1981), pp. 22–33.

McMillan, J.F., 'Thomas Innes and the Bull "Unigenitus" ', *Innes Review* 33 (1982), pp. 23–30.

McMillan, J.F., 'Jansenists and Anti-Jansenists in Eighteenth Century Scotland: The Unigenitus Quarrels on the Scottish Catholic Mission, 1732–1746', *Innes Review* 39 (1988), pp. 12–45.

McNeill, W.A., 'Documents Illustrative of the History of the Scots College, Paris', *Innes Review* 15 (1964), pp. 66–85.

McRoberts, D., 'The Scottish Catholic Archives, 1560–1976', *Innes Review* 26 (1977), pp. 59–128.

Mason, R.A., 'Scotching the Brut: Politics, History and National Myth in Sixteenth–Century Britain', *Scotland and England 1286–1815*, (Ed. R.A. Mason) (Edinburgh 1987)

Montagu, V.M., 'The Scottish College in Paris', *The Scottish Historical Review* Vol 4 (1907), pp. 399–416.

Oliphant, T.L.K., *The Jacobite Lairds of Gask* (London 1870)

Paul, J.B. (Ed.), *The Scots Peerage, founded on Wood's edition of Sir Robert Douglas's Peerage of Scotland, containing an historical and genealogical account of the nobility of that kingdom*, 8 Volumes (Edinburgh 1904–1911)

Prebble, J., *Culloden* (London 1961)

Prevost, M. & D'Arrat R. (Eds), *Dictionnaire de Biographie Française* Vol VI (Paris 1954)

Raunié, E., *Épitaphies du Vieux Paris Recueil Général des Inscriptions Funéraires des églises, couvents, hospices, cimetières et charniers depuis le moyen âge jusqu'à la fin du XVIIIe siècle*, Tom III (Paris 1901)

Ritzler, R. & Sefrin, P., *Hierarchia Catholica Medii et Recentioris Aevi*, Vol 6 (Padua 1958)

Saint-Clair, R.W., *The Saint-Clairs of the Isles etc* (Auckland, N.Z. 1898)

The Scots College Rome, a tribute of the Scots College Society (London & Edinburgh 1930)

Simpson, G.G., 'Letters of Father Thomas Innes about the Archives of the Church of Glasgow', *Innes Review* 13 (1962), pp. 62–70.

Stuart, J. (Ed.), 'Papers by Father Innes', *The Miscellany of the Spalding* Club, Vol 2 (Aberdeen 1842), pp. 351–380.

Tait. A., *Tait's Roman Account of Britain and Ireland in Answer to Father Innes & c, Edinburgh: 1741, Tracts Illustrative of the Traditionary & Historical Antiquities of Scotland* (Edinburgh)

Tayler, A. & H., *Jacobites of Aberdeenshire and Banffshire in the Forty-five*, 2nd Ed (Aberdeen 1928)

Tayler, A. & H., *Jacobites of Aberdeenshire and Banffshire in the Rising of 1715* (Edinburgh & London 1734)

Tayler, H., *Lady Nithsdale and her Family* (London 1939)

Taylor, M., *The Scots College in Spain* (Valladolid 1971)

Terry, C.S. (Ed.), *The Jacobites and the Union, being a narrative of the movements of 1708, 1715, 1719 by several contemporary hands* (Cambridge 1922)

The Register of the Privy Council of Scotland (Edinburgh 1877–1933)

Waddell, A., *Waddell's Remarks on Innes' Critical Essay on the Ancient Inhabitants of Scotland, Edinburgh: 1733. Tracts Illustrative of the Traditionary & Historical Antiquities of Scotland* (Edinburgh)

Waterworth, J., *The Canons and Decrees of the Sacred and Oecumenical Council of Trent, celebrated under the Sovereign Pontiffs, Paul III, Julius III and Pius IV* (London & New York 1848)

Appendix 1: Known Bursars of Grisy

	Assigned	*Demitted*
William de Camera	1384	
Geoffrey Norman		1467
William Winchester	2 Sept 1467	
William Forrester	2 Sept 1486	1502
John Hervey	30 Aug 1502	
George Lokert	15 Jan 1526	
William Cranston	(1549)	
John Stuart	(1549)	
John Mattheison	(1549)	
John Rule	(1549)	
John Hay		
Thomas Makeson		1556
Thomas Wynterhop	27 May 1556	
David Henderson	(1558)	
John Scot	(1558)	
George Critton		1600
William Lumsden	3 Sept 1600	
Michael Christy		1609
William Lumsden	19 May 1609	
Robert Pendrick		1627
William Bellenden	14 April 1627	
Alexander Pendrick		1637
David Chambers	24 Sept 1637	1639
John Heries	7 Oct 1637	1638
Patrick Con	21 Jan 1638	1639
John Black	19 Aug 1638	1639

Appendix 2: Partially Reconstructed Register of the Scots College Paris

Italicised Names = those who were ordained priests.
    + = those who became bishops.
    * = members of the peerage.
    # = those who became clan chieftains.

Principalship of William Lumsden 1604–

1. *David Chambers* (possible), son of Patrick Chambers of Fintry, Aberdeen diocese, studied Aberdeen University, convert, ordained prob Paris c.1609, Principal of College 1637–1641, died 17/18 Jan 1641.

2. William Lumsden, cleric, Aberdeen diocese, recd. burse 19 May 1609.

3. William Fraser, probably younger son of the second Laird of Techmuiry. diocese of Aberdeen, entered Scots College Paris 1 July 1611, died at Paris 8 February 1661.

College under Care of Robert Philip & Aex Pendrick — 1617

1617   5 Theological students in the college.

Principalship of Alexander Pendrick 1617–1637

4. George Con, (possible), son of Patrick Con of Achry & Isabella Chyn, Aberdeen diocese, entered Rome 1619, left Rome 1619, died 10 January 1640.

5. *Patrick Gordon*, of Letterfourie, Aberdeen diocese, Rome 1616–1619, entered Scots College Paris 1619, ordained Paris c. 1626, died 8 July 1653.

6. Robert (Andrew) Maclean, from Dumfries, diocese of Galloway, born 1604,left Scots College Paris for Douai in 1621, went to Würzburg May 1623, died before September 1628.

7. *Andrew Leslie* (possible), diocese of Moray, born 1597. seminary of Braunsberg 1613–1618, entered Rome 1618, left Rome for France 1621, ordained Paris? c.1625, later Jesuit, died 1654.

8. Hugh Ferguson, diocese of Ross, came from Douai about Pentecost 1622, but sent back again after two months.

9. John Gordon, from Boghole, Nairnshire, diocese of Moray, left from Paris for Douai at age of 15 in 1623. On account of plague, he was sent back, but died on the way in August 1626.

1623   2 students in the college

10. James Grant, from Strathspey, diocese of Moray, entered Douai 28 July 1620, and after recuperation from exhaustion in Scotland was sent back 15 May 1625. He died in the Scots College, Paris 1626.

11. John Abercromby, born c.1613 son of a page of Kirk of Rayne, Aberdeen diocese, left for Douai 7 April 1627.

12. A. Gordon?, arrived Paris 7 December 1627.

13. J. Alexander?, arrived Paris 7 December 1627.

14. *Thomas Chambers* Snr, diocese of Aberdeen, born 1604, seminary of Braunsberg 1619–1625, probably at Scots College Paris before entering Rome 21 Oct 1629, ordained Rome c.1632, died 8 March 1661.

15. *George Leith*, diocese of Aberdeen, entered Rome 1634, ordained 1641, Principal of Scots College Paris 1641–1655.

Pricipalship of David Chambers 1637–1641

16. *William Ballantine*, diocese of Galloway, born 1618, convert, student at Paris before entering Rome in 1641, ordained Rome on 3 Dec 1645, Prefect of the Mission 13 Oct 1653, died Elgin 2 Sept 1661.

17. *James Crichton*, diocese of Glasgow, student at Paris before entering Rome in 1642, ordained Rome, left Rome 1645 and served on mission, apostatised 1655/6, repented 1660, died June 1660.

18. *James Ramsay*, entered Rome 1643, ordained c.1647, became Curé of Bourguignon, France, died 6 July 1684.

19. *Thomas Lumsden*, diocese of Aberdeen, at Scots College Paris before entering Rome 1644, ordained Rome 1645, died 28 June 1671.

20. *Robert Barclay*, son of David Barclay of Mathers and Elizabeth Livingston, diocese of Aberdeen, graduated Aberdeen University 1633, all ecclesiastical studies in Scots College Paris before 1647, Principal of Scots College, Paris 1655–1682. Died 7 Feb 1682.

1638   10 or 12 students in the college.

21. John Heries, from Kirkudbright, Galloway diocese, received bursary 7 October 1637, resigned bursary before 21 January 1638.

22. Patrick Con, diocese of Aberdeen, born 1610, received bursary as tonsured cleric 21 January 1638, renounced bursary 1 September 1638, died Paris 21 November 1694.

23. *John Black*, received bursary 19 August 1638, renounced bursary 31 August 1638, became Chaplain to Nuns at Chantilly, near Paris.

24. _____ Forrester, son of William Forrester, Canongate, Edinburgh, diocese of St Andrews, entered October 1638. Very short stay. Became a soldier.

Principalship of George Leith 1641–1655
(Gilbert Blackhall Principal 1655)

25. John Leith, son of John Leith and Margaret Mortimer, diocese of Aberdeen, at Rome, then entered Douai 1637, left for Scots College Paris 14 August 1643.

26. *John Menzies*, son of Thomas Menzies of Balgownie & Margaret Gordon, diocese of Aberdeen, born 1727, at Scots College Paris 1643–1645, at Madrid 1645–1647, became Canon of St Geneviève 1649.

27. James Bethune, son of Dr James Bethune and Janet Goldman, diocese of St Andrews, born c.1631, at college c.1645–48, married Elizabeth Blair (the couple had 10 children), 'practised medicine wt very good success at Coupar in Fyfe' c. 1655–1685, died before 1690.

28. John Abercromby, left college for Ratisbon September 1646, but went to Würzburg where he took the habit.

29. *David (Placid) Keith*, left college for Ratisbon September 1646, but went to Würzburg where he took the habit, in Poland 1662 (?).

30. Patrick Lumsden, son of William Lumsden & Helen Barclay, Aberdeen diocese, born 1626, at Douai 1641–1646, entered Paris 1646.

31. *Alexander Leith*, convert, son of Patrick Leith of Harthill & Anne Abercromby, born 1628, was in Scots College Paris 1646, entered Douai 10 Mar 1649, ordained 1667, joined Jesuits.

32. Patrick Gordon, had begun Philosophy by 1654.

Principalship of Robert Barclay 1655–1682

33. Alexander Gordon, convert, ecclesiastical student, entered 15 Nov 1655.

34. George Baillie, left Scots College Paris March 1656, entered Rome 1656, left Rome 1656.

35. William Hay alias Colinson, Aberdeen diocese, left Scots College Paris March 1656, entered Rome 1656, left Rome 1 May 1659.

36. *Gilbert Gray*, son of John Gray, born 1624, Dunkeld diocese, left Scots College Paris 1657, entered Rome 1657, ordained Rome 1662, apostatised, died 1678.

37. Gilbert Menzies, Aberdeen diocese, left Scots College Paris 1657, entered Rome 1657, left Rome 1662.

38. James Tyrie, Brechin diocese, entered Paris August 1656, left October 1659, entered Rome 1659, left October 1662, apostatised, later taught in St Andrews University.

1657   7 students in the college

39. James Francis Abercromby, diocese of St Andrews, left Paris after Philosophy 1658/9, entered Rome 1664, left on account of bad health, and died on the way home.

40. *John Strachan*, born c.1635, Regent in Aberdeen University 1651–1655,convert, left Scots College Paris 1659, joined Jesuits, ordained Naples c.1667, Rector of Scots College, Rome 30 Nov 1670–10 Feb 1671. Died Rome 10 Feb 1671.

41. *George (Benedict) Hay or Colinson*, of Dalgety, Aberdeen diocese, left Scots College Paris 21 October 1661, entered Rome 1661, left 1665. Became a Benedictine, transferred to Ratisbon c. 1673 (?).

42. *Alexander Irvine*, son of Alexander Irvine of Belty & Isabella Irvine, born 1640, Aberdeen diocese, at Douai 1656–1662, entered Scots College Paris 1662, ordained Paris 1667, died 16 September 1706.

43   *Alexander Burnet*, diocese of Aberdeen, Scots College Paris 1662–1667, ordained deacon in Paris, Scots College Rome 1667–1671, ordained priest Rome, died 1675.

44. *Alexander P. Leslie*, son of Alexander Leslie and Agnes Gordon, born 1650, diocese of Moray, entered 1663, ordained Paris 1672. Visitator. Died 6 May 1702.

45. Robert Barclay, son of Colonel David Barclay & Catherine Gordon, diocese of Moray, born 1648, non-Catholic, left college 1665, became Quaker Apologist. Died 1690.

46. *John Irvine*, son of John Irvine of Belty, entered Rome 1662, left 1665/7, entered Scots College Paris 1665/7, ordained Paris 1667.

47. *Robert Monro*, born 1645, diocese of Ross, convert, entered Douai 17 May 1663, Scots College Paris February 1666–February 1668, ordained in Rome c. 1671, Martyr 28 January 1704.

48. *John Irvine* (Cabrach), son of Francis Irvine & Margaret Leith, diocese of Aberdeen, born 1652/4, entered Scots College Paris 1666, left 1671, entered Rome 1671, ordained Rome c. 1677, died 19 May 1717.

49. *John Davidson*, diocese of Aberdeen, left Scots College Paris 1667, entered Scots College Rome 1667, dismissed 1671, but became a Dominican and was missionary in Scotland.

50. *Louis Innes*, son of James Innes & Jane Robertson, diocese of Aberdeen, born 1651, educated Scots College Paris, ordained Paris c.1676, Prefect of Studies 1680–1682, Principal of College 1682–1713, Almoner to James Edward Stuart 1713–1718, Almoner to Queen Marie D'Este, died 11 February 1738.

51. *Charles Whyteford*, son of Colonel Walter Whyteford, grandson of David, Bishop of Brechin, born c.1649, educated at Scots College Paris, ordained Paris c.1676, Procurator of College 1696–1689, Principal of College 1713–1738. Died 25 December 1738.

52. *Thomas (Placid) Fleming*, diocese of Glasgow, born October 1642, convert, left Scots College Paris 1668, ordained as Benedictine priest 1671, became Abbot of Ratisbon, died Ratisbon 8 January 1720.

53. *George Gordon*, diocese of Aberdeen, educated at Scots College Paris, ordained Paris 1674, died 29 May 1695.

1669   12 students in the college

54. *Robert Davidson*, diocese of St Andrews, left Scots College Paris, entered Rome 21 October 1672, ordained Rome c.1677, died Leith 13 May 1711.

55. *Alexander Christie*, (possible), son of Alexander Christie, diocese of St Andrews, left Scots College Paris 1674, entered Rome 1674, ordained Rome, died Dunkirk April 1715.

56. Thomas Strachan, left Scots College Paris 1675.

57. *Richard (Augustine) Hay*, son of George Hay & Jean Spottiswood, born Edinburgh 16 August 1661, convert, went to Scots College Paris June 1673, left August 1677, ordained (as Augustinian) Chartres 22 Sept 1685.

58. William Fraser, son of Alexander Fraser of Techmuiry & Janet Fraser, daughter of 10th Lord Saltoun, in Scots College Paris 1677 and 1678. Died 1735/6.

59. _____ Maxwell, son of John Maxwell, in Scots College Paris 1677.

60. John Stewart, son of Patrick Stewart of Boggs & Anna Gordon, in Scots College Paris 1677, married before Nov 1697 Jean Gordon of Farskane.

61. Robert Douglas of Bridgford, diocese of Aberdeen, in Scots College Paris 1677, left 1680.

62. John Muirhead, son of Muirhead of Lachab, was in Scots College Paris 1677, died March 1681.

63. *Angus Macdonald*, eldest son of Roderick Macdonald & _____ Macdonald, of Glenaladale, diocese of Argyle, entered Scots College Paris August 1678. Ordained Paris 1682. Died Inverness 6 January 1684.

64. Patrick Ogilvie, son of Walter Ogilvie of Raggall & Anna Gordon, diocese of Aberdeen, entered Scots College Paris 1678, married Elizabeth _____, 2 sons, died 1732.

65. James Gordon, son of John Gordon of Letterfourie & Janet Seton, born 1660, entered Scots College Paris 1678, married Glicerie Dunbar, killed 6 at Sheriffmuir, died 1748.

66. John Gordon of Beldornie, diocese of Aberdeen, entered Scots College Paris 1678.

67. James_____, nephew of Alexander Dunbar, Prefect of the Scottish Mission, was in Scots College Paris

68. *Thomas Innes*, son of James Innes & Jane Robertson, diocese of Aberdeen, born 1662, entered Scots College Paris 1679, ordained Paris 10 March 1691, M.A. Paris 1694, Prefect of Studies 1718–1727, Vice-Principal of College 1727, author of *Critical Essay on the Ancient Inhabitants of Scotland* and *The Civil and Ecclesiastical History of Scotland*, died 8 February 1744.

69. +*James Gordon*, son of Patrick Gordon of Glastirum, diocese of Aberdeen, born in Enzie 1664, entered Scots College Paris 1679, went to Louvain and returned to Scots College Paris 1683, ordained Paris 1692, ordained Bishop 11 April 1706, succeeded Bishop Nicolson 1718, died Thornhill near Drummond Castle 1 March 1746.

70. *Alexander Gordon*, born 1655, like James Gordon, he seems to have entered Scots College Paris, then gone to Louvain, and returned to Scots College Paris in 1683, ordained Paris c.1683, died Paris 30 November 1724.

71. Charles Gordon of Achanacy, diocese of Aberdeen, entered Scots College Paris 1680.

72. James St Clair, son of James St Clair of Roslin & Jean Spottiswood, diocese of St Andrews, born 8th March 1671, entered Scots College Paris in 1680s, became Page of Honour to Queen Marie and Cornet of her Guards in Parker's Company, killed at the Battle of the Boyne 1690.

73. John Blaccader, son of Archibald Blaccader who lived in Cadiz, was in Scots College Paris 1681, left 1683.

Principalship of Louis Innes (1682–1713)

74. Alexander Davidson, left Scots College Paris 1683.

75. *George Adamson*, from Grange in Strathbogie, diocese of Moray, entered Paris April 1683, entered Rome 1690, ordained Rome c.1697, Prefect of Studies Paris 1697–1703, died Strathbogie 29 May 1707.

76. Adam Strachan, ecclesiastical student, entered Paris 20 May 1683, left unordained 1687.

77. Robert Maxwell, son of John(?) Maxwell, was in the college in 1683.

78. John Urquhart, son of Adam Urquhart of Meldrum & Lady Mary Gordon, diocese of Aberdeen, born 1668, entered Scots College Paris 1682, left 1684, married Jean Campbell, imprisoned for a day in July 1689 on suspicion of anti-Government sympathies, apparently apostatised, died 1726.

79. George Con, entered 1683, left Sept 1685.

80. James Barclay, left Scots College Paris 1684.

81. Alexander St Clair, son of James St Clair of Roslin & Jean Spottiswood, diocese of St Andrews, entered Scots College Paris October 1684, married Jean Semple.

82. Alexander Gordon, son of Lord Alexander Gordon of Auchintoul & Isobel Gray, diocese of Aberdeen, born 27 December 1669, entered Scots College Paris 1684, later Major-General in Russian army, married (1) _____ Gordon, daughter of Gen. Patrick Gordon, married (2) Margaret Moncrief, led centre at Sherrifmuir, wrote *History of Peter the Great*, died July 1752.

83. George Gordon, son of Lord Alexander of Auchintoul & Isobel Gray, diocese of Aberdeen, entered Scots College Paris 1684, married Barbara Mackenzie, died at sea 1746.

84. John Byers, son of Byers of Coatts, diocese of St Andrews, entered Scots College Paris 1684, still there 1688.

85. Robert Gordon, sent to Paris by Alexander Dunbar in 1684.

86. _____Leslie, brother to Fetternear, diocese of Aberdeen, entered Scots College Paris 1684.

87. *Lord James Drummond, son of James Drummond, first titular Duke of Perth and Jane Douglas, diocese of St Andrews, born in or before February 1673, entered Scots College Paris 1686, married Jean Gordon, died Paris 9 April 1720.

88. Alexander Leslie, son of Walter Leslie, born in Paris, entered Scots College Paris 1686, died in the college May 1691.

89. Alexander Clerk, from Edinburgh, diocese of St Andrews, ecclesiastical student, left Scots College Paris 1687.

90. Patrick Dixon, son of James Dixon, ecclesiastical student, left Scots College Paris 1687.

91. _____ Innes, left Scots College Paris 1687.

92. Thomas Irvine, son of Dr Irvine, from Edinburgh, diocese of St Andrews, entered Scots College Paris 1687, expelled 1687.

93. +*John Wallace*, son of Patrick Wallace, Provost of Arbroath, diocese of St Andrews, baptised Arbroath 8 April 1654, Episcopalian Minister, then convert, stayed in Scots College Paris as a gentleman boarder from at least 1687. After many years there decided to become a priest, left college 1706, ordained priest Preshome 1708, consecrated bishop Edinburgh 1720, died Edinburgh 30 June 1733.

94. _____ Balentin, in Scots College Paris 1687, left 1688.

95. James Brown, son of Hugh Brown, from Edinburgh, diocese of St Andrews, born c.1675, entered Scots College Paris 1687.

96. James Urquhart, in Scots College Paris 1687, still there 1692.

97. *Lord John Fleming, 6th Earl Wigton, son of William Fleming 5th Earl & Henrietta Seton, born c. 1673, diocese of Galloway, entered Scots College Paris May 1687, married (1) Margaret Lindsay 14 March 1698, (2) Mary Keith 8 February 1711, (3) Euphame Lockhart, died Edinburgh 10 February 1744.

98. *Charles Fleming, son of William Fleming 5th Earl & Henrietta Seton, born c. 1675, diocese of Galloway, entered Scots College Paris May 1687, died unmarried Cumbernauld 16 May 1747.

99. *Alexander Drummond*, diocese of Glasgow, convert, born 1668 educated Scots College Paris, deacon Paris 24 Sept 1695, priest Paris c.1696, died 25 May 1742.

100. James Petrie, diocese of Dunkeld, entered Scots College Paris August 1688, entered Rome 3 May 1689, left same year.

101. John Pringle, diocese of St Andrews, entered Scots College Paris August 1688, entered Rome 3 May 1689, left 22 September 1692, unordained.

102. _____ Lockhart(?), Cleghorn's son, in Scots College Paris 1689.

103. _____ Rigge, convert, formerly a minister, left Scots College Paris 1689 to be a soldier in Ireland.

104. John MacLean, diocese of Argyll, left Scots College Paris for Rome 3 March 1690, entered Rome 10 April 1690, but left before the end of September.

105. George Panton, entered Scots College Paris 1691, left 1703 for Douai, but was refused admittance.

106. *John Gordon*, son of James Gordon & Helen Gordon, diocese of Moray, born 1672, convert, tonsured Paris 23 September 1695, left & entered Rome 6 Nov 1697, left 20 September 1701 & re-entered Paris, ordained Paris c. 1708, died 11 February 1720.

107. John Dunbar, son of Thomas Dunbar & Anne Polson, diocese of Moray, tonsured Paris 23 September 1695.

108. Gilbert Wauchope, nineteenth child and ninth son of Andrew Wauchope of Niddrie-Marischal & Margaret Gilmour, born 9 January 1684, diocese of St Andrews, ecclesiastical student, entered Scots College Paris June 1693, left 1704, re-entered as medical student 1706, became doctor of medicine, died 15 May 1747.

109. James Kennedy, born in Brussels, was student in Scots College Paris 1694.

110. *Peter Fraser*, convert, entered Scots College Paris, entered 1696, left college 1702, ordained Scothouse 11 March 1704, died Morar 9 March 1731.

1697   4 students in the college

111. *George Dalgleish*, son of Colin Douglas & Elizabeth Irvine, diocese of Ross, born 1681, entered Scots College Paris 1697, left for Rome & entered 30 October 1698, left Rome 24 April 1706, back in Scots College Paris from May 1706 until October 1706 though for reasons of expediency not called a student, ordained Scothouse 15 August 1707, died Morar 29 April 1731.

112. George Ross, son of Alexander Ross of Pitkery & Joanna Monrho, diocese of Ross, born 1677, entered Scots College Paris 1697, left & entered Rome 30 October 1698, left 20 February 1700, unordained.

113. +*Alexander Smith*, born c.1683 at Fochabers, diocese of Moray, entered Scots College Paris 1698, ordained Preshome 1712, Procurator of Scots College Paris 1718–1730, Bishop 1735, died Edinburgh 21 August 1767.

114. *George Innes*, son of Charles Innes & Claudia Irvine, born July 1683, was in Scots College Paris by 1698, ordained Paris 1712, Rector of Morar 1714, Rector of Scalan 1717–1721, Prefect of Studies Paris 1727–1738, Principal 1738–1752, died 29 April 1752.

115. *Lord Edward Drummond, son of James Drummond 1st Duke of Perth & Mary Gordon, his 3rd wife, later 6th Duke of Perth, born 1690, entered Scots College Paris 1698, aged 8, married Anne Elisabeth Middleton 25 November 1709, died Paris 6 February 1760.

116. *William Drummond, son of James Drummond 1st Duke of Perth & Mary Gordon, his 3rd wife, younger brother of above, entered Scots College Paris 1698, died young at St Germains.

117. George Napier, son of Napier of Wrighthouse, entered Scots College Paris 1698, very young.

1699   11 students in the college

118. _____ Syms, in Scots College Paris 1699.

119. John Caryll, son of John Caryll 2nd Baron of Durford & Elizabeth Harrington, great nephew of Lord Caryll, Secretary of State, baptised West Grimstead 28 December 1687, entered Scots College Paris end of 1699, married Lady Mary Mackenzie, died April 1718, buried at Harting.

120. _____ Drummond, convert, nephew of Abbot Cooke, entered Scots College Paris 1699, made first communion April 1699.

121. *Gregor MacGregor*, son of Malcolm MacGregor & Mary Gordon, diocese of Aberdeen, born 1682, Scots College Paris July 1699–May 1700, entered Rome 6 June 1700, expelled 12 May 1705, Scots College Paris 1705–January 1706, joined Benedictines, ordained Würzburg c.1708.

122. Alexander Mackintosh, ecclesiastical student, Scots College Paris 1700–1703, went to Rome but did not enter on account of scruples, came back to Paris in starving condition 1704.

123. Ranald Macdonald, educated Scots College Paris, ordained deacon Paris, died in Holland 4 July 1711.

124. *Peter Reid*, convert, son of Alexander Reid & Isabella Blebars, diocese of Brechin, born 1678, entered Scots College Paris 1701, left for Rome & entered 14 November 1702, ordained Rome c. 1706, died Preshome 27 November 1726.

125. Paul Gray, nephew of Louis Innes, entered Scots College Paris 1701

126. Neal Beaton, probably ecclesiastic, Highlander, entered Scots College Paris 1702, left 1703, but was received back in December 1703, left March 1704.

127. John Drummond, son of Ludovic Drummond, was in Scots College Paris 1702, still there 1706.

128. James Drummond, son of Ludovic Drummond, was in Scots College Paris 1702, left 1704.

129. Rorie Mackenzie, left Scots College Paris 1703.

130. Robert Ross, ecclesiastic, entered Scots College Paris 1703, left for Rome 1703, but was not recommended by Paris College.

131. Thomas Abercromby, left Scots College Paris 1704.

132. Francis Bowers, son of Alexander Bowers & Carol Starlin, diocese of Brechin, entered Scots College Paris 1704, left for Rome & entered 27 October 1705, left 3 April 1711 unordained.

133. *Robert Gordon*, born 1687 or 1688, son of William Gordon of Bogy, merchant in Aberdeen and Isabella Davidson, diocese of Aberdeen, entered Scots College Paris 1704, left for Rome Sept 1705, ordained probably 28 Oct 1711, Prefect of Studies, Paris 1712–1718 and 1753–1756, died Paris 23 Mar 1763.

134. *Angus MacLachlan*, diocese of Argyll, at Scots College Paris 1704–1712, ordained Paris 1712, died March 1760.

135. Lewis Innes, son Francis Innes & Jean Maitland, entered 1704 or beginning of 1705, left 1709.

136. Gregory Farquharson, 4th son of Charles Bui Farquharson, entered Scots College Paris 1707, died 1746.

137. Lewis Gray, nephew of Louis Innes entered Scots College Paris 1707, left college 1709.

138. *James (Francis) Stevens*, son of William Stevens & Elizabeth Faulds, diocese of Glasgow, born 1685, entered Rome 26 March 1703, left 8 July 1707, entered Scots College Paris July 1707, left April 1710, became a Lazarist, and is listed with priests in Memorabilia.

139. Archibald Anderson, nephew of Bishop Nicolson, entered Scots College Paris 1708, left in August 1718 as Deacon, but was never ordained for heath reasons, died 1773/4.

140. Lewis James Gray, died in the college 31 July 1708.

141. John Joseph Veillan, diocese of St Andrews, convert, cleric, left 1716, died Edinburgh 18 October 1719.

142. *George Gordon*, son of William Gordon (known as Bogy), diocese of Aberdeen, born 1701, entered Scots College Paris 1712, ordained Paris 1726.

Principalship of Charles Whyteford (1713–1738)

143. Patrick Gordon, eldest son of James Gordon of Letterfourie & Glicerie Dunbar, diocese of Aberdeen, entered Scots College Paris 1713, left July 1716.

144. Eowell Macdonnell, was student in Scots College Paris 1714.

145. Benbecula's son was student in Scots College Paris 1715.

146. *Charles Stewart, Lord Linton, later 5th Earl of Traquair, son of Charles 4th Earl & Mary Maxwell, diocese of Glasgow, entered Scots College Paris 1715, married Theresa Conyers, died Edinburgh 24 April 1764.

147. *John Stewart, later 6th Earl of Traquair, son of Charles 4th Earl & Mary Maxwell, diocese of Glasgow, entered Scots College Paris 1715, married Christian Anstruther, died Paris 28 March 1779.

148. Patrick Young, entered Scots College Paris 1715, still there 1726.

149. George Gordon, son of Alexander Gordon & Anne Lumsdel, diocese of Moray, born 1694, left Scots College Rome as a subdeacon on account of health. After two years in Scots College Paris, was sent to Scotland because of bad health, but returned to Paris against orders July 1720, and died in the college on 27 Nov 1721.

150. James Innes, son of Francis Innes & Jean Maitland, diocese of Aberdeen, ecclesiastical student, entered Scots College Paris 1716.

151. *Colin Campbell*, of Lochnell, diocese of Argyll, born 1689, convert, entered Scots College Paris September 1716, ordained Paris 1722, instigator of Jansenist problems, killed at Culloden 1746.

152. *James Tyrie*, son of David Tyrie of Dennedir & Ann Menzies, diocese of Aberdeen, born 6 November 1700, entered Scots College Paris 1716, left for Rome & entered 7 April 1717, ordained Rome 1725, apostatised.

153. *John Stuart, son of James Stuart, 1st Earl of Bute & Christian Dundas, his second wife, diocese of the Isles, born at Rothesay 6 September 1700, convert, entered Scots College Paris 1717, died at Rome 1738.

154. Aeneas MacDonald, probably ecclesiastical student, left for health reasons 1722.

155. _____ Brown, son of James Brown, entered Scots College Paris 1720.

156. John Dixon, diocese of St Andrews, entered Scots College Paris 1720, died in college (acolyte) 31 August 1728.

157. John Farquharson, 2nd son of Robert Farquharson of Achriachan & _____ Stewart, diocese of Moray, born at Achriachan 25 August 1710, entered Scots College Paris 1721, expelled 1732, entered French military service, married Mary Elizabeth Vaniere.

158. Robert Dugud, son of Alexander Dugud, late of Bitby, entered Scots College Paris 1721, left for Ratisbon 1723.

159. John Gordon of Glencat, son of John Gordon & Jean Gordon, born 1704, entered Scots College Paris 1721, ordained Deacon in Paris, expelled 1730. Apostatised, published book against Church, recanted 1742 & became an agent for the Bishops in London, died London 2 Nov 1770.

160. Aeneas Macdonald, 10th son of Ranald Macdonald & _____ Cameron, diocese of Argyll, entered Scots College Paris 1721, left 17 March 1727, became banker in Paris, one of seven men of Moidart, killed in French Revolution in 1790.

161. *James Drummond, 3rd Duke of Perth, son of James Drummond 2nd Duke & Jean Gordon, diocese of St Andrews, born 11 May 1713, entered Scots College Paris 1721, died at sea 13 May 1746.

162. *John Drummond, later 4th Duke of Perth, son of James Drummond 2nd Duke & Jean Gordon, diocese of St Andrews, born in France 1714, entered Scots College Paris 1721, died 28 September 1747.

163. *Andrew Riddoch*, born 1700, is in Scots College Paris by 1721, left, returned October 1734, ordained Paris 1740, died 11 July 1772.

164. _____ Riddoch, a second student called Riddoch, probably a brother of the previous was in Scots College Paris 1721.

165. John Perkins, in Scots College Paris 1721.

1721   12 students in the college

1722   9 students in the college

166. John Grant, entered Scots College Paris 1722, described as very young and 'not fit for Syntax'.

167. Andrew Parkins, son of Isaac Parkins & Anne Wauchop, left Scots College Paris for Ratisbon 1723, studied Philosophy at Erfurt, professed Ratisbon 1726, died 10 July 1728.

1723   8 students in the college

168. *George Duncan*, son of John Duncan & Catherine _____, born Edinburgh, diocese of St Andrews, entered Scots College Paris 1724, tonsure Paris Advent 1725, left college Sept 1726, ordained Scalan 1732, Rector of Scalan 1758, died 21 November Edinburgh 1761.

169. *Alexander Gordon*, of Coffurich, born 3 November 1710, entered Scots College Paris 1724, subdeacon Paris, deacon Scalan 22 June 1734, ordained priest Scalan 21 September 1734. Died Edinburgh 9 November 1793.

170. *John Gordon*, son of Peter Gordon (of Enzie), born August 1706, entered Scots College Paris 1724, expelled, 1732, but ordained at Scalan 1734, later defected and married.

171. *William Farquharson*, son of Robert Farquharson of Achriachan & _____ Stewart, diocese of Moray, born 1712, date of entry to Scots College Paris not known, expelled 1732, but ordained at Troyes 24 September 1735.

172. John Stuart, (related to family of Lesmurdy), entered Scots College Paris 1725.

1727   11 students at beginning of year, 9 students at end.

173. *Alan Macdonald*, son of Alexander Macdonald of Stonybridge & Ziles Macdonald, diocese of the Isles, born c. 1696, entered Scots College Rome 13 November 1715, left 23 September 1721, came to Paris in 1727, and although not formally received as a student of Scots College Paris, was housed by the college and lived in the college by day where he ate and studied for at least four months from 17 February until 10 June. Left for Rome, but was not received there, went to Madrid, left for Douai 1728, and was finally ordained priest in Scotland in 1736. Was chaplain to Prince Charles in the '45, and afterwards imprisoned and banished for life. He, however, returned to Scotland in 1748, and worked in both Highlands and Lowlands until his death in Edinburgh on 17 May 1781.

174. William Lindsay, left Scots College Paris 29 August 1727.

175. *John Gordon*, son of George Gordon of Dorlaithers & Barbara Mackenzie, born 21 July 1713, entered Scots College Paris 1727, ordained Paris 1743, Principal of College 1752–1777, died Paris 23 April 1777.

176. John Augustine Arthur, a student, died in the College 9 January 1729.

1729   6 students in the college

177. *John McKenzie*, son of George McKenzie & Helen Milne, diocese of Aberdeen, convert, entered Scots College Paris 1729, received tonsure & 4 minor orders at Troyes 5 July 1733, ordained priest Paris 1737, Prefect of Studies 1738–1743, defected 1745, married, repented & entered La Trappe.

178. Alexander Gordon, 4th son of James Gordon of Letterfourie & Glicerie Dunbar, diocese of Aberdeen, born 1714, entered Scots College Paris 1730, married Helen Russell 1778, died 16 January 1797.

179. James Campbell, brother of Colin, convert, entered Scots College Paris 1730.

180. James Gordon, son of George Gordon of Glastirum, born c.1719,great nephew of Bishop Gordon entered Scots College Paris c.1730, married (1) Mary Hay, died 22 February 1783.

181. Alexander Bowers, nephew of Patrick Bowers ordained Rome, was in Scots College Paris 1731.

182. *William Duthie*, son of John Duthie & Mary Henderson, diocese of Aberdeen, entered Scots College Paris after November 1731, received tonsure & 4 minor orders at Troyes 5 July 1733, ordained Paris 1737, Rector of Scalan 1741–1758, Prefect of Studies Paris 1761–1766, died 7 Jan 1785.

1732   2 students in the college

183. William Douglas, entered Scots College Paris by December 1732, still there 1733.

184. John Gordon of Beldornie, son of J. Gordon of Beldornie & Mary Gordon, was in Scots College Paris by 1735.

185. George Gordon, son of J. Gordon of Beldornie & Mary Gordon, was in Scots College Paris by 1735, left 1742, became apprentice to ship-carpenter in Leith.

186. James Falconer, ecclesiastical student, entered Scots College Paris 1736, expelled 1740, apostatised 1743.

187. Neil MacEachan, son of Alexander MacEachan of Howbeg, diocese of the Isles, ecclesiastical student, born 1719 entered Scots College Paris 1736, left September 1737, married 1763, died Sancerre 1788.

188. Alexander Colbert, probably son of John Colbert or Cuthbert of Castlehill and Jean Hay, diocese of Moray, entered 1736, later known as L'Abbé Colbert. Died in France in September 1782.

189. Charles Farquhar, ecclesiastical student, entered Scots College Paris 1737, expelled 1740.

190. Alexander Drummond, entered Scots College Paris 1738.

191. William Stuart, entered Scots College Paris 1738.

192. Robert Grant, entered Scots College Paris 1738.

193. John McDonald, Highlander, from Highland seminary, entered Scots College Paris 1738.

194. _____ Symour, Highlander, from Highland seminary, entered Scots College Paris 1738, left 1744.

1738   14 students in the college

Principalship of George Innes (1738–1752)

195. # Ranald Macdonald, son of Ranald Macdonald, 15th chief of Clanranald & Margaret Macleod, entered Scots College Paris February 1739, left February 1742, married (1) Mary Hamilton (2) Flora Mackinnon.

196. # Alastair Ruadh Macdonnell, son of John Macdonnell, 12th chief of Glengarry, & Margaret Mackenzie, born 1725 entered Scots College Paris 1740, died unmarried 1761.

197. Lewis Innes, son of James Innes, nephew of Principal George Innes, diocese of Aberdeen, entered Scots College Paris August 1741. His son William became a priest.

198. John Drummond, son of Westerfeddels, was in Scots College Paris 1741, left 1742.

199. John Cairny, left Scots College Paris February 1742.

1742   6 students in the college

200. +*Seignelay Colbert*, son of George Colbert or Cuthbert of Castlehill and Mary Mackintosh, diocese of Moray, born 1736, entered Scots College Paris 1747, left September 1761 (?), ordained France 1762, Bishop of Rodez 2 April 1781, died London 14 January 1813.

201. Alexander Bowers, son of Alexander Bowers of Methie, entered Scots College Paris 1748.

202. William Gordon is in Scots College Paris by 1749.

203. *Alexander Gordon*, from Newmills near Keith, diocese of Aberdeen, was in Scots College Paris by 1749, ordained Paris c. 1764, Prefect of Studies, Procurator, Principal 1777–1792, died Traquair 1 October 1818.

204. 'Bucktie' was student in Scots College Paris in 1749.

205. Bishop Macdonald's nephew was student in Scots College Paris in 1749.

206. Robert Gray, ecclesiastical student, was in Scots College Paris in 1749, died in the college 21 April 1758.

207. _____ Drummond, son of Dr John Drummond entered Scots College Paris 1752.

Principalship of John Gordon (1752–1777)

208. Andrew Gordon, nephew of John Gordon of Glencat, had left Scots College Paris by 1755.

209. John Macdonnell, diocese of Ross, born 1734, entered Rome 22 February 1751, left 14 August 1755, entered Scots College Paris 1755, left for health reasons & became a soldier.

210. *Alexander Geddes*, son of Alexander Geddes & Janet Mitchel, born at Pathhead near Preshome 1737, diocese of Aberdeen, entered Scots College Paris 1758, ordained Paris 1764, dismissed from the mission 1779, died London 26 February 1802.

211. *Henry Innes*, son of James Innes, born at Ballogie 1748, diocese of Aberdeen, entered Scots College Paris c.1759, ordained Paris c.1771, Prefect of Studies, Procurator, died Ballogie 11 November 1833.

212. Ewan _____, was to be received back 1760.

213. John Duff, entered Scots College Paris 1761.

214. James Gordon of Auchleuchries died in Scots College Paris 3 September 1762.

215. *John Baptist Gordon*, born Newmill near Keith c.1749, diocese of Aberdeen, entered Scots College Paris c. 1762, left for Valladolid 1770, ordained Valladolid 21 September 1771, died in mental hospital.

216. *James Hugh Macdonald*, born Guidal in Morar, diocese of Argyll, entered Scots College Paris 1764, ordained Paris 1770, taught in Buorblach 1770–1772.

217. *Alexander Innes*, son of James Innes, diocese of Aberdeen, born 1750, entered Scots College Paris July 1764, ordained Paris 1777, Prefect of Studies 1781–1792, Procurator 1792, died 14 September 1803.

218. Andrew Fletcher, entered Scots College Paris October 1766, left September 1769.

219. *Alexander Macdonald*, son of Archibald MacDonald, cadet of Keppoch, born in Clianaig, Glen Spean December 1753, diocese of Argyll, entered Scots College Paris 1767, left for Valladolid 1770, ordained Valladolid 1776, died Halifax, Nova Scotia 15 April 1816.

220. _____ Gordon, of Auchleuchries left Scots College Paris 1770.

221. *Peter Hay*, was probably in Scots College Paris by 1770, ordained Paris 1777, Prefect of Studies, died Auchinhalrig 17 December 1783.

1770   7 ecclesiastical students in the college

Principalship of Alexander Gordon (1777–1792)

222. James Hay, from Stobhall, diocese of Dunkeld, entered Scots College Paris October 1777, left 15 Nov 1782.

223. Nathan Selkirk, diocese of Galloway, ecclesiastical student, entered Scots College Paris October 1777.

224. *James Cattanach*, diocese of Galloway, entered Scots College Paris 1777/8, ordained Paris September 1788, died Campbeltown 3 December 1836.

225. Neil MacLeod, was in the college 1786, left the college 15 July 1789.

226. Donald Macdonald, was in the college 1786, left 15 July 1790.

227. Alexander Macnab, was in the college 1786, left 15 July, 1790.

228. Charles Carmichael, was in the college 1786, left 6 Aug 1791.

1787   6 students in the college

1788   5 students in the college (after James Cattanach had gone to the Scottish mission)

229. Walter Stuart, was in the college 1789, and still there throughout 1791

230. M. Cuisinier, was in the college 1789, and still there throughout 1791

231. M. Portier, was in the college 1789, and still there throughout 1791

232. George Blount, entered 29 Oct 1790, left 14 Aug 1791.

233. Jean or Benjamin Forbes, born in France, mother was English, entered 1 Sept 1791.

1791   2 students in the college.

Index of Names

Abercorn, Lady 34
Abercromby, James Francis 208
Abercromby, John, Student in 1627 8, 206
Abercromby, John, Student in 1646 208
Abercromby, Thomas 213
Adamson, George 6, 8f, 11, 20, 68, 70, 105, 210
Alexander, J. 207
Alexander I, King of Scots 36
Alexander VII., Pope 46, 102
Algeo, Thomas 34
Anderson, Archibald 152, 214
Anderson, Patrick S.J. 46
Anderson, William 168, 183
Anne of Brittany, Queen of France 177, 186, 188
Anne, Queen of Britain 83f
Archibald, David 48
Arthur, John Augustine 130, 152, 216
Atterbury, Francis, Bishop of Rochester 179f, 183f

Balgonie, Lady 43
Baillie, George 42, 208
Ballentin 65, 211
Ballentine, William 20, 31, 37f, 40f, 50, 67, 195, 207
Baluze, Étienne 181, 183
Banks, Alice 48
Barberigo, Marcantonio, Cardinal 74
Barberini, Francesco, Cardinal 37,44
Barberini, Maffeo, Cardinal 28, 30
Barclay, David, Colonel 36, 41, 42
Barclay, James 210
Barclay, Robert, Principal 12, 14, 20, 23f, 31f, 36–53, 57, 66, 76, 86, 104, 128, 177, 195, 197, 207
Barclay, Robert, Quaker 12, 36, 208
Beaton, James, Archbishop 1, 3f, 6, 11f, 23, 29, 47, 173, 177f., 191f.
Beaton, Neil 12, 213
Bellenden, William 205
Benedict XIII, Pope 120f
Berkeley, Theobald de 36
Berniers, Père 105
Betham, Dr 60f
Bethune, George 12
Bethune, James 12, 207
Berwick, Duke of 83f
Bigné, Père 105
Bisset, George S.J. (*alias* Talbot, Gilbert) 43– 45, 47
Blaccader, John 14, 210
Black, John 30, 205, 207

Blackwood, Henry 4
Blakhal, Gilbert, Principal 20, 30, 32–33, 52, 178, 189
Blount, George 219
Boece, Hector 4, 88
Bolingbroke, Henry St John 84
Borghese, Camillo, Cardinal (later Pope Paul V) 6
Bossuet, Jacques Bénigne, Bishop of Troyes 123, 131, 141
Bowers, Alexander 160, 216
Bowers, Francis 213
Breadalbane, Earl of 82
Brockie, Thomas 114, 116, 143
Brodie, Alexander 61f
Broghill, Lord 41
Brown, Gilbert 178, 191
Brown, Hew 9
Brown, James 9, 65, 211
Brown, Richard 215
Bruce, Robert, King of Scots 1, 121
Buchanan, George 4, 88
Bur, Alexander, Bishop of Moray 2
Burnet, Alexander 39, 67, 208
Burnet, David 20f, 45, 49, 51, 59, 104, 178, 189
Byers, John 58, 65, 211

Cahassy, James 21, 58
Caille, Honoré 181
Caillot, Maurice 190f
Cairney, John 138, 217
Camera, William de 2, 205
Cameron, Alexander, Bishop 188
Cameron, Allan 88
Cameron, Captain 85
Cameron of Lochiel 91
Campbell, Archibald, Bishop 183
Campbell, Colin 14, 88f, 94, 104, 109f, 114f, 117ff, 123, 127, 131, 135, 139, 142f, 156, 166, 196, 214
Campbell, Sir Duncan 14
Campbell, General 90
Campbell, James 14, 115ff, 123f, 156, 216
Canaries, James 74
Carmichael, Charles 219
Carnegie, James 20, 105, 107f, 115, 122, 128, 133f, 149f, 152
Carpentier, M. 187
Carruthers, Andrew, Bishop 51, 189
Carte, Thomas 179, 184, 192
Caryll, Lord John, Baron of Dunford 9, 12, 19, 24, 73, 179, 185

Subject Index

Augustinian(s) 63, 74

Banished Priests 37–39, 66–67, 94–95, 160, 162
Benedictine(s) 33, 45, 63, 76, 104, 108f
Buorblach, seminary 218
Buildings of the College 1, 4, 24f, 30, 46–48, 64, 159, 167

Carthusian Prior(s) 15, 29, 44f, 51, 69, 72, 76, 112, 135ff, 149f, 154, 156, 161, 170–173
Carthusians 16, 32, 47, 57, 72, 75, 177, 181, 186
Culloden, battle 89, 92ff

Discipline 40, 51, 65, 136, 153f, 159, 162, 167
Dominican(s) 41, 121
Douai, seminary 33, 42, 47

Falkirk, battle 93
Finance 1, 23f, 47f, 58, 61f, 68, 82, 124, 143, 154, 167, 170
Franciscan(s) 29, 49, 50, 52

Gallicanism 122, 126, 137, 197
Guidal, seminary 24, 155

Health 152, 157, 166f
Holyrood 62f, 80, 91

Jacobitism 15, 76, 80–98, 159, 161f, 166, 174, 193, 196, 197f
Jansenism 75, 94, 102–144, 159, 161f, 166, 174, 193, 196, 197f
Jesuit(s) 10f, 15f, 29, 32ff, 39f, 42ff, 46, 49, 51, 58f, 62, 67, 74f, 107, 109, 120, 125, 128

La Trappe 157
Lazarists (Vincentians) 76

Madird cf Scots College, Spain
Molinism 102, 104, 120
Morar, seminary 149, 155f, 162, 196

Navarre, College of, seminary 180

Oath, missionary 34, 46
Oratorians 29

Penal laws & Persecution 37, 62, 66, 80, 160, Presbyterians 14, 62, 63,
Prestonpans, battle 96
Propaganda 37–41, 46f, 49f, 58, 67, 74, 110, 118, 129, 133, 135, 138, 160f

Ratisbon, Scots monastery 152
Recollects (Friars of branch of Franciscans) 73
Rome, Scots College, seminary 6, 10f, 33f, 38, 42, 44ff, 49, 51f, 57, 72, 74, 76, 81, 162

St Nicolas du Chardonnet, seminary 36, 38, 137
Scalan, seminary 24, 76, 149, 152, 155f, 158, 162, 170, 196
Sheriffmuir, battle 84–87
Spain, Scots College, seminary 33, 50, 52, 162
Spies 41, 115

Trent, Council of 7, 22

Unigenitus 102–110, 116–135, 139, 141, 144, 196f

Vatican Council, Second 103
Visitation of the College 50, 75, 105, 134, 135, 150
  of the Highlands & Islands 182
  of Scotland 39, 52

Würzburg, Scots monastery 33, 118

Contention betw. Scot Bps & Principals:
(money)   167
1761
1770 some cash withdrawn fm Nissei
     crash of E. India Co.
     knock down house after accidt

1762 Bp blame staff for apostacies

Hay v Gordon (Alexandr)
        John Gordon (Princ's brother)
     had lost his regn.
_____

(1)   great debate as to where obligation 1
              maintenance lay.
      Alex Gordon — Scot. Nissn
      Bp Hay   — his brother, Alx
         Re Paris-educe: priests did not
              take Nisn Oath
(2)   another debate — Hay wanted
      Henry Innes, College Procurator, to return
      to Scot. Nissn
                                        169
      1783 Hay refuses to send any more
           students to Pai:
           complaints about boarders &
           Princ's violent temper

p170 . Princ. Gordon withholds moves

p170

Kr. Rev.
_____
expected religious orders wd. be suppressed
and College's ecclesiastical superior 171
the Prior y the Carthusian.
Princ Gordon converted Papal Nuncio &
But ambassador Cnt. wt. Bps &:
Selling the property & moving elsewhere:
172. Bps had no jurisd jurisdiction over the
College, & no legal standing in France.
Princ. Gordon had all rights & privileges
of a Scots citizen, and a legal posture.
Sale of College needed permission of
French Parliament.
172. 1791. 23 Dec. Bp Geddes in
arr. in Paris. Paris May 1792
Geddes leaves Paris May 1792
174. - 1792 Aug. college twice
Invaded by armed banditti
174. 1793 Oct. Alex Innes prisoner
at Colge — condemned to death in
1794. 27 July. grave dgr. fall of Robespierre
Innes reprieved
1792 Alex Gordon left Paris
with Book of Arisy & Statuts